COMPLETE DEFENSE TO QUEEN PAWN OPENINGS

ABOUT THE AUTHOR

Eric Schiller, widely considered one of the world's foremost chess analysts, writers and teachers, is internationally recognized for his definitive works on openings. He is the author of 80 chess books including Cardoza Publishing's definitive series on openings, *World Champion Openings, Standard Chess Openings*, and *Unorthodox Chess Openings*—an exhaustive opening library of more than 1700 pages. He's also the author of *Encyclopedia of Chess Wisdom, Gambit Opening Repertoire for White, Gambit Opening Repertoire for Black, Complete Defense to King Pawn Openings, Complete Defense to Queen Pawn Openings*, and multiple other chess titles for Cardoza Publishing. (For listings of all chess titles published by Cardoza Publishing, go online to www.cardozapub.com.)

Eric Schiller is a National and Life Master, an International Arbiter of F.I.D.E., and the official trainer for many of America's top young players. He has also presided over world championship matches dating back to 1983. Eric Schiller's web site is www.chessworks.com.

COMPLETE DEFENSE TO QUEEN PAWN OPENINGS

Eric Schiller

Cardoza Publishing

To Tarrasch Fans Everywhere

FIRST EDITION

Copyright © 1998 by Eric Schiller
- All Rights Reserved -

Library of Congress Catalogue Card No: 97-67065
ISBN: 0-940685-80-9

CARDOZA PUBLISHING
P.O. Box 1500 Cooper Station, New York, NY 10276
Phone (718)743-5229 • Fax (718)743-8284
Email: Cardozapub@aol.com
Web Site- www.cardozapub.com

Write for you free catalogue of gaming and chess books, equipment, software and computer games.

TABLE OF CONTENTS

INTRODUCTION

This aggressive counterattacking repertoire covers Black opening systems against virtually every chess opening except for 1.e4 (including most flank games), based on the exciting and powerful Tarrasch Defense, an opening that helped bring Championship titles to Kasparov and Spassky.

This book contains everything you need to know, even if you have never played the Tarrasch before, or haven't even heard of it! Every important concept is presented so that without memorizing any of the moves, you will still have a deep understanding of the opening and can use it to immediate advantage at the board. Once you learn the lines, your opponents will have a hard time making any progress against your solid opening play, and you will be able to take advantage of their positional weaknesses.

The Tarrasch has a long and rich history of success at all levels of play and is ideal for players who like counterattacking openings that allow Black to achieve an early equality or even an outright advantage in the first few moves. This flexibility is reflected in the strategic handling of the openings, where understanding of general ideas is much more important than memorizing specific moves.

All of the important strategic and tactical ideas of the openings, and all of the latest theoretical opinions have been checked and evaluated, and the moves we recommend for Black should hold up even against the most experienced opponents. Complete games are also presented to give a full picture of the openings shown, from the first moves right through the endgame.

You will learn enough of the general principles of the openings that you'll be able to play well at the start of the game even without detailed knowledge. Once you learn to achieve good positions from the start, and control the flow of the opening, many of your opponents will start to crumble and you'll have all you need to bring home the mate!

THE TARRASCH DEFENSE

The **Tarrasch Defense** is a variation belonging to the Queen's Gambit Declined. It is a flexible formation that can be used to meet just about any move order used by White. It normally is reached by 1.d4 d5; 2.c4 e6; 3.Nc3 c5. We'll look at transpositional paths later on.

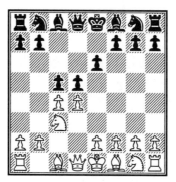

In the Tarrasch, Black challenges the center immediately. White now has to constantly consider the consequences of captures in the center. Usually White exchanges the c-pawn for Black's d-pawn, and later the White d-pawn can be exchanged for the Black c-pawn.

This gives Black an isolated d-pawn, which we will discuss in detail later. For now, let's consider the typical pawn structure that arises after an exchange of pawns at d5.

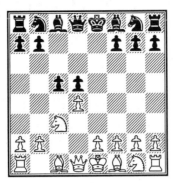

There is a lot of tension in the center. White can capture at c5 or Black can capture at d4, in either case setting up the isolated d-pawn for Black. It is important to note, however, that clarification of the situation does not usually take place in the first few moves. When a central tension is resolved, then it is possible to concentrate on plans which are appropriate to the central situation. While the center remains fluid, it is harder to find the correct plan because the central situation can change quickly. So usually this pawn center stays intact until move 9, when both sides have competed development.

While the Tarrasch Defense is used primarily by advanced players, this is mostly a result of the tendency for teachers of young chessplayers to avoid openings which involve isolated pawns, on the grounds that they are difficult to defend. Therefore it is only when players graduate to higher levels of competition that they begin to encounter the defense.

Many great players have used the Tarrasch Defense. You will meet some of them in the section on Heroes in the Tarrasch Defense. For now, all that need be said is that World Champions such as Garry Kasparov and Boris Spassky relied on the Tarrasch to get to the top.

The Tarrasch appeals to players with a strong fighting spirit. Tactics can dominate the middlegame, with long combinations involving temporary and permanent sacrifices. The stronger the endgame skills, the better, since the Tarrasch, often leads to endgames which are difficult to win, or even draw (some of the time)! As you play the Tarrasch your understanding of many endgames, especially those with rooks and minor pieces, will broaden and deepen, making you a better overall player.

HOW TO STUDY THE TARRASCH DEFENSE

The best way to learn the Tarrasch Defense is to study the games of the masters, looking for typical positional and tactical ideas. There are so many transpositional paths that viewing the opening as a tree of variations does not make as much sense. You have to learn from experience, of course, and it is always better if the experience, especially a loss, comes in a game you don't play yourself!

The games in this book illustrate a variety of themes and many are among the most instructive games in the Tarrasch canon. They are organized by variation. You should play each game all the way to the end in order to see how various positional factors bring about a won, lost, or drawn game.

Pay particular attention to the endgames. In order to play the Tarrasch well you need to know which endgames can be drawn and which are hopeless. Sometimes you can afford even to give away your precious d-pawn if the resulting endgame can be held. These illustrative games will give you a good idea of the possibilities.

The Tarrasch Defense is easy to learn because there are only a few types of structures that can arise, most of them involving isolated d-pawns or a small chain with pawns at c6 and d5.

OVERVIEW

1.d4

The Tarrasch Defense can be reached from just about any opening except for 1.e4. The highly transpositional nature of the opening requires less memorization and places a premium on understanding important strategic concepts and typical tactical devices. Naturally, White does not have to play straight into the main lines of the Tarrasch, so we must examine all the other reasonable options.

In this book we will try to adopt the Tarrasch formations wherever we can by playing ...d5, ...e6 and ...c5 in rapid succession. Against some of White's alternative strategies, this is not always the most efficient plan in terms of achieving equality. However, it is easier to play familiar positions, and to the extent that you sometimes get less in the opening, you receive benefits in the middlegame where your experience provides a great deal of assistance.

All of the lines in this book have been thoroughly tested and White cannot achieve more than a very minimal advantage. There are no openings that can absolutely guarantee an equal position for Black, since the advantage of the first move takes time to overcome. The opening repertoire provided in this book is as good as any alternative system, and has a number of significant advantages.

The most important aspect of the Tarrasch Defense is the isolated d-pawn which appears in many variations. As you learn how to handle the "isolani", you will be able to apply your knowledge in almost every game. Your experience in typical endgames will also provide an edge. Our repertoire maximizes the use of familiar patterns and structures, so you can get up to speed quickly.

1...d5.

The best defenses for Black prevent White from taking control of the center early in the game. 1...d5 prevents 2.e4, and therefore is one of the best moves. It is strongly recommended that you adopt this move order, even though others are available. After 1...e6 White can force you into a French Defense with 2.e4, which is only acceptable to Francophiles. Often 1...Nf6 can reach Tarrasch positions, but usually only when White fails to take advantage of precise move orders that render this strategy risky. In any case, 1...Nf6 invites many alternatives by White, such as the Trompovsky Attack (2.Bg5) which is very popular these days.

2.c4.

OVERVIEW

There are several options for White here. In the analysis sections of the book we will look at the most popular alternatives to 2.c4. For really strange moves you should consult *Unorthodox Chess Openings*, but we will cover everything which is seen in serious games.

2.Nf3 is the most popular alternative, and we devote three games to handling the variations where White refrains from an early c4. The Torre Attack, London System, and Colle System are not particularly ambitious openings for White, and Black can achieve a comfortable game without difficulty.

2.Nc3 is the harmless Veresov Attack. I used to play it but eventually gave it up because there is no way to get an advantage for White. If you play the Caro-Kann, then 2...c6 is a good reply, transposing to the main lines after 3.e4. Similarly, the French is available after 2...e6. In this book we will concentrate on a quite different approach with the gambit line 2...e5 which is very obscure but nevertheless seems to be quite sound.

2.e4 is the Blackmar Diemer Gambit. Black can get a good game by either accepting or declining the offer of a pawn. French and Caro-Kann players will already be used to this approach, as the gambit is played in several forms against those opening. I'll show you a simple and solid reaction.

    2...e6.

This is the only move to head for Tarrasch territory. Black supports the pawn at d5 and opens a line for the bishop at f8 in support of ...c5, which is the next move in our strategy.

3.Nc3.

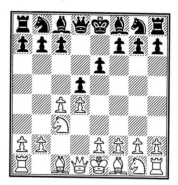

White should bring out a knight here, and it doesn't make much of a difference which one is developed first.

3.Nf3 gives White a few additional options later in the game and sidesteps a gambit line for Black which does not enter into our repertoire. Often this position is reached when the game starts with 1.c4 or 1.Nf3.

3...c5.

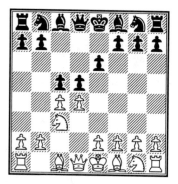

This is the defining move of the Tarrasch Defense. From here on, both sides must contemplate the effects of pawn exchanges in the center. Black now has a clear plan for development. The knights will come to c6 and f6, the bishop moves from f8 to e7, and kingside castling follows. The role of the bishop at c8 depends on White's plans. Usually White will exchange at d5, opening up a line for the bishop to move to g4, f5, or e6.

4.cxd5.

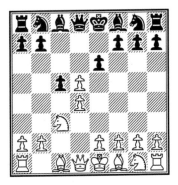

This is the normal reply. White will weaken Black's central pawn formation and spend most of the game trying to win the d-pawn. Don't worry, this plan rarely succeeds without giving Black more than enough counterplay, as we will see in our illustrative games.

4.e3 is the primary alternative. This leads to a somewhat dull, symmetrical play in the opening, but the game can explode in fireworks later, as you can see in the game Rotlevi–Rubinstein, one of the finest masterpieces. In any case, by locking the bishop at c1 behind the e-pawn, White gives up any hope of building an attack and Black can develop in an atmosphere of peace and quiet.

4...exd5.

We now see that Black has a semi–open e-file ready to use once Black manages to castle and bring the rook to e8.

5.Nf3.

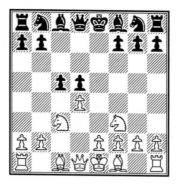

The only logical move, really.

5.e3 leads to a particularly poor form of the opening for White. Just compare the power of the bishop at c8 to the shut–in at c1!

5.dxc5 is the Tarrasch Gambit, and while it is not completely harmless, Black obtains a superior game with correct play.

5.e4 is the unsound Marshall Gambit. A solid defense is presented in our illustrative game.

5...Nc6.

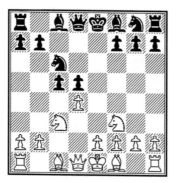

In the Tarrasch, you usually develop your knights in alphabetical order. If Black plays casually with 5...Nf6, White gets a good game with 6.Bg5!, as I found out to my discomfort against British Grandmaster Tony Miles many years ago.

6.g3.

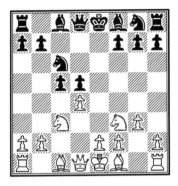

This is the most logical formation. The bishop will come to g2 and put additional pressure at d5.

6.Bg5 Be7; 7.Bxe7 Ngxe7 is nothing special for White, but you should make certain that you are familiar with the theory and ideas as explained in our illustrative game.

6.Bf4 is completely harmless. The bishop does not operate effectively from this square.

6...Nf6.

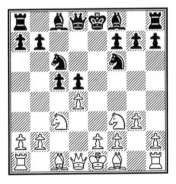

Notice how our opening follows the classical wisdom of developing a few pawns in the center and then bringing out knights before bishops!

7.Bg2.

The position of the bishop at g2 gives Black two strategic possibilities. Since the bishop no longer protects the pawn at e2, that pawn can easily become a target. This is especially true in the main lines. In addition, Black can set up a battery of bishop and queen on the c8–h3 diagonal and play ...Bh3 as part of a kingside attack. However, the bishop not only aims at d5, but can also place annoying pressure at c6 and b7. That is why it is considered a particularly powerful weapon. Once in a while, it can maneuver into a position to attack the Black kingside, as seen in Kasparov–Gavrikov, page 42.

7...Be7.

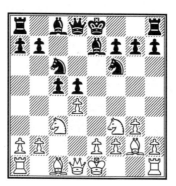

Some players try to delay this, so that if White captures at c5, no tempo is lost. That is logical, but impractical, since White need not capture there at all. It is time to get ready to castle, and in any case there really aren't any acceptable alternatives. It is much too early to determine the best square for the bishop at c8, and if you bring it to the wrong square, you would still have to give up a tempo to reposition it later.

8.0–0 0–0.

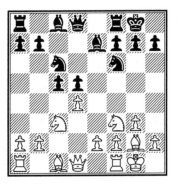

Not much to say about castling. It's available and it is good, so just do it! Here White has a wide range of possibilities. These will be examined in individual games but here is a quick overview.

9.Bg5.

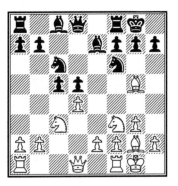

White places pressure at f6, and thereby undermines the support of the weak pawn at d5. This move, and the immediate capture at c5, are the most promising continuations for White and one of the two is almost always the choice of a top player.

Black can respond with one of three strategies: a central exchange, advance of the c-pawn or passive defense with ...Be6. All three are playable and when you have played the Tarrasch for over a decade, as I have, you may wish to explore all three. Defending the ...Be6 lines requires a lot of endgame skill, so it is not for amateurs. The ...c4 lines are very sharp and to be honest, White should be able to gain an advantage against it. So we will stick with the central exchange ...cxd4, which is the traditional main line and bears the greatest similarity to other lines in our repertoire.

9.dxc5.

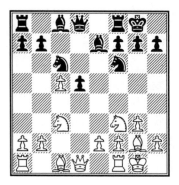

This is equal in popularity to the Bg5 line, and after Black recaptures at c5. White usually play 10.Bg5. The old line with 9...d4 is now considered refuted, and I haven't played it in a dozen years, when the line I considered Black's last, best hope was refuted in a game I played in an international tournament in London. The advance of the d-pawn is a key part of Black's strategy, but there is no need to sacrifice a pawn to achieve it.

9.b3.

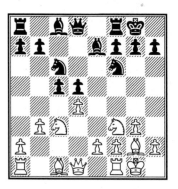

The queenside fianchetto was popular until the mid–1980s, when Garry Kasparov won convincing games as Black during his World Championship ascent. This variation can be a lot of fun for Black, as you can see in my game against Meins.

9.Be3.

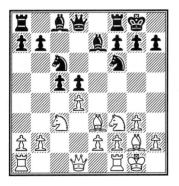

This is an odd–looking move but the idea is to place as much pressure as possible at c5. Black can get a reasonable game by placing either bishop or knight at g4. The capture at d4 can be played, but by contrast with the 9.Bg5 cxd4; 10.Nxd4 h6; 11.Be3 line, which is the principal variation of the Tarrasch, Black suffers from the lack of "luft" for the king, and back rank mates can become a problem.

9.Bf4.

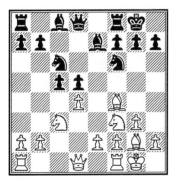

The bishop does not belong here and Black can play an early ...Bd6 if the need arises to defend the dark squares. By developing the bishop from c8 and placing a rook there, typical Tarrasch strategy, Black gets a good game.

No other moves need to be taken seriously and require special preparation. Just bring a rook to e8 and c8, after moving the bishop from c8 to some useful square. Moves such as ...Ne4 and ...Qa5 can be played where appropriate. Just head for the normal pawn structures, capturing at d4 when the time is right.

STRATEGIC GOALS OF THE OPENING

All good chessplayers understand the basic ideas which underlie sound opening play. They are not always easy to articulate, and it must never be forgotten that principles often come into conflict, and should never be followed unthinkingly. Consider them as mere guidelines or good advice, and follow them as often as you can.

Black's goals in the Tarrasch Defense are very simple. First of all, Black will develop pieces as quickly as possible. First we place three pawns in or near the center at d5, e6, and c5. Let's concentrate on the Black side. We will ignore White's formation, for the moment.

Next, the knights are developed.

Then the dark–squared bishop moves to allow castling.

After castling the position, the light–squared bishop can be determined. Usually by this time White has played cxd5 and we have answered with ...exd5.

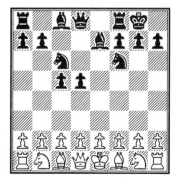

The result is a flexible piece formation which can be used to attack on all three areas of the board. On the queenside the c-file is used either to advance the c-pawn or as a highway for rooks headed to the seventh rank. In the center, d4 is the target. Either Black will advance an isolated d-pawn to d4, or will try to aim pieces at a White pawn on that square, using a knight at c6 and bishop at f6, b6 or a7. In most cases, Black can use the e4–square for a knight, pointing at the vulnerable f2–squares.

On the kingside, many attacking formations are possible. Black can use the dark squared bishop on the b8-h2 diagonal or a7–g1 diagonal. Knights operate from e4 and e5, and the queen usually enters at h4 or f6. Rooks can join the action via ...Rc6 (or 36)–g6 but also commonly attack from the side on the seventh rank.

Black has a flexible position with comfortable development. Therefore it is important to keep the pieces well coordinated throughout the opening and early middlegame. Sometimes this may involve sacrificing a pawn, and as a general rule it is better to give up a pawn than to fall into a passive defense.

THE ISOLATED D-PAWN

Much has been written on the most famous "isolani" of all, the isolated d-pawn. Siegbert Tarrasch was convinced that the traditional evaluation of an isolated pawn, that it is a major weakness, was wrong and that the isolated pawn was in fact a strong weapon. Let's first look at the pawn structure by itself.

If the game came down to a king and pawn endgame, Black would be in real trouble. The pawn at d5 is weak, and can easily be blockaded by an enemy king at d4. In fact, the blockade is the best-known strategy for operating against an isolated d-pawn is to blockade it with a piece, usually a knight.

When there is a White piece at d4, the Black pawn cannot advance the pawn from d5 and White can aim other pieces at it. Extreme views have been expressed on the subject of the "isolani". The great Hypermodern strategist Aron Nimzowitsch considered the blockade to be a potent weapon against the isolani, rendering it very weak. For Tarrasch, on the other hand, the isolani is a source of dynamic strength, because it cramps the enemy position. In any case, there is no doubt that the isolani has "the lust to expand". It wants to move forward whenever possible. Modern thinking holds that the isolani is neither good nor bad in isolation, but must be judged depending on the surrounding circumstances.

Dynamic players such as Korchnoi and Kasparov have been willing, and even eager, to accept an isolated d-pawn, while more positional players such as Karpov and Andersson are reluctant to play with an isolani and are more often found battling against it. In any case, there is hardly a Grandmaster who lacks a strong feeling one way or another!

From our point of view, as Black, the isolani provides us with many tactical and strategic possibilities. In the worst case, it will sit passively at d5 until it is swept off the board by the White army. Even then, however, many of the resulting endgames are merely drawn, and not lost, as we will see in examples later in the book.

THE BEST SQUARES FOR YOUR PIECES

As Black in the Tarrasch Defense you have a clear picture of how your forces are going to be deployed. We already discussed Black's ideal formation. Here it is again.

King

The King should be castled on the kingside after the pawn trio (e6, d5, c5), knights, and dark–squared bishops have been developed. Generally, you will want to keep the king at g8 and not hide it in the corner at h8 because there it is further from the center. Since many Tarrasch games make the transition into the endgame phase, your king must be able to return to the center quickly once enough pieces have been removed from the board to make it safe to do so.

Queen

The queen should not be developed until it can perform a genuinely useful function. Usually a5, c7 and e7 can be used as a home for the queen, while both f6 and b6 can be considered as temporary resting places. Since endgames with an isolated d-pawn can be difficult to defend, it is better to keep the queens on the board in the early middlegame. An exchange of queens is only recommended if you are going to receive some tangible value, such as material or the repair of your own pawn structure.

Rooks

The placement of the rooks is one of the trickiest questions in chess, and in the Tarrasch both sides must wrestle with this difficult puzzle. After castling, the rooks are usually at a8. Leaving aside the queen and minor pieces, which are developed early in the game, we have the following structure.

It is clear that rooks should be on the c–, d–, and e-files as these files are either open or contain a weak pawn which might be a target for enemy operations. Unfortunately, each side has only two rooks, and three files are therefore one too many. The queen can help out, but often she is off on other errands. Careful study of the illustrative games will give you a good idea of the possibilities.

Bishops

Bishops are a pleasure to deal with in the Tarrasch. Both bishops have an easy time developing.

The dark–squared bishop belongs at e7, and even if it has to capture a White pawn at c5 (a result of d4xc5) it often retreats to e7 when attacked. The c5 square is no place for a bishop, since it can be attacked by Rc1, Qc2, Na4 or Ne4. The bishop, which starts the game at c8, is often known as a "bad" bishop in the Queen's Gambit Declined because 2...e6 limit its powers. In the Tarrasch the e-pawn is usually removed by an early central exchange, and the bishop can be stationed at e6, in defense of the center, or at g4, attacking either a knight at f3 or a pawn at e2. When supported by a queen at d7 or c8, the bishop can go to h3 to attack an enemy bishop at g2. The bishop sometimes goes to f5 to attack a White knight at e4.

The light-squared bishop should only sit at e6 if the defense of the pawn at d5 is essential. This is usually the result of an error on Black's part, since passive defense is not part of the strategy of the Tarrasch. If the Black pawn has advanced from d5 to d4, however, then a bishop at e6 enjoys a wide perspective on both sides of the board and can be quite strong.

The bishop goes directly to g4, to pressure an enemy pawn at e2.

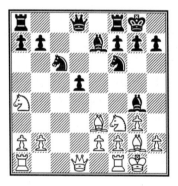

Even if there is a knight at f3, it is still uncomfortable for White, because the knight at f3 helps to support the center. Black now has the option of capturing it. In addition, Black can establish a battery of queen and knight, taking control of the h3-square.

Knights

In the Tarrasch Defense, the Black knights are quickly placed on c6 and f6, and these are their best positions, keeping pressure at d4 and e4. The knight at c6 is often captured by a White knight at e5, bringing the pawn from b7 to a more vulnerable position at c6.

The backward pawn at c6 is not a real weakness, but White can easily control c5 and occupy it with a minor piece. This gives White important control over enemy territory.

Pawns

Each advance of a pawn creates weaknesses in the pawn structure, which can be exploited by enemy pieces. Black must be especially careful to pay heed to this during the opening, as pawn weaknesses on the flanks can give White more targets, and defending those targets may leave Black without enough firepower to protect the isolated d-pawn.

Note that all of the general remarks about the Tarrasch Defense refer to the main lines where White exchanges the c-pawn for Black's e-pawn by capturing cxd5 early in the game.

The a-pawn belongs at home throughout the opening and early middlegame. Advance it only when White has a pawn at b3, or when you have no other choice. This applies to the normal variations. In special cases, such as the Symmetrical Variation, there may be a useful role for this pawn at a6.

Just leave the b-pawn alone unless you have a very good reason for moving it. The control of the c6–square is of great importance, as we have seen in our discussion of Tarrasch strategy.

The use of the c-pawn is partly a matter of style. In the approach to the Tarrasch Defense advocated in this book, the pawn rarely advances to c4. I personally enjoy using the riskier lines with ...c4 in my own games, and that system will be explored in detail in a forthcoming book, but here we will stick with the traditional strategy of central exchange with ...cxd4.

The famous isolated d-pawn has already been discussed in detail, as it is the heart and soul of the Tarrasch Defense. Remember that you must not treat it as a weakling requiring constant care. It is a weapon, and you want to use it to pierce White's defensive armor. Advance to d4 and gain more space for your pieces. Get the pawn to d3 and you will either challenge White's e-pawn or severely cramp White's position. If the pawn reaches d2, you are usually winning!

The e-pawn normally disappears early in the game, but can magically reappear later if White is allowed to capture a bishop or knight at e6 and force the recapture with the f-pawn. In this case the e-pawn will be very weak, and you will have to keep a close eye on it.

Don't move the f-pawn! It must stay in place to defend the castled king and also to cover e6, in case you decide to place a bishop there.

In the Tarrasch Defense, you do not fianchetto a bishop at g7 under any normal situations, so keep the pawn on that square.

As a general rule, White is not able to launch a kingside attack in the Tarrasch Defense, at least in the normal lines where White fianchettoes a bishop at g2. Therefore advancing the h-pawn to h6 does not create a major weakness, and this is often a useful move to battle for control for the g5–square. A pawn at h6 also allows the king to escape from the back rank, and there are a lot of tactical tricks that are no longer available to White.

TYPICAL STRATEGIES AND TACTICS

In this section we examine typical tactical devices available to both sides. These patterns can often turn up in the early middlegame, so it is a good idea to pay close attention to these positions as well as those you encounter as you work your way through the illustrative games. The following games illustrate a wide range of tactical devices. They are presented in full, so that you can see how each position arose from the Tarrasch structure. You can use these positions as targets, when searching for candidate moves in your games. Also note the mistake which leads to the target position.

It is worth reviewing these positions from time to time, especially before going into battle in tournament competition. Whenever you fall into a trap, or execute on against your opponent, write it out and include it in a notebook. Treat those games just as you do the examples presented below.

TACTICS FOR BLACK

We will first look at tactics from the Black side, beginning with the game, Demetriescu-Nagy as our first example.

DEMETRIESCU VS. NAGY
Postal, 1936

The advance of Black's d-pawn to d3 can be used to clear the d4 square for occupation by a knight. If it does so while attacking an enemy piece, it is a powerful combinational device.

1.c4 e6; 2.d4 d5; 3.Nc3 c5; 4.cxd5 exd5; 5.Nf3 Nc6; 6.g3 Nf6; 7.Bg2 Be7; 8.0-0 0-0; 9.dxc5 d4; 10.Na4 Bf5; 11.Bd2 Be4; 12.Nh4? This seriously weakens f3, h3, and g2.

12...Bxg2; 13.Nxg2 Ne4; 14.Qc2!

14...d3! Black wins a piece. **15.exd3 Nd4; 16.Qd1 Nxd2; 17.Qxd2? Nf3+!** Black won.

BURN VS. LASKER
Hastings, 1895

This is a classic example from one of the greatest tournaments of all time. Black uses a demolition sacrifice to strip away the pawn barrier on the a7-g1 diagonal.

1.d4 d5; 2.c4 e6; 3.Nf3 Nf6; 4.Nc3 c5; 5.e3 Nc6; 6.cxd5 exd5; 7.Bd3 a6; 8.dxc5 Bxc5; 9.0-0 0-0; 10.Bd2 Re8; 11.Rc1 Ba7; 12.Ne2 Bg4; 13.Bc3 Ne4; 14.Ng3.

The White king seems to have plenty of defenses, but the pressure at e3 and f2 is too great. **14...Nxf2; 15.Rxf2 Rxe3; 16.Nf5 Rxf3; 17.gxf3 Bxf5; 18.Bxf5 Qg5+; 19.Bg4 h5; 20.Qd2 Be3.** Black won.

HANSEN VS. NIELSEN
Alborg, 1947

When White moves the knight from f3 to e5, this undermines the support of d4. This can be exploited, especially when the White king is at g1 and the f-pawn has been advanced.

1.d4 d5; 2.c4 e6; 3.Nc3 c5; 4.cxd5 exd5; 5.Nf3 Nc6; 6.g3 Nf6; 7.Bg2 Be7; 8.0-0 0-0; 9.Bg5 Be6; 10.Rc1 c4; 11.Ne5 Rc8; 12.f4.

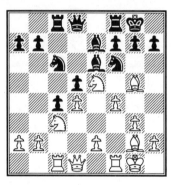

The d4–square is weaker than it looks! **12...Nxd4; 13.Bxf6** (13.Qxd4?? Bc5) **13...gxf6; 14.Nf3 Nf5; 15.Qd2 Bc5+. Black won.**

LEMPEREUR VS. FAVRE
Chamberg, 1978

The a8-h1 diagonal is usually pretty secure for White, but sometimes the departure of the knight from f3 opens up tactics.

1.Nf3 d5; 2.g3 c5; 3.Bg2 Nc6; 4.d4 e6; 5.0-0 Nf6; 6.c4 Be7; 7.cxd5 exd5; 8.Nc3 0-0; 9.dxc5 d4; 10.Na4 Bf5; 11.Bf4 Be4; 12.Ne5??

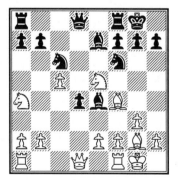

White forgets that Black can use the d5 square for the queen. **12...Bxg2; 13.Kxg2 Nxe5. Black won.** If 14.Bxe5, then 14...Qd5+.

NOGUEIRAS VS. VERA
Havana, 1982

The f2-square is always a target. The typical attack involves a knight at g4, or, better, e4, and a bishop or queen on the a7-g1 diagonal. **1.d4 d5; 2.c4 e6; 3.Nc3 c5; 4.cxd5 exd5; 5.Nf3 Nc6; 6.g3 Nf6; 7.Bg2 Be7; 8.0–0 0–0; 9.Be3 Bg4; 10.h3 Bxf3; 11.Bxf3 Qd7; 12.Bg2 Rad8; 13.Bg5 Ne4; 14.Bxe7 Qxe7; 15.dxc5 Qxc5; 16.Rc1.**

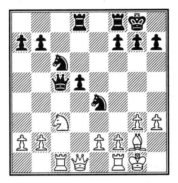

The pin on the f-pawn leads to material gain for Black. **16...Nxg3; 17.Ne4 Qxc1; 18.Qxc1 Nxe2+. Black won.**

MASMEIJER VS. WEYERSTRASS
Match, 1983

Here is another example of the weakness of f2. The rook at f1 sometimes has defensive duties at f2 and along the back rank, in which case it is hard to perform both jobs effectively.

1.d4 e6; 2.c4 d5; 3.Nc3 c5; 4.cxd5 exd5; 5.Nf3 Nc6; 6.g3 Nf6; 7.Bg2 Be7; 8.0–0 0–0; 9.Bg5 Be6; 10.dxc5 Bxc5; 11.Rc1 Bb6; 12.a3 h6; 13.Bxf6 Qxf6; 14.Na4 Rfd8; 15.b4 Rac8; 16.Qd3 Ne5.

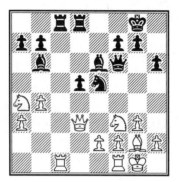

The rook at f1 is overworked. It needs to defend its colleague at c1, but must also guard f2. **17.Nxe5 Bxf2+!!; 18.Rxf2 Rxc1+; 19.Bf1 Qxe5; 20.Rf4 Bh3. Black won.**

STORLAND VS. BOE
Randaberg, 1988

The sacrifice of the exchange at a8 is not a common theme, but it does turn up when Black has compensating play in the center and on the queenside. In this example, Black exploits several themes to gain the advantage, but the focus, perhaps surprisingly from the diagrammed position, is at e2.

1.d4 d5; 2.c4 e6; 3.Nc3 c5; 4.cxd5 exd5; 5.g3 Nc6; 6.Nf3 Nf6; 7.Bg2 Be7; 8.0-0 0-0; 9.Bg5 cxd4; 10.Nxd4 h6; 11.Bf4 Qb6; 12.Ndb5??

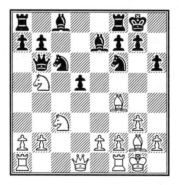

The position of the knight is precarious. Infiltration at c7 looks possible but Black has some resources that show just how bad White's situation really is. **12...d4!; 13.Nc7 dxc3; 14.Nxa8 Qxb2; 15.Nc7 Rd8;**

16.Qb3 Nd4; 17.Qxb2 cxb2; 18.Rab1 Nxe2+; 19.Kh1 Nxf4; 20.Rxb2 Nxg2. **Black won.**

SCHUBERT VS. SCHLECHTER
Vienna, 1915

The White pawn at e2 is always a target, even when it seems to be well protected. The e3-square can also play an important role. In this next example, both come into play.

1.d4 d5; 2.Nf3 c5; 3.c4 e6; 4.cxd5 exd5; 5.Nc3 Nf6; 6.g3 Nc6; 7.Bg2 Be6; 8.0-0 Be7; 9.Bg5 0-0; 10.dxc5 Bxc5; 11.Rc1 Be7; 12.Nd4 h6; 13.Be3 Ng4; 14.Nxe6 fxe6.

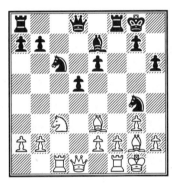

White impulsively exchanged his knight for the bishop at e6. The temptation of the bishop pair was great, but Black has a very strong center. The open f-file is the source of counterplay.

15.Bh3 Nxe3! The e-pawn falls with check, but does not significantly alter the picture. **16.Bxe6+ Kh8; 17.fxe3 Bg5!** Sooner or later the e-pawn must fall. **18.Nxd5 Qd6; 19.Bh3 Rxf1+; 20.Kxf1 Rd8; 21.Bg2 Ne7; 22.h4 Nxd5; 23.Bxd5 Bxe3; 24.Rc3 Qxg3. Black won.**

SMEJKAL VS. MARJANOVIC
Vrsac, 1977

As in most openings, it is easy for Black to go wrong and get stuck in an ugly, passive position. It is important to know some defensive plans that can be employed. Often, the d-pawn must be sacrificed while a solid defense is erected. Here is an instructive example.

1.c4 e6; 2.Nf3 d5; 3.d4 c5; 4.cxd5 exd5; 5.g3 Nc6; 6.Bg2 Nf6; 7.0-0 Be7; 8.Nc3 0-0; 9.Bg5 cxd4; 10.Nxd4 h6; 11.Be3 Bg4; 12.Qa4 Qd7; 13.Rfd1 Bh3; 14.Bh1 Rfd8; 15.Nb3 Qf5; 16.Qb5 Rd7; 17.Nd4.

White achieved most of the necessary goals in the opening. Development is completed with Rac1, and there is pressure at c6 and d5.

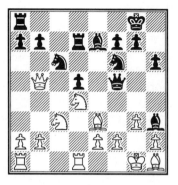

Still, Black is able to set up a viable defense.
17...Nxd4; 18.Rxd4 Rad8; 19.Rad1 b6!

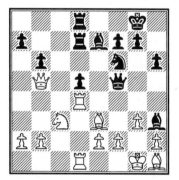

This is the key move in the defensive plan. **20.Bxd5 Bc5; 21.Be4.** White has no advantage after. **21...Nxe4; 22.Rxd7 Rxd7; 23.Qxd7 Qxd7; 24.Rxd7 Bxd7; 25.Nxe4 Be7** since the bishop pair is as valuable as White's extra pawn. **Drawn.**

LANGE VS. MULLER
Postal, 1989

When Black has a bishop at f6, the a1-h8 diagonal can be the source of great counterplay, especially when supported by a knight at e4, as here. **1.Nf3 d5; 2.c4 e6; 3.g3 Nf6; 4.Bg2 c5; 5.cxd5 exd5; 6.0-0 Be7; 7.d4 0-0; 8.Nc3 Nc6; 9.b3 Ne4; 10.Bb2 Bf6; 11.Na4 Re8.**

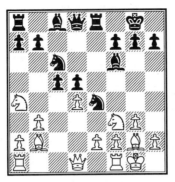

It is not easy to see just how weak the c3–square really is! **12.dxc5??
Bxb2; 13.Nxb2 Nc3; 14.Qd2 Nxe2+; 15.Kh1 Bg4!** Now f3 comes
under attack as well. **16.Rfe1 Qf6; 17.Rxe2 Bxf3; 18.Ree1 Re4;
19.Nd3 Rae8; 20.Nf4 Qb2. Black won.**

HALLGRIMSSON VS. LAREN
Postal, 1990

White's bishop at e3 can be an inviting target, even when the g4-
square is covered and inaccessible to the Black knight.

**1.d4 d5; 2.c4 e6; 3.Nc3 c5; 4.cxd5 exd5; 5.Nf3 Nc6; 6.g3 Nf6;
7.Bg2 Be7; 8.0–0 0–0; 9.Bg5 cxd4; 10.Nxd4 Re8; 11.h3 h6; 12.Be3
Bd6; 13.a3.**

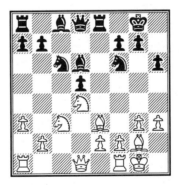

The bishop at e3 is defended only by the f-pawn, inviting
13...Bxg3! 14.Bxh6 Bc7; 15.Bc1 Nxd4; 16.Qxd4 Qd6. Black won.

GILLEFALK VS. LARSSON
Unknown, 1992

Along White's second rank, both b2 and e2 often act as targets.
1.d4 d5; 2.c4 e6; 3.Nf3 c5; 4.cxd5 exd5; 5.g3 Nc6; 6.Bg2 Nf6; 7.0-0 Be7; 8.Nc3 0-0; 9.Bg5 cxd4; 10.Nxd4 h6; 11.Bf4 Bg4; 12.Qa4 Qd7; 13.Rfd1 Rfd8; 14.Ndb5.

Black can use a temporary pawn sacrifice to get to the weak squares along the seventh rank. **14...d4; 15.Bxc6 Qxc6; 16.Nxd4 Qb6; 17.Ndb5 Bh3; 18.Nc7 Ng4; 19.e3 Qxb2; 20.Ne4 Qe2. Black won.**

TACTICS FOR WHITE

Now we turn our attention to White's viewpoint, and see what the thinking is from that side of the board.

KASPAROV VS. GAVRIKOV
Frunze, 1981

Need some fuel for your nightmares? This game, one of the greatest demolitions of the Tarrasch of all time, should be studied time and time again to observe the many different tactics Kasparov employs. There are many lessons here, but one of the most important is the need to keep control of c6.

1.d4 d5; 2.c4 e6; 3.Nf3 c5; 4.cxd5 exd5; 5.g3 Nc6; 6.Bg2 Nf6; 7.0-0 Be7; 8.dxc5 Bxc5; 9.Bg5 0-0; 10.Nc3 d4; 11.Bxf6 Qxf6; 12.Nd5 Qd8; 13.Nd2 a6? This attempt to preserve the bishop by retreating to a7 has been discredited.

14.Rc1 Ba7; 15.Nc4 Rb8; 16.Nf4 b5.

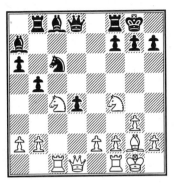

Black looks solid, but c6 is a weakness for White to exploit.
17.Nd6! Qxd6; 18.Rxc6 Qd8; 19.Qc2 a5; 20.Rc1 Re8; 21.Bd5.

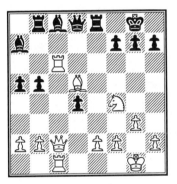

The bishop at g2 rarely gets to participate in a kingside attack, but in this game Kasparov uses the powerful cleric to rip apart Black's position. Just watch the bishop constantly shift and find new targets.
21...Bb6; 22.Qb3 Re7; 23.Bf3 Re5; 24.Bh5! g6.

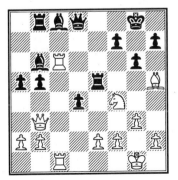

Now there is devastation on the light squares. **25.Bxg6!! hxg6; 26.Rxg6+ Kf8; 27.Rh6 Ke7; 28.Rcc6 Rf5; 29.Qf3 Bc7; 30.Qe4+ Re5; 31.Ng6+ fxg6; 32.Rh7+ Kf8; 33.Qxg6. White won.**

SZYPULSKI VS. ZOLNIEROWICZ
Polish Championship, 1996

Black's kingside is often left without a lot of defense, and even with no weaknesses in the pawn structure, White can sometimes exploit this.

1.d4 e6; 2.Nf3 d5; 3.c4 c5; 4.cxd5 exd5; 5.g3 Nf6; 6.Bg2 Be7; 7.0-0 0-0; 8.dxc5 Bxc5; 9.Nc3 Nc6; 10.a3 a6; 11.b4 Ba7; 12.Bb2 Re8; 13.Rc1 Bg4; 14.Na4 Ne4; 15.Nc5 Nxc5; 16.bxc5 Qe7.

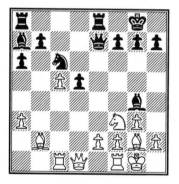

White does not seem to have a kingside attack, but the position holds more than meets the eye. **17.Qxd5 Qxe2; 18.Bxg7 Ne7.** If 18...Kxg7, then 19.Qg5f. **19.Qg5 Bxf3; 20.Bf6+. White won.**

MARSHALL VS. CORZO
Havana, 1913

Every beginner is taught to castle early in the game. Here is a reminder of what happens when you don't!

1.d4 d5; 2.c4 e6; 3.Nc3 c5; 4.cxd5 exd5; 5.Nf3 Nc6; 6.g3 Nf6; 7.Bg2 Be7; 8.0-0 h6?; 9.Bf4 Be6; 10.dxc5 Bxc5; 11.Rc1.

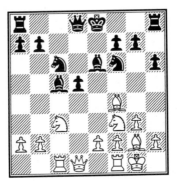

Black neglects castling and makes superficial developing moves. **11...a6; 12.Ne5 Bd6; 13.Qa4 Rc8; 14.Nxc6 Rxc6; 15.Nxd5 Nxd5; 16.Rxc6 Bxf4.**

Black didn't want to lose minor material, but now he must part with the queen. **17.Rc8+. White won.**

CASAS VS. PIAZZINI

Argentina, 1950

We must keep an eye on a number of critical squares in the Tarrasch. Along the c-file, both c6 and c5 are of importance. The latter is especially vulnerable, since we rarely want to weaken the queenside with ...b6.

1.d4 d5; 2.c4 e6; 3.Nc3 c5; 4.cxd5 exd5; 5.Nf3 Nc6; 6.g3 Nf6; 7.Bg2 Be7; 8.0-0 0-0; 9.dxc5 d4; 10.Na4 Bf5; 11.Bf4 Be4; 12.Rc1 Qd5; 13.Ne1 Bxg2; 14.Nxg2 Ne4; 15.a3 Nxc5; 16.Nxc5 Bxc5.

The bishop at c5 is insufficiently defended. **17.e4. White won.**

PALM VS. GEROLD
Postal, 1973

Since White has many opportunities to capture a bishop at e6 with a knight, forcing our f-pawn to move, we need to keep an eye on the potential vulnerability of the g6-square, which is exploited in this example.

1.c4 Nf6; 2.Nf3 e6; 3.g3 c5; 4.Bg2 d5; 5.cxd5 exd5; 6.0-0 Nc6; 7.d4 Be7; 8.Nc3 0-0; 9.Bg5 cxd4; 10.Nxd4 h6; 11.Be3 Re8; 12.Qa4 Na5; 13.Rad1 Bd7; 14.Qc2 Be6.

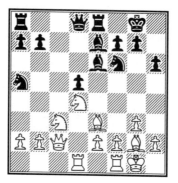

This is one position where the exchange at e6 cannot be offered safely. The g6 square becomes too vulnerable.

15.Nxe6 fxe; 16.Qg6 Kh8; 17.Ne4 Rf8; 18.Bxh6 gxh6; 19.Qxh6+ Nh7; 20.Qxe6. White won.

ASTOLFI VS. BRETON
Toulouse, 1990

We have already seen Kasparov take advantage of the weakness at c6. Here an amateur player provides an instructive lesson on the same theme.

1.d4 d5; 2.c4 e6; 3.Nc3 c5; 4.cxd5 exd5; 5.Nf3 Nc6; 6.g3 Nf6; 7.Bg2 Be7; 8.0-0 0-0; 9.Bg5 cxd4; 10.Nxd4 h6; 11.Bf4 a6; 12.Rc1 Be6; 13.Na4 Qa5.

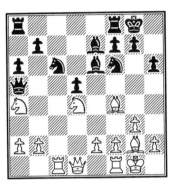

White now uses an exchange sacrifice to win material.

14.Rxc6! Bd7. 14...bxc6; 15.Nxc6 and the queen cannot protect the bishop at e7. 15.Bc7 Qb4; 16.a3. White won.

VAN DER BOOGAARD VS. KRUIZINGA
Postal, 1991

Although the isolated d-pawn can sometimes be sacrificed, it should not be allowed to drop off the board without compensation. White has many tricks, but the usual formula is to capture the supporting knight at f6 and a grab at d5.

1.d4 d5; 2.c4 e6; 3.Nc3 c5; 4.cxd5 exd5; 5.Nf3 Nc6; 6.g3 Nf6; 7.Bg2 Be7; 8.0-0 0-0; 9.Bg5 cxd4; 10.Nxd4 h6; 11.Be3 Qa5; 12.Qb3 Rd8; 13.Rfd1 Nxd4; 14.Bxd4 Bc5.

This allows the d-pawn to fall without compensation.

15.Bxf6. Black resigned, but after **15...gxf6; 16.Nxd5 Qa6; 17.Qc3,** Black's position is hopeless. **White won.**

TRANSPOSITIONAL POSSIBILITIES

1.d4

This is the traditional way of starting the game that ends up in the Tarrasch Defense. We'll consider several different paths, discussing the benefits and drawbacks of each. There are huge numbers of possible move orders, but the Tarrasch is hard to avoid. 1.c4 e6 is a perfectly reasonable method of reaching the Tarrasch, one I often use myself.

The only extra preparation needed is to take care to have a plan if White absolutely refuses to play the d-pawn to d4 choosing to place it at d3 instead. Then we have positions which usually arise from the Reti Opening or English Opening, but that is pretty much unavoidable after 1.c4 if White wants to stick to the flank formulas. Now 2.Nc3 (2.d4 d5; 3.Nc3 c5 arrives at the same position) 2...d5; 3.d4 c5 rejoins the main line at White's fourth move.

1.Nf3 d5; 2.g3 c5; 3.Bg2 Nc6; 4.d4 is a reversed Gruenfeld Defense. It can transpose to the Tarrasch after 4...e6; 5.0-0 Nf6; 6.c4 Be7; 7.cxd5 exd5; 8.Nc3 0-0.

1.g3 is rarely used to reach a Tarrasch, though it is possible. 1...d5. (1...e5 is the problem move. After that a Tarrasch is out of the question.) 2.Nf3 c5; 3.Bg2 Nc6; 4.d4 e6; 5.0-0 Nf6; 6.c4 Be7; 7.cxd5 exd5; 8.Nc3 0-0.

1.b3 (or 1.Nf3 and 2.b3), on the other hand, easily slips into the Tarrasch mold. For example, 1.b3 d5; 2.Nf3 c5; 3.Bb2 Nc6; 4.g3 Nf6; 5.Bg2 e6; 6.0-0.

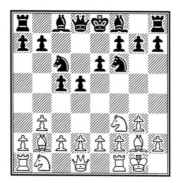

White is playing in true hypermodern style, refusing to occupy the center with pawns. Nevertheless, soon this must change. After 6...Be7. White can play 7.c4 0-0; 8.cxd5 and then on 8...exd5; 9.d4 we reach the Larsen Variation of the Classical Tarrasch (9.b3).

Jumping from the hypermodern to more traditional styles, 1.e4 seems a very strange way to start toward a Tarrasch. In fact, the pawn almost always stays at e2 or e3. But there is a twist to this story. Here, it is White who wants to play the Tarrasch, with an extra move. Believe it or not, this can be achieved in a very normal opening–the Caro–Kann Defense. 1...c6; 2.d4 d5; 3.exd5 cxd5; 4.c4. This is the Panov Attack. 4...Nf6; 5.Nc3 g6. (Black also plays 6...e6 and 6...Nc6.) 6.Nf3 Bg7; 7.Be2 0-0; 8.0-0 Nc6.

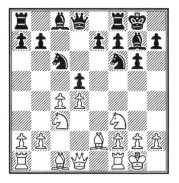

Now we have the Tarrasch Defense with colors reversed. The problem is that since Black has not yet made the fundamental choice of plans that is usually made at move 9, there really isn't a useful move. The position is about equal, which means that White has lost some of the opening advantage that comes with the privilege of moving first.

1...d5.

1...Nf6 is rarely used to set up a Tarrasch formation, since White can easily prevent it. Nevertheless, it is possible to reach the desired position: 2.c4 e6; 3.g3. This is the Catalan Opening, and it is not too difficult for the game to be led into Tarrasch territory.

3.Nf3 d5; 4.cxd5 exd5; 5.Bg5 is a quite different story.

This plan forces the game into the Exchange Variation of the Queen's Gambit Declined, not a particular favorite among Tarrasch fans. 3...d5; 4.Bg2 Be7; 5.Nf3 0-0; 6.0-0 c5; 7.cxd5 exd5; 8.Nc3 Nc6.

1. d4 e6; 2.c4 d5; 3.Nc3 c5 is a direct transposition to the Tarrasch, rejoining the main line at move 4. The drawback to the plan is that instead of 2.c4, White can play 2.e4, and then Black has been forced into the French Defense. That's fine, if you like playing the French, but those of us who enjoy the Tarrasch rarely feel comfortable when our bishop at c8 has no scope.

1...c5; 2.Nf3. Normally White plays 2.d5 here, leading to the Old Benoni Defense. 2...Nf6; 3.g3 Nc6; 4.Bg2 d5; 5.0-0 e6; 6.c4 Be7; 7.cxd5 exd5. (7...Nxd5 leads to the Semi–Tarrasch, in the lines known as the Keres–Parma Attack.)

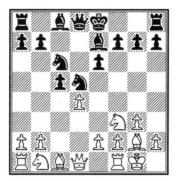

Here it is White who has an isolated pawn, instead of Black. Leaving this choice in Black's hands is, to my mind, an unacceptable situation for White. It is as if White gave Black the option of playing offense or defense! 8.Nc3 0–0 is another path.

2.c4.

2.Nf3 e6. (2...c5 is often avoided because Black is in effect playing a Queen's Gambit down a full tempo. Nevertheless, the only way White can take advantage of this is by capturing at c5, and Tarrasch himself proved long ago that Black has nothing to fear after 3.dxc5 e6.) 3.c4 c5; 4.cxd5 exd5 rejoins the 1.d4 d5; 2.c4 e6; 3.Nf3 c5; 4.cxd5 exd5 line at move 5.

2.g3 is not a common move order, because Black can set up a solid position with an early ...c6, defending the d5 pawn. 2...Nf6; 3.Bg2 e6; 4.c4 Be7; 5.Nf3. This transposes to the Catalan move order discussed under 1.d4 Nf6; 2.c4 e6; 3.g3. We reach the Classical Tarrasch with 5...0–0; 6.0–0 c5; 7.cxd5 exd5; 8.Nc3.

2...e6.

2...Nf6? 3.cxd5 Nxd5 is known to be better for White.
3.Nc3.

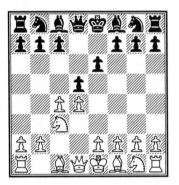

3.Nf3 is sometimes played in order to avoid the Schara Gambit. (1.d4 d5; 2.c4 e6; 3.Nc3 c5; 4.cxd5 cxd4, which is the subject of analysis in my *Gambit Opening Repertoire for Black.*) 3...c5; 4.cxd5 exd5; 5.g3 (5.Nc3 Nc6; 6.g3 Nf6; 7.Bg2 Be7; 8.0-0 0-0 is the third most common move order, but it drops to less than 4% of my Tarrasch database) 5...Nc6. (5...Nf6 is possible here, even though it is generally considered appropriate to develop the knights in "alphabetical order." The knight at b8 should move to c6 before the knight at g8 goes to f6. The difference is only significant when White already has a knight at c3, since there is additional pressure on the pawn at d5. 6.Bg2 Be7; 7.0-0 0-0; 8.Nc3 Nc6 has been played 43 times.) 6.Bg2 Nf6; 7.0-0 Be7; 8.Nc3 0-0 is the second most popular move order, seen almost 7% of the time.

3...c5.

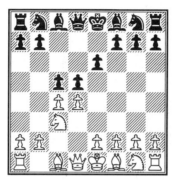

4.cxd5. The advantage of this move is quite simple. By capturing immediately, White insures that Black will have to recapture with the pawn. If the exchange is delayed, Black can often recapture with a knight from f6, and that leads to the Semi–Tarrasch Opening. The important difference is that, it is White, not Black, who must accept the isolated pawn.

Although this is far and away the most popular route, it does have one significant drawback. Black can reply not by recapturing at d5, but instead by capturing the White pawn at d4, leading to the sharp Schara Gambit. This possibility alone is enough to deter many players from adopting the canonical move order.

4...exd5.

The crucial lines of the Schara Gambit are not part of our repertoire, but let's see what "trouble" White can get into. 4...cxd4; 5.Qa4+ (5.Qxd4 Nc6; 6.Qd1 exd5; 7.Qxd5 Be6; 8.Qxd8+ Rxd8; 9.e3 Nb4; 10.Bb5+ Ke7; 11.Kf1 g5 has not been clearly evaluated. Black's king is safe and the minor pieces can play active roles which provide compensation for the pawn) 5...Bd7; 6.Qxd4 exd5; 7.Qxd5 Nc6; 8.Nf3 Nf6; 9.Qd1 Bc5; 10.e3 Qe7; 11.Be2 g5; 12.0–0 g4; 13.Nd4 0–0–0.

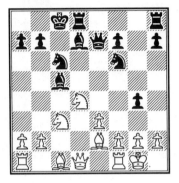

This is a messy position and both sides can aim for the enemy king. Not the sort of brawl a quiet positional player likes.

5.Nf3.

5.g3 Nf6; 6.Bg2 Nc6; 7.Nf3 Be7; 8.0–0 0–0 can also be used, but it is a less flexible move order.

5...Nc6.

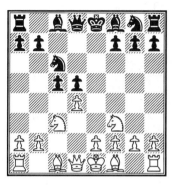

5...Nf6 is a mistake. After 6.Bg5! Black is under pressure. **6.g3.**

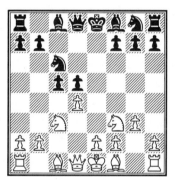

For many decades this has been considered the true test of the Tarrasch Defense. White logically stations the bishop at g2, where it can take aim at the isolated pawn at d5. **6...Nf6.**

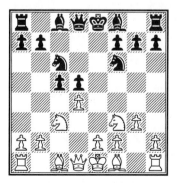

A straightforward move, adding to the defense of the pawn at d5. **7.Bg2.** At this point the next few moves are relatively automatic. **7...Be7; 8.0–0 0–0.**

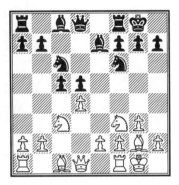

And here we are! The path we took as our main line was seen in over 500 games, more than one third of our collection. That may not seem like much, but the second most popular order was seen in only 7% of the games. So we take this as our canonical move order, the one we'll use as a reference. The story does not end here, however.

White has many choices at the next turn, and some of those may "collect" transpositions that diverged from our main line a long time ago. For example, at many points White can play dxc5, and Black can capture with the bishop. Then we would reach the position seen via our normal move order and one more move–pair.

9.dxc5 Bxc5.

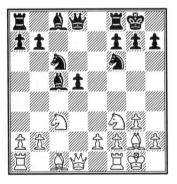

The mysteries of this position have been probed in hundreds of games, as we'll see later in the sections on the Classical Tarrasch Defense.

CLASSICAL TARRASCH

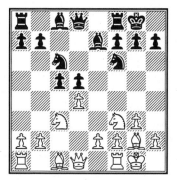

1.d4	d5
2.c4	e6
3.Nc3	c5
4.cxd5	exd5
5.Nf3	Nc6
6.g3	Nf6
7.Bg2	Be7
8.0–0	0–0

The Classical Variations are by far the most common. As we have already seen, they can be reached by many different move orders. This is especially true of the lines with dxc5 or b3 for White.

In this section, we will consider the following plans for White.

1. White plays 9.Bg5
2. White plays 9.dxc5
3. White plays 9.b3
4. White plays 9.Bf4
5. White plays 9.Be3, and other moves

White plays 9.Bg5

1.d4 d5; 2.c4 e6; 3.Nc3 c5; 4.cxd5 exd5; 5.Nf3 Nc6; 6.g3 Nf6; 7.Bg2 Be7; 8.0-0 0-0; 9.Bg5.

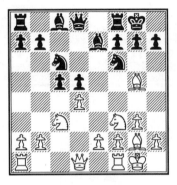

This move is very popular because it works to undermine the support of the critical d5–square. White's goal is simple: to win the d-pawn. The simple threat is Bxf6 followed by Nxd5.

Black has three different replies. We will adopt the central exchange strategy, which is most consistent with the Tarrasch strategy. The alternatives are the advance of the c-pawn to c4, which is considered very risky, and the passive line with 9...Be6, which leads to an endgame in which Black is fighting for a draw.

After 9...cxd4, play usually continues **10.Nxd4 h6; 11.Be3 Re8**, after which White has many different moves. We will examine all of the major plans in these illustrative games, and in the game Vadasz–Nunn in the Heroes chapter. The plans include developing the queen at b3, c2 or a4 developing a rook at c1 capturing one of the knights or advancing the a-pawn.

Overview of White's plans:

> 1) 12.Rc1 is Kramnik vs. Illescas Cordoba
> 2) 12.Qb3 is Karpov vs. Kasparov
> 3) 12.Qa4 is Belyavsky vs. Kasparov
> 4) 12.Qc2 is Belyavsky vs. Kasparov
> 5) 12.a3 is Smyslov vs. Kasparov
> 6) 11.Bxf6 is Seirawan vs. Kasparov
> 7) 12.Nxc6 is Vadasz vs. Nunn (Heroes Chapter)

KRAMNIK VS. ILLESCAS CORDOBA
Linares, 1994

1.c4 c5; 2.Nf3 Nf6; 3.Nc3 e6; 4.g3 Nc6; 5.Bg2 d5; 6.cxd5 exd5; 7.d4 Be7; 8.0–0 0–0; 9.Bg5 cxd4; 10.Nxd4 h6; 11.Be3 Re8; 12.Rc1.

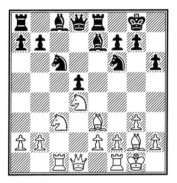

Since the c-file is where the action is, White wastes no time and brings the powerful rook to the open file. There is no immediate threat, and Black can prepare to operate on the e-file with **12...Bf8.**

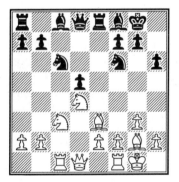

White has many plans here. In general, White is going to try to place a knight at c5, and can exchange at c6 to create a big hole at c5. Our bishop at f8 keeps an eye on the square, but sooner or later White will be able to achieve the goal. We will concentrate on the immediate application of the strategy, moving the knight from c3 to a4, where it can get to c5 in one leap.

13.Na4.

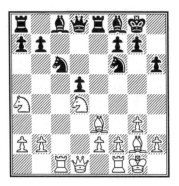

This is a very topical move and was chosen by Burgess & Pedersen as the most promising line for White in their book, *The Queen's Gambit for the Attacking Player.*

We must consider a number of alternatives, however. White can capture on c6, take control of b4 by advancing the a-pawn, develop a rook at e1 for eventual support of the pawn at e2, or initiate queenside play with Nb5 or Qb3.

A) 13.Nxc6 bxc6; 14.Na4 Ng4!? This forces White to occupy c5 with the bishop, giving special flavor to the middlegame. 15.Bc5 (Others are inconsequential. 15.Bd4 Bd7; 16.Nc5 Bxc5 is fine for Black) 15 ...Bxc5. Black does not have to capture, but it is not a bad idea. 16.Nxc5 Qf6; 17.h3 Ne5; 18.e4 Rb8!; 19.b3 Rb5. Black has active play to compensate for the weak center. Timman–Gligoric, Niksic 1978.

B) 13.a3 is preferred by Karpov. This interesting plan is discussed in Heyl–Kahane in the Into the Future chapter.

C) 13.Re1 Bg4; 14.h3 Bh5; 15.Nf5 Bg6 is solid for Black.

D) 13.Ncb5 Bd7; 14.Nxc6 bxc6; 15.Nd4 c5; 16.Nb3 c4; 17.Nd2 gives Black the opportunity to blast open the position with an exchange sacrifice.

After 17...Rxe3; 18.fxe3 Bc5; 19.Kh1 Be6, White was at a loss for a good plan. The game continued 20.Rf3 Ng4; 21.e4 Qg5; 22.exd5 Bxd5; 23.e4 Be6; 24.Qe2 Rd8; 25.Rf4 Nf2+; 26.Rxf2 Bxf2; 27.Rd1 Bg4; 28.Bf3 Rxd2; 29.Rxd2 Bxf3+. White resigned, Doroshkievich–Riabchonok, Soviet Union 1969. Better is 20.e4! After 20...Be3, the position is unclear.

E) 13.Qb3 Na5; 14.Qc2 Bg4; 15.h3 Bh5; 16.b3 Ba3; 17.Rcd1 Bg6; 18.Qd2 Bb4; 19.Qb2 Rc8; 20.Ndb5 Rxe3; 21.fxe3 Qe7; 22.Nxd5 Nxd5; 23.Bxd5 a6; 24.a3 was drawn in Urban–Mintschev, European Postal Championship 1990.

13...Bd7. This is not the only move. You might consider the following as an alternative.

A) 13...Ng4! Is a good move if you want variety. 14.Nxc6 bxc6; 15.Bd4 Bd7; 16.Nc5 Bf5; 17.Re1 Qg5; 18.e4 dxe4; 19.Nxe4 Bxe4; 20.Rxe4 Rxe4; 21.Bxe4 was agreed drawn in Robatsch–Anikayev, Sochi 1974, and it is not clear where and how White should improve.

B) 13...Nxd4; 14.Bxd4 Bg4; 15.Re1 Bb4; 16.Nc3 Bxc3; 17.Bxc3 Ne4; 18.Bd4 Be6 gave Black a solid position in Muller–Weiss, Wurttemberg 1992.

14.Nc5. 14.Nxc6 bxc6; 15.Bc5 Bxc5; 16.Nxc5 Bg4; 17.Re1 is better for White, according to Hübner.

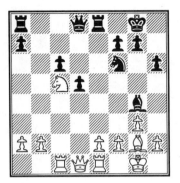

This is such a typical Tarrasch position that it is hard to believe that White has much. Black can just play on the b-file and or challenge the knight with Nd7. I'd be uncomfortable defending against a positional master such as Karpov, but otherwise the position ought to be playable over the board. When White occupies c5 immediately with the knight, we have the following picture.

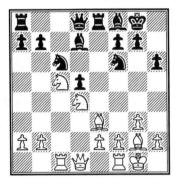

Black must play carefully here. Let's look at one way to go wrong. **14...Na5?!** is an instructive error. The knight winds up retreating to c6 a few moves later, an admission that the strategy has failed. In the Tarrasch you should not play ...Na5 unless you have a very concrete plan in mind. Fortunately, there are two alternative plans which I think are playable.

a) 14...Nxd4; 15.Bxd4 Bc6. Although it is passive, Black's position seems solid enough. 16.e3 Ne4; 17.b4 a5; 18.a3 axb4; 19.axb4 Bb5; 20.Re1 b6; 21.Nxe4 dxe4; 22.Bf1 Bxf1; 23.Rxf1 Re6 led to a draw in Schmidt–Kato, Tokyo 1990.

b) 14...Bxc5; 15.Nxc6 bxc6; 16.Bxc5 is better for White, according to Ftacnik, but after 16...Ne4 I don't see anything special.

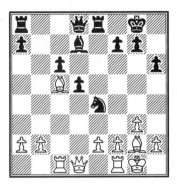

Black can continue with ...Qa5, ...Rab8. The center is solid and White's bishop at g2 is useless.

15.b3 Rc8; 16.Nxd7 Qxd7; 17.Qd3 Nc6; 18.Nxc6 bxc6.

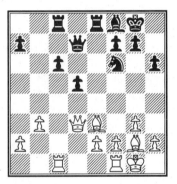

White's bishop pair and superior pawn structure provide a significant advantage. Perhaps Black can hold with perfect play, but life will be a struggle. **19.Rfd1 Qb7; 20.Bc5 Bxc5; 21.Rxc5 Qe7; 22.Rc2 Qa3; 23.e3 Red8; 24.Qf5 Rb8?!** 24...Qd6!? is more to the point. **25.Rxc6 Qxa2; 26.Rxf6 gxf6; 27.Bxd5 Rxd5; 28.Rxd5 Qxb3; 29.Qg4+?** 29.Kg2! White is better. **29...Kh7; 30.Rd6 Qb1+; 31.Kg2 Qg6; 32.Qf3 Kg7; 33.Ra6 Rb5;** 33...Rb4; 34.Rxa7 Qe4 is a tough draw, Black should hold the rook and pawn endgame. **34.Rxa7 Rf5; 35.Qe2 Qh5; 36.g4 Qg6; 37.Rxf7+ Kxf7; 38.Qc4+. Black resigned.**

What conclusions can we draw from this game? It was sloppily played by Black, and Illescas claimed that after White's 22nd move Black should be able to hold. Indeed, White's position is nothing special, and with correct play Black can hold. If this represents the worst for Black, there is no reason to avoid the line. 13...Ng4 requires further tests, and there are many plans for Black to explore at move 14.

KARPOV VS. KASPAROV
World Championship, 1984

1.d4 d5; 2.c4 e6; 3.Nf3 c5; 4.cxd5 exd5; 5.g3 Nf6; 6.Bg2 Be7; 7.0–0 0–0; 8.Nc3 Nc6; 9.Bg5 cxd4; 10.Nxd4 h6; 11.Be3 Re8; 12.Qb3.

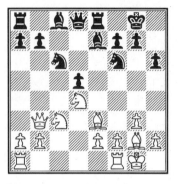

It is time for White to deploy the heavy artillery, and this move effectively adds pressure to d5, the weak point in Black's position.

12...Na5. In contrast to the previous game, the knight move actually accomplishes something. **13.Qc2 Bg4.** Logical, because it places counter–pressure at e2, the typical plan for Black in such structures.

Nevertheless, serious consideration should be given to occupying c4 with the knight. 13...Nc4 has been dismissed, but it may be playable after all, thanks to a plan involving the advance of the g-pawn if White occupies f4 with a bishop.

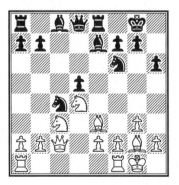

A) 14.Bf4 g5!?; 15.Bc1 Bg4; 16.Nf5 Bf8; 17.b3 Nd6; 18.Nxd6 Qxd6; 19.Bb2 Qe6; 20.Rad1 Rad8; 21.Nb5 Bg7; 22.Nd4 Qa6 with plenty of play for Black, and not much for White, Schirm–Borik, Bundesliga 1988.

B) 14.Nf5 Nxe3; 15.Nxe3 Be6; 16.Rad1 d4; 17.Qa4 Qb6; 18.Ned5 Bxd5; 19.Nxd5 Nxd5; 20.Bxd5 Bf6 is solid enough for Black, Schwanek–Almada, Mendoza 1985.

C) 14.Bc1 is best handled with 14...Bg4!

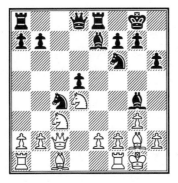

Black obtains an active position with this move. This situation is complicated and we should analyze concrete variations here. White can play on either flank or in the center. So many ways to go wrong!

C1) After 15.Rd1 Rc8, White can try 16.h3 (16.b3 is slow. 16...Nd6; 17.Bb2 Nde4; 18.Qd3 Bb4; 19.Nxe4 dxe4; 20.Qb5 Qe7; 21.Nf5 Bxf5; 22.Qxf5 Bc3 with a solid position for Black, Werner–Schubert, Germany 1984) 16...Bh5. (16...Bd7 is probably playable, for example 17.Nxd5 Ne3!; 18.Bxe3 Rxc2; 19.Nxc2 Bd6 and I'd rather have the queen.) 17.Nf5 Bc5; 18.g4 (18.Nxd5 Rxe2; 19.Nde7+ Bxe7; 20.Rxd8+ Bxd8 is better for Black, according to Ugrinovic) 18...Bg6; 19.Bxd5 Qc7; 20.Bg2 h5!

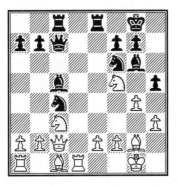

This strong move gives Black the initiative needed to justify the investment of a pawn. Watch how the kingside gets cracked open. 21.Nd5 Nxd5; 22.Rxd5 hxg4; 23.hxg4 Bxf5; 24.gxf5 Nb6; 25.Rxc5

Qxc5; 26.Qxc5 Rxc5 and Black won in Muco–Ivanovic, Siaperas 1990.

C2) 15.Nf5 Bb4; 16.a3 Bxf5; 17.Qxf5 Bxc3; 18.bxc3 Qa5 gives Black effective knights and White's bishop pair confers no advantage.

C3) 15.b3 Na3!; 16.Qd2 Rc8; 17.Bxa3 Bxa3; 18.Ndb5 Bc5; 19.Nxd5 Nxd5; 20.Qxd5 Qxd5; 21.Bxd5 Bxe2 is even.

C4) 15.h3 does not have much of an effect. 15...Bh5; 16.b3 Bc5; 17.Qd1 Bb4; 18.Ncb5 Nd6; 19.Nxd6 Qxd6; 20.Bb2 Rad8; 21.a3 Bc5; 22.Re1 a6; 23.Nf5 Qe6. Black has strong pressure against White's weaknesses, Tesic–Dabetic, Yugoslav Team Championship 1995.

By the way, 13...b6 is perhaps worthy of further investigation.

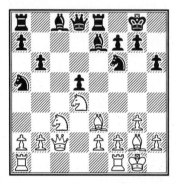

14.Rfd1 Bc5; 15.Nf5 Re5; 16.Nd4 Rxe3; 17.fxe3 Nc4; 18.Nxd5 Nxd5; 19.Qxc4 Nxe3; 20.Qd3 Nxd1; 21.Rxd1 Rb8; 22.b4 Bxd4+; 23.Qxd4 Qxd4+; 24.Rxd4 Be6 and the endgame was eventually drawn in Krasenkov–Iuldachev, Voskresensk 1992.

So we see that Black has some interesting options at move 13. Still, developing the bishop at g4 is in keeping with our overall strategy of pressure at e2, so let's return to it as our main line.

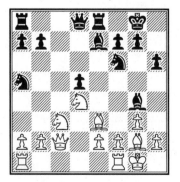

14.Nf5. Grandmaster Lajos Portisch's move, which has been very effective for White. Kasparov has played both sides of the position, so many of its secrets have been exposed. White has tried many less radical moves. In each case Black has sufficient resources. The most obvious alternatives are attacking the bishop with h3 or moving one of the rooks to d1.

14.h3. Challenging the bishop has a downside, in that Black can later create a queen and bishop battery to attack it. Because of this, the bishop usually retreats to d7. 14...Bd7; 15.Rad1 Qc8 is a very interesting line, for example 16.Kh2 Nc6; 17.Nxd5?! (17.Nxc6 bxc6; 18.Na4 would be stronger, leading to typical position. 18...Bf5; 19.Qc3 might encourage a sacrifice with 19...Rb8; 20.Bxa7 Bb4; 21.Qf3 Rb7; 22.Bd4 Ne4 and Black has a very active position) 17...Nxd5; 18.Bxd5 Bxh3; 19.Nxc6 bxc6; 20.Bxc6 Bxf1; 21.Rxf1 Bd6; 22.Qa4 Rxe3; 23.fxe3 Rb8; 24.Qc4 Kh8; 25.Rxf7 Rb4; 26.Qd5 Rh4+; 27.Kg1 Bxg3; 28.Qc5 Rh1+. White resigned, Vukic–Novoselski, Kragujevac 1984.

So let's try moving a rook to d1. But which one? That's always a tough choice for White. 14.Rfd1 plans to station rooks at c1 and d1, leaving the e-pawn unsupported.

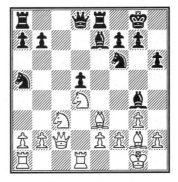

14...Rc8; 15.Nf5 (15.h3 Bd7; 16.Nb3 Nc4; 17.Bd4 b5 gave Black a good position in Kahn–Lengyel, Balatonbereny 1995) 15...Bb4 places pressure on the White queenside. Here are three continuations:

A) 16.a3 is a poor move. 16...Bxc3; 17.bxc3 Qd7; 18.Nd4 Nc4; 19.Bc1 Re7; 20.a4 Rce8; 21.Bf1 Bh3; 22.Ba3 Bxf1; 23.Rxf1 Qh3; 24.e3 Ng4; 25.f3 Nxa3 and White resigned in Savva–Yasin, Haifa 1989.

B) 16.Bd4 Rxe2; 17.Qd3 Bxc3; 18.Bxc3 Re8; 19.Bf3 d4? Sometimes simple is good. (19...Bxf3; 20.Qxf3 Re6; 21.Ne3 Nc4!; 22.Nxd5 Nxd5; 23.Rxd5 Qe7 would have been fine for Black.) 20.Bxd4 Bxf3; 21.Qxf3 Re6; 22.Bc3 Qb6; 23.Bxf6. White won. Nasybullin–Savva, Manila Olympiad 1992.

69

CARDOZA PUBLISHING • ERIC SCHILLER

C) 16.h3 Bxf5; 17.Qxf5 Bxc3; 18.bxc3 is Van Wely–Brinck Claussen, Lyngby 1989.

Black has some reason to be satisfied with the position, because the power of the bishop pair is offset by the weakness at c3 and a strong post for the knight at c4.

14.Rad1 might be the right choice, keeping open an option of defending the e-pawn with a rook at e1.

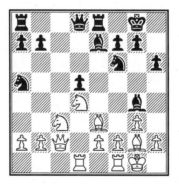

14...Rc8 is the obvious reply, and again White has a choice. Most of the themes have already been seen, but we should pay some attention to the plan where White drives our bishop back and attacks on the kingside. First we will consider three minor alternatives.

A) 15.Qd3 Bb4; 16.Ndb5 Nc4; 17.Bc1 a6; 18.Nd4 Bxc3; 19.bxc3 Qa5; 20.h3 Bh5; 21.g4 Bg6; 22.Nf5 Qxa2; 23.Bxd5 Nxd5; 24.Qxd5 Qxe2; 25.Qxb7 Bxf5; 26.gxf5 Ne5; 27.Qg2 Nf3+; 28.Kh1 Nh4; 29.Qg4 Rc4; 30.Qxe2 Rxe2 and Black was better in Skalkotas–Seitaj, Novi Sad Olympiad 1990.

B) 15.Nf5 Bb4; 16.Bd4 Nc4; 17.Nxg7 Kxg7; 18.Nxd5 Ne5; 19.Qb3 Bc5; 20.Bxc5 Rxc5; 21.Nxf6 Qxf6 and White did not have nearly enough compensation for the piece in Gronn–Grant, Gausdal (Troll Masters) 1992.

C) 15.f3 Bh5; 16.Bh3 Bg6 is also fine for Black, Preuschoff–Steinbrecht, Porz 1989.

D) 15.h3 Bh5; 16.g4 (16.a3 is also handled by 16...Bg6) 16...Bg6. This position has been doing well for White, but I think that is only due to an inaccurate play later on. 17.Nf5 Bb4; 18.Bd4 Ne4; 19.Qa4 Bxc3; 20.Bxc3.

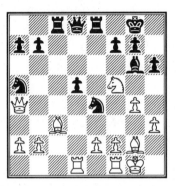

We have a position that has been reached several times. Black must tread carefully. 20...Bxf5; 21.gxf5 was seen in Kortchnoi–Ivkov, Rovinj 1970, and now with 21...Nc4; 22.Qxa7 Qc7. Black would have a promising game, despite the pawn deficit. Still, Black may be able to do even better with 20...Nc4! This has not been played, but it looks very promising, for example: 21.Qxa7 Bxf5. (21...Nxc3; 22.bxc3 Bxf5; 23.gxf5 Rxe2; 24.Qxb7 Nd2; 25.Rfe1 Rxe1+; 26.Rxe1 Rxc3; 27.Bxd5 and White is better.) 22.gxf5 Qc7 and Black's position looks good enough to be worth a pawn. Or 21.Bxe4 Rxe4; 22.Nd4 Qb6; 23.Qb3 Qc7; 24.Nb5 Qb8 and Black's pieces are more active.

In any case, 14.Nf5 is considered the critical line. Black responds with the natural **14...Rc8**.

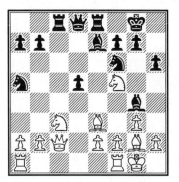

Black has tried many plans, but this one, chosen by Kasparov, is probably best here. Whether Black can achieve full equality is open to question, but White's advantage, if any, is minimal against best play. Still, I'd feel more comfortable in the line with 13...Nc4 that we looked at earlier.

15.Bd4.

15.Nxe7+ is also good. Karpov used it effectively to defeat Kasparov, but in their next encounter switched to the text. 15...Rxe7 16.Rad1 Qe8. (16...Rd7! would have limited White's advantage and after ...Be6 Black would have a solid, if passive, position. This is how Black should handle the position. Kasparov's move is too ambitious. He hopes to sacrifice at e3, but Karpov isn't going to allow it. Watching the game in Moscow, I was similarly optimistic about Black's position.)

17.h3 Bh5. The bishop must keep pressure on e2, as otherwise the a-pawn will drop for nothing. 18.Bxd5 Bg6; 19.Qc1 Nxd5; 20.Rxd5 Nc4; 21.Bd4 Rec7. (21...b5!? might be better.) 22.b3 (22.Qf4! would have been wiser, since after 22...a6; 23.e4 b5; 24.Re1 Black does not seem to have a good plan) 22...Nb6; 23.Re5 Qd7; 24.Qe3 f6; 25.Rc5 Rxc5; 26.Bxc5 Qxh3; 27.Rd1.

White does not have much to work with, but Karpov is capable of exploiting even the smallest positional advantages, and ground Kasparov down: 27...h5; 28.Rd4 Nd7; 29.Bd6 Bf7; 30.Nd5 Bxd5; 31.Rxd5 a6; 32.Bf4 Nf8; 33.Qd3 Qg4; 34.f3 Qg6; 35.Kf2 Rc2; 36.Qe3 Rc8; 37.Qe7 b5; 38.Rd8 Rxd8; 39.Qxd8 Qf7; 40.Bd6 g5; 41.Qa8 Kg7; 42.Qxa6. White won. Karpov–Kasparov, World Championship, Game 7, 1984.

15...Bc5; 16.Bxc5 Rxc5.

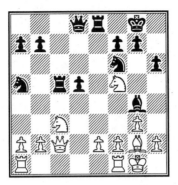

17.Ne3! 17.b4? Bxf5!; 18.Qxf5 Rxc3; 19.bxa5 Qxa5 and Black is much better. **17...Be6; 18.Rad1.** 18.b4 is still ineffective: 18...Rc7; 19.bxa5 d4; 20.Ned1 dxc3; 21.Nxc3 Qd4 and White is in trouble.
18...Qc8; 19.Qa4 Rd8; 20.Rd3 a6; 21.Rfd1 Nc4; 22.Nxc4 Rxc4.

23.Qa5. 23.Qb3 Qc5; 24.Qxb7 Rb4; 25.Qxa6 is also good, Voss–Steinbrecht, Porz 1990.

23...Rc5. 23...Rd7! is a better defense. It was suggested by Yusupov, commenting on this game, and had a small test later. 24.Rd4 b5 secures some necessary space on the queenside. 25.Rxc4 dxc4; 26.Rf1 Rd6 was agreed drawn in Morovic–Salazar, Santiago Zonal 1989.

24.Qb6 Rd7; 25.Rd4 Qc7; 26.Qxc7 Rdxc7; 27.h3. 27.Nxd5 Nxd5; 28.Bxd5 Bxd5; 29.Rxd5 Rxd5; 30.Rxd5 Rc2 is no worse for Black in the endgame. White must be patient.

27...h5.

Black suffers from the weak d-pawn, which must be passively defended. Against a lesser player, Black might be able to stubbornly resist, but Karpov knows how to play these positions very well. **28.a3 g6; 29.e3.** White is in no rush. Karpov slowly improves the position. **29...Kg7; 30.Kh2 Rc4; 31.Bf3 b5; 32.Kg2 R7c5; 33.Rxc4 Rxc4.** 33...dxc4; 34.Rd6 and the weak base of the pawn chain comes under attack.

34.Rd4 Kf8; 35.Be2 Rxd4? Kasparov should really have known that the rooks must stay on the board to preserve drawing chances. That is what most of us thought in the press room, and this move came as a bit of a surprise.

36.exd4.

Black has a bad bishop in the endgame. If the knights were gone passive defense is possible. With knights, Black's disadvantage is larger. **36...Ke7; 37.Na2!** The knight heads for b4. **37...Bc8; 38.Nb4 Kd6; 39.f3 Ng8; 40.h4 Nh6; 41.Kf2 Nf5!** Kasparov uses active defense to limit the damage.

42.Nc2 f6? Another slip, at the worst possible time. Kasparov sealed this move at adjournment. Had the adjournment come one move earlier, he would have found the best line to fight for a draw. 42...Nh6! followed by ...Bf5 was the correct plan. **43.Bd3 g5; 44.Bxf5 Bxf5; 45.Ne3 Bb1; 46.b4 gxh4?**

This allows Karpov to sacrifice a pawn to gain a study–like win. **47.Ng2!! hxg3+; 48.Kxg3 Ke6; 49.Nf4+ Kf5; 50.Nxh5.**

This endgame is a win for White, who has a knight much stronger than the enemy bishop. **50...Ke6; 51.Nf4+ Kd6; 52.Kg4 Bc2; 53.Kh5 Bd1; 54.Kg6 Ke7.** 54...Bxf3; 55.Kxf6 is a simple win. White will place a knight at f5 and bring the king in. The plan is slow, but inevitable. **55.Nxd5+ Ke6; 56.Nc7+ Kd7; 57.Nxa6 Bxf3; 58.Kxf6 Kd6; 59.Kf5 Kd5; 60.Kf4 Bh1; 61.Ke3 Kc4; 62.Nc5 Bc6; 63.Nd3 Bg2; 64.Ne5+ Kc3; 65.Ng6!** Karpov's technique is superb.

65...Kc4. The king cannot go after the a-pawn! 65...Kb3; 66.Nf4 Bb7; 67.d5 Kxa3; 68.d6 Bc6; 69.Nd5! Kb3; 70.Kd4 Bd7; 71.Kc5. White wins with Nb6 followed by d7. **66.Ne7 Bb7; 67.Nf5 Bg2; 68.Nd6+ Kb3; 69.Nxb5 Ka4; 70.Nd6. White won.**

BELYAVSKY VS. KASPAROV
Candidates Match, 1983

1.d4 d5; 2.c4 e6; 3.Nc3 c5; 4.cxd5 exd5; 5.Nf3 Nc6; 6.g3 Nf6; 7.Bg2 Be7; 8.0–0 0–0; 9.Bg5 cxd4; 10.Nxd4 h6; 11.Be3 Re8; 12.Qa4.

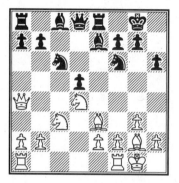

White applied direct pressure at c6, and plans to bring a rook to d1, where it is poised to take aim at d5. This was once considered strong, but Kasparov helped to reduce the reputation of the move. On the other hand, in the only game we have played so far, he crushed me with it! **12...Bd7.** Black takes care of the problem at c6, but d5 loses the support of the queen. **13.Rad1.** The pawn at d5 is sufficiently defended, though it may not seem that way. White's attempt to capture it will fail. There are other rook moves and the retreat of the queen to be considered as well.

A) 13.Nxd5 Nxd5; 14.Bxd5 is refuted by 14...Na5!

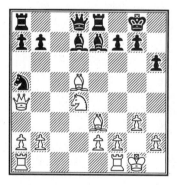

This gives Black an initiative. 15.Qd1 Bh3; 16.Bg2 Bxg2; 17.Kxg2 Nc4; 18.Bc1. White pieces are forced to retreat to hold on to the pawn. (18.b3 Nxe3+; 19.fxe3 Bg5 is better for Black.) 18...Bf6; 19.e3

Re4; 20.b3 Bxd4; 21.exd4 Rxd4; 22.Qe2 Qd5+; 23.Qf3 Qxf3+; 24.Kxf3 Nd2+; 25.Bxd2 Rxd2 and Black has a better endgame, Littke–Allen, World Under 20 Championship 1992.

B) 13.Rfd1 should also be countered by 13...Na5.

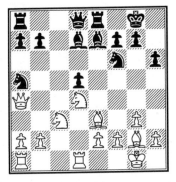

14.Qc2 Nc4!; 15.Bf4 Rc8; 16.Nxd5 Ne3; 17.Qxc8! is given as unclear by Kasparov. 17...Bxc8; 18.Nxe3 Qb6; 19.Nc4 Qa6 is not easy to evaluate. White has enough material–rook, knight and pawn–to justify the investment of a queen, especially since the pieces are well posted. On the other hand, Black has a solid position and the only problematic piece is the bishop at c8.

C) 13.Qb3 Na5; 14.Qc2 (14.Qd1 Nc4; 15.Nxd5 Nxd5; 16.Bxd5 Nxe3; 17.fxe3 Bf6 and the bishop pair and superior pawn structure is worth more than White's useless extra pawn, Tatenhorst–Dankert, Hamburg 1986) 14...Rc8; 15.Rad1 Nc4; 16.Bc1 Bb4; 17.Nxd5 Ne3. (17...Nxd5; 18.Bxd5 Qe7; 19.Qb3 Nb6; 20.Bxb7 Rc7; 21.Qf3 Bh3 recovers the exchange, but things get complicated after 22.Nc6! Qf8; 23.Ba6 Bxf1; 24.Kxf1 Qc5; 25.Nxb4 Qxb4 and White has two pawns and a bishop for the rook, Chiong–Zolnierowicz, Bern 1991.)

18.Nxf6+ gxf6; 19.Qb3 Nxd1; 20.Rxd1 Bf8; 21.Bxb7 Rc5 leads to an interesting battle, for example 22.Bd5 Qe7; 23.Bf4 Rd8; 24.h4 Ba4; 25.Qxa4 Rcxd5; 26.e3 Qe4; 27.Qc6 f5; 28.Rc1 Bg7; 29.Bxh6 Bxd4; 30.exd4 Rxd4; 31.Qxe4 fxe4. Quinteros–Frey, Lone Pine 1977.

An interesting endgame in which Black has slightly more winning chances than White, though the game ended in a draw,.

D) 13.Rac1 Na5; 14.Qc2 Nc4; 15.Nxd5 Rc8; 16.Qb3 Nxe3; 17.Nxe3 Bc5 gives Black good counterplay. 18.Rcd1 b6; 19.Rd3 Ne4; 20.Qd1 Qf6; 21.Nb3 Ba4; 22.Qb1 and here 22...Bxb3; 23.axb3 Nxf2; 24.Rxf2 Qg5; 25.Rf1 Rxe3; 26.Rxe3 Qxe3+; 27.Kh1 Qxb3 gave Black a clear advantage in Tatenhorst–Schwagli, Bern 1994.

So White has nothing better than bringing the rook from a1 to d1.

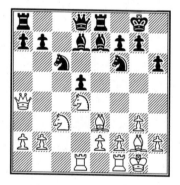

13...Nb4. This is not the only move, but it is the most active and most popular choice.

14.Qb3 a5; 15.Rd2?!

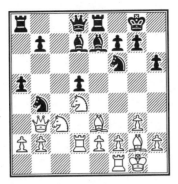

White sensibly defends the b-pawn and targets the weak d-pawn. The only problem is that White is really obliged here to stop the further advance of the a-pawn. Once again capturing at d5 fails.

A) 15.Nxd5 Nbxd5; 16.Bxd5 Nxd5; 17.Qxd5 Bh3; 18.Qxb7 Bxf1; 19.Rxf1 Rb8; 20.Qa7 Ra8; 21.Qb7 Bf6 is acceptable for White only if the queens stay on the board for a while. Black is certainly not worse, however, as all of the pieces have room to roam. Vaganian–Ivkov, Odessa 1975 eventually ended in a draw.

B) 15.a4! is the most logical reply.

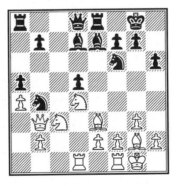

This is the correct move, and Black has tried many different plans. I believe that 15...Rc8 leads to the most complex and rewarding play, and have confidence in the Black side. 15...Rc8 is the normal reply.

B1) 16.Rd2 Bc5. (16...Bg4; 17.h3 Bh5; 18.Nf5 Bc5; 19.Nxd5 Nfxd5; 20.Bxd5 Qf6; 21.Bxc5 Rxc5; 22.Ne3 Nxd5; 23.Nxd5 Qe6; 24.Qxb7 Bxe2; 25.Re1 Bf3; 26.Red1 Qe1+; 27.Kh2 Bxd1. Black won. Issakainen–Shevelev, Jyvaskyla 1994.) 17.h3 (17.Rfd1 Rxe3; 18.fxe3 Qe7; 19.e4 dxe4; 20.e3 Be6, now pieces start flying off the board:

21.Nxe6 Bxe3+; 22.Kh1 Bxd2; 23.Rxd2 Qxe6; 24.Qxe6 fxe6; 25.Bxe4 Nxe4; 26.Nxe4 Nd5 and Black was better in Manor–Johanson, Lyon Zonal 1990) 17...Qb6; 18.Kh2 Ne4; 19.Nxe4 dxe4; 20.Rfd1 Qf6; 21.Nb5 Bxb5; 22.axb5 b6; 23.Bxc5 Rxc5; 24.Rd6 Qe5; 25.Rxb6 Rxb5; 26.Rxb5 Qxb5 was agreed drawn in Schussler–Olafsson, Gausdal Zonal 1985.

B2) 16.Ndb5 Be6; 17.Bd4 and here 17...Ne4 is the most intriguing line. 18.Nxe4 dxe4; 19.Qe3 Bg5.

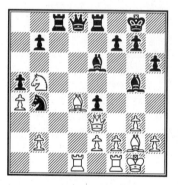

This position has been reached several times, and is critical to the evaluation of the line. The capture of the pawn at e4 is nothing to worry about. 20.Qxe4 Bb3; 21.Qxb7 Bxd1; 22.Rxd1 Rxe2; 23.Nc3 Re7; 24.Qf3 Nc2!; 25.Qf5 (25.Bxg7? Re1+! This was the point behind ...Nc2!; 26.Rxe1 Nxe1; 27.Qe4 Nxg2; 28.Be5 f6; 29.Bd4 Ne1 and White cannot regain enough material) 25...Nxd4; 26.Rxd4 Re1+; 27.Bf1 Qxd4!; 28.Qxc8+ Bd8 and White did not have enough compensation for the pawn in Paunovic–Todorovic, Yugoslavia 1988.

Therefore White sometimes tries to challenge the bishop at g5. 20.f4 leads to 20...exf3; 21.Qxf3 Bd5; 22.Qf2 Rc2; 23.Nc3 Bb3; 24.h4 Qxd4; 25.Rxd4 Be3; 26.Qxe3 Rxe3; 27.Be4 Nc6; 28.Bxc2 Nxd4; 29.Bxb3 Nxb3 and Black was at least equal in Fedorowicz–S.Arkell, London 1988.

B3) 16.Nc2 is a reasonable try.

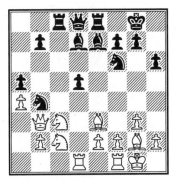

White challenges the knight at b4. This makes some sense, though it does give up the nice outpost at d4. 16...b5! The pin on the knight at c3 makes this possible. 17.Nxb4 bxa4; 18.Nxa4 Bxb4; 19.Nc3 Bxc3; 20.bxc3.

Black's advanced a-pawn provides a serious advantage. 20...a4!; 21.Qa2 Bb5. Capturing at c3 also looks good. 22.Bxd5 Qe7; 23.c4 Nxd5; 24.cxd5 Qe4; 25.Rd4 Qc2; 26.Qxc2 Rxc2. The remainder of the game is worth looking at, just to see how bishops of opposite color do not always manage to draw when rooks are on the board! 27.Rb1 Bd7; 28.Rb7 Bh3; 29.Rd1 a3; 30.d6 a2; 31.g4 Bxg4; 32.f3 Rxe3; 33.fxg4 Rd2; 34.Ra1 Rexe2; 35.d7 Kf8; 36.Ra7 Ke7; 37.h3 g6; 38.Kf1 Rf2+; 39.Kg1 Rg2+; 40.Kf1 Rdf2+; 41.Ke1 Rg1+; 42.Kxf2 Rxa1 and White resigned in Ristic–Petursson, Smederevska Palanka 1984.

15...a4!

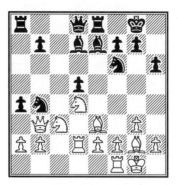

This advance strengthens Black's initiative. **16.Qd1 a3; 17.Qb1.** 17.Qb3 Qa5; 18.bxa3 Qxa3; 19.Nxd5 Nfxd5; 20.Bxd5 Nxd5; 21.Qxd5 Bh3! gives Black enough counterplay.

17...Bf8.17...Bc5 is an interesting alternative. 18.bxa3 Rxe3!; 19.fxe3 Rxa3; 20.Qb2 Qe7; 21.Kh1 Ra6; 22.a3 Qxe3; 23.axb4 Bxd4 but White has a strong resource: 24.Nd1! Bxb2; 25.Nxe3 Bc3; 26.Rd3 Bxb4; 27.Nxd5. White is better. **18.bxa3 Rxa3; 19.Qb2.** 19.Ndb5 Bxb5; 20.Nxb5 Raxe3; 21.fxe3 Qb6; 22.Nd4 Rxe3 and Black has compensation for the exchange.

19...Qa8.

20.Nb3?! 20.Ndb5 Bxb5; 21.Nxb5 Rxa2; 22.Qb3 would maintain equality, according to Kasparov. **20...Bc6; 21.Bd4.** 21.Nc5 d4; 22.Bxd4 Bxg2; 23.Kxg2 b6+ wins a piece.

21...Ne4; 22.Nxe4 dxe4; 23.Ra1? 23.Nc5! was the best try. 23...Nxa2. (23...e3; 24.Bxc6 exf2+; 25.Bxf2 Nxc6 is better for Black.) 24.Ra1 Qa5; 25.Nxe4! Bxe4; 26.Rxa2 Bxg2; 27.Kxg2 Qd5+; 28.Kg1 Rb3 with a minimal advantage for Black, according to Kasparov.

23...Bd5; 24.Qb1 b6; 25.e3 Nd3; 26.Rd1.

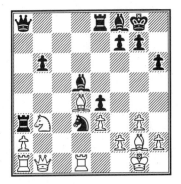

Now Kasparov pushes the b-pawn to forward to b4, securing more space. **26...b5; 27.Bf1 b4; 28.Bxd3.** Belyavsky tries to get rid of the invasive knight, but now the light squares are too weak. **28...exd3; 29.Qxd3 Rxa2; 30.Rxa2 Qxa2; 31.Nc5 Bf3! 32.Ra1 Qd5; 33.Qb3 Qh5; 34.Nd3 Bd6; 35.Ne1 Bb7; 36.Rc1 Qf5; 37.Rd1 Bf8; 38.Qb1** White lost on time in this fairly hopeless position. **Black won.**

BELYAVSKY VS. KASPAROV
Candidates (6th game), 1983

1.d4 d5; 2.c4 e6; 3.Nc3 c5; 4.cxd5 exd5; 5.Nf3 Nc6; 6.g3 Nf6; 7.Bg2 Be7; 8.0–0 0–0; 9.Bg5 cxd4; 10.Nxd4 h6; 11.Be3 Re8; 12.Qc2.

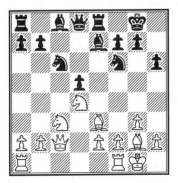

This is an unpretentious variation. White simply prepares to develop the rooks. **12...Bg4.** As usual, this move is an essential part of Black's strategy to target e2. **13.Rfd1.** Besides 13.Rfd1, there are two other significant plans.

With 13.Rad1, White forgoes play on the c-file. **13...Qd7; 14.Nxc6.**

(14.Nb3 Be6; 15.Nc5 Bxc5; 16.Bxc5 Rac8; 17.Qa4 a6; 18.Qf4 Qd8; 19.Bd4 Nxd4; 20.Rxd4 Qc7; 21.Qxc7 Rxc7 and Black winds up in a typical slightly worse endgame. It is very difficult for White to win without help, and none was provided by Black in the following example. 22.Rfd1 Rd7; 23.e3 Red8; 24.Kf1 Kf8; 25.Ke1 Ke7; 26.R1d2 Rd6; 27.Kd1 R6d7; 28.Kc1 Rd6; 29.b3 R8d7; 30.Kb2 Rd8; 31.h3 g6; 32.g4 R8d7; 33.f4 Rd8; 34.Bf3 b5; 35.Rg2 Ne8; 36.Rgd2 Nc7; 37.h4 f6; 38.Rg2 Bf7; 39.Rgd2 Be6; 40.a3 Bf7; 41.Rg2 Rh8; 42.Rgd2 Rhd8; 43.R4d3 Be6; 44.Ne2 was eventually drawn in Cooper–Anderton, Chester 1979.

Now Black de-isolates the d-pawn with 14...bxc6; 15.Bd4 Nh7; 16.Na4. (16.f3 Bh3; 17.e4 c5; 18.Bf2 Bxg2; 19.Kxg2 d4; 20.Nd5 Ng5; 21.f4 Qh3+; 22.Kh1 Nf3; 23.Bg1 Nxg1; 24.Rxg1 Rac8; 25.g4 Qf3+; 26.Qg2 Qxg2+; 27.Kxg2 Bf8 and Black went on to draw in Loginov–Ehlvest, Volgodonsk 1983.)

Black should avoid 16...Ng5?; 17.f3 Bh3; 18.Bxh3 Qxh3; 19.Qxc6 Bc5; 20.Bf2 Rac8; 21.Qxd5 Rxe2; 22.Nxc5 Rxc5; 23.Qd8+ Kh7; 24.Qd3+ Rf5; 25.f4 and Black resigned in Stefansson–Johannesson, Reykjavik 1990.

16...Bf6! looks best to me, for example 17.f3 (17.Rfe1 Rab8; 18.Nc5 Qe7) 17...Bxd4+; 18.Rxd4 Bh3; 19.Bxh3 (19.Nc5 Qe7! threatens ...Re3+!) 19...Qxh3 and Black is doing fine, for example 20.Qxc6 Rac8; 21.Qxd5?? Rxe2 and Black wins.

13.h3 is another sensible move.

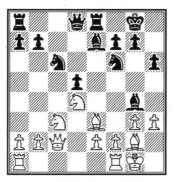

13...Bd7. Black can also play the bishop to e6, but this line is more interesting.

A) 14.Rfd1 Qc8; 15.Kh2 Bc5; 16.Rac1 Nxd4?!; 17.Bxd4 Bxd4 (17...Bf5 comes into consideration). 18.Rxd4 was better for White in Aseyev–Frois, Linares Open 1996. Black has a better line. 16...b6! 17.Nxd5 Nxd5; 18.Bxd5 Nb4; 19.Qb3 Nxd5; 20.Qxd5 a5 (20...Bxh3? overlooks White's main threat. 21.b4) 21.Qg2 (21.h4 Bg4 and e2 is coming under a lot of pressure) 21...Qa6.

B) 14.Rad1 Qc8; 15.Kh2 Bf8; 16.Rfe1 Re5; 17.Rh1 Rh5; 18.Kg1 Bxh3; 19.Bf3 Re5; 20.Nxc6 bxc6; 21.Bd4 Bf5! Black already has leverage. 22.e4 Rxe4; 23.Nxe4 Nxe4; 24.Qe2 c5; 25.Be3 Qe6; 26.Kg2 d4; 27.Bc1 Re8. Black won, Belyavsky–Illescas, Linares 1990.

C) 14.Nxd5? allows 14...Nxd5; 15.Bxd5 Nb4! and Black will exchange the knight for the bishop and then grab the pawn, with the bishop pair and a better game. **13...Bf8** is a typical move in such positions, but 13...Qd7 might be more effective.

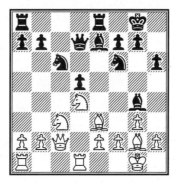

This is a highly consistent continuation, preparing to double on the d-file. 14.Nb3 (14.Rac1 Bh3; 15.Bh1 Rac8; 16.Nxc6 bxc6; 17.Bd4

Nh7 is given by Kasparov, who notes that the knight will redeploy at e6 via g5) 14...Rac8 is best, leading to unclear complications.

A) 15.Nxd5 Nxd5; 16.Rd2 Nxe3; 17.fxe3 (17.Rxd7? loses to 17...Nxc2) 17...Qe6 and I think Black has enough compensation. More testing is 16.Bxd5 but 16...Nb4; 17.Qe4 Nxd5; 18.Rxd5 Bf6; 19.Rxd7 Rxe4; 20.Rxb7 Bxe2; 21.Rxa7 Bxb2 provides enough compensation, according to Kasparov.

B) 15.Rac1 is calmer. 15...Bd6; 16.a3 (16.Nc5 Bxc5; 17.Bxc5!? is an interesting alternative) 16...Be5; 17.Nc5 Qe7; 18.Nxd5 Nxd5; 19.Rxd5 b6 is unclear, according to Kasparov.

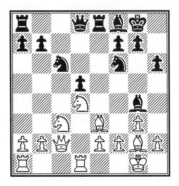

14.Rac1.

14.h3 Bd7 does not work so well with the bishop at f8. 15.Nxd5 Nxd5; 16.Bxd5 Nb4; 17.Bxf7+! Kxf7; 18.Qb3+ Kg6; 19.a3 and now Black must settle for 19...Kh7. (19...Nc6; 20.Qd3+ Kf6; 21.Nxc6 Bxc6; 22.Qc3+ Kg6; 23.Rxd8 Raxd8; 24.b4 and White is clearly better.) 20.axb4 Bxh3; 21.Ra5 Qe7; 22.Nf3 Qxb4; 23.Qxb4 Bxb4; 24.Rb5 a5; 25.Rxb7 Rab8; 26.Rxb8 Rxb8; 27.Ne5 with a winning endgame for White, Tazelaar–Etman, Postal 1990. Better is 14...Bh5 and 15...Bg6.

14...Rc8.

14...Qa5; 15.Qb3! puts too much pressure on the weak light squares d5 and b7.

15.Nxc6. 15.Qa4 is critical, according to Kasparov.

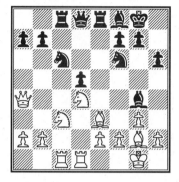

15...Na5 is considered best, but White seems to get an advantage after. 16.Nxd5 (16.Nb3!? Nc4; 17.Nxd5 is probably also a bit better for White) 16...Nxd5 17.Rxc8 Bxc8; 18.Bxd5 Rxe3; 19.Nb5 (19.Bxf7+ Kxf7; 20.fxe3 Bh3 is less clear) 19...Qb6; 20.fxe3 Qxe3+; 21.Kh1 Be6; 22.Bxe6 Qxe6; 23.Qc2 and White has a material advantage.

Why not 15...Nxd4; 16.Bxd4 Bxe2? I don't see anything special for White here, even if Black's pawns are vulnerable. After all, Black has an extra pawn, for the moment. Play will probably continue 17.Nxe2 Rxe2; 18.Rxc8 Qxc8; 19.Bxf6 gxf6; 20.Bxd5 Bc5. Black is not worse here.

15...bxc6.

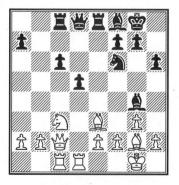

16.Bd4. 16.Bxa7 c5; 17.Bxd5 (17.Nxd5 Nxd5; 18.Rxd5 Qa5; 19.Bxc5 Rxe2; 20.Qc4 Rxc5!; 21.Rxc5 Qxc5 wins for Black) 17...Qa5; 18.Qa4 Qxa4; 19.Nxa4 Bxe2; 20.Rd2 Nxd5; 21.Rxd5 Ra8 and there is no disputing Black's advantage. **16...Bb4; 17.Rd2 Qe7; 18.a3 Ba5!;**

19.b4. This move would have been more effective had White first kicked the bishop with h3. **19...Bb6; 20.e3 Qe6; 21.Qb2.** 21.Na4 Ne4; 22.Rd3 (22.Bxe4 dxe4; 23.Bxb6 axb6; 24.Nxb6 Rcd8) 22...Ng5 gives Black a strong attack. **21...Bxd4; 22.Rxd4.** 22.exd4 is, according to Konikowski, the only way to play for the advantage, but Kasparov noted that Black can gain strong kingside counterplay with 22...Bh3. **22...c5; 23.bxc5 Rxc5; 24.Ne2 Rec8; 25.Rxc5 Rxc5.**

26.Nf4. 26.h3 is an alternative. 26...Bf5; 27.Nf4 Qc8; 28.Bxd5 Rc1+; 29.Kg2 Nxd5; 30.Nxd5 Bxh3+; 31.Kh2 Kh7!; 32.Ne7 Qa8; 33.e4 (33.Kxh3 Qh1+; 34.Kg4 Rc5 would give Black sufficient compensation) 33...Rc7; 34.Nd5 Rb7; 35.Qc2 Be6; 36.e5+ Kh8; 37.Nc7 Qc8; 38.Qd3 Rb8 is even, according to Belyavsky. **26...Qc8; 27.h3 Rc1+; 28.Kh2 Rc2; 29.Qb3 Bf5; 30.Kg1 Rc1+; 31.Rd1 Be4.** White would probably be better after exchanging at e4, but a draw was agreed.

SMYSLOV VS. KASPAROV
Vilnius (Candidates), 1984

1.d4 d5; 2.Nf3 c5; 3.c4 e6; 4.cxd5 exd5; 5.g3 Nf6; 6.Bg2 Be7; 7.0–0 0–0; 8.Nc3 Nc6; 9.Bg5 cxd4; 10.Nxd4 h6; 11.Be3 Re8; 12.a3.

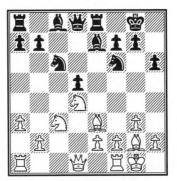

This is Smyslov's Variation. Smyslov has invented many strategies in the openings by advancing a rook pawn, for example the ...h6 systems in the Closed Spanish as Black, and the a3 system as White in the same opening!

This is an example of prophylactic play, as advocated by the great Aron Nimzowitsch. You may notice that in many variations Black places a knight at b4, attacking d5, c2 and other important light squares. Since White has a lead in development, this is a good time to take over the b4-square. In the short term, the move also makes available a2 for the White queen, a distant post which nevertheless aims at d5.

12...Be6. With the weakening of the light squares on the queenside, this square is a natural post for the bishop. Black can try to maneuver a knight to c4, for example, without having to worry about the advance of the b-pawn to b3, because then the pawn at a3 would be insufficiently defended. Nevertheless, Kasparov soon changes his mind and moves the bishop to g4, suggesting that this is the proper strategy in the immediate circumstances too. Both lines are fully playable.

12...Bg4; 13.Qb3 (13.Qc2 Qd7; 14.Nxc6 bxc6; 15.Na4 Bh3; 16.Bd4 Bxg2; 17.Kxg2 Ne4; 18.f4 c5; 19.Bf2 Rac8; 20.Rac1 Qc6; 21.Kg1 Bf6; 22.b3 Nxf2; 23.Kxf2 Bd4+; 24.Kg2 c4; 25.bxc4 dxc4+; 26.Rf3 Be3; 27.Rd1 c3; 28.Rd3 Bd2; 29.Nxc3 Rxe2+; 30.Kf1 Rxh2; 31.Qb3 Qc5; 32.Nd1 Re8; 33.Rfe3 Bxe3; 34.Nxe3 Rxe3 and White resigned in Manhood–Bruere, Postal 1991) 13...Na5; 14.Qa2 and here:

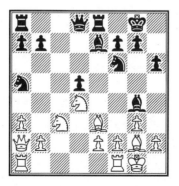

A) 14...Nc4; 15.Nxd5 (15.Nc2 led to an interesting struggle after 15...Nxe3; 16.Nxe3 d4! Play continued 17.Nxg4 Nxg4; 18.Nd5 Bd6; 19.Rad1 Qg5; 20.b4 a5; 21.Qb2 axb4; 22.axb4 Bb8; 23.b5 Re5; 24.f4 Qh5; 25.h3 Rxd5; 26.hxg4 Rxb5; 27.Qxd4 Qg6; 28.Be4 Ba7; 29.Qxa7

Rxa7; 30.Bxg6 fxg6; 31.Rd8+ Kf7; 32.Rd7+ Ke6; 33.Rfd1 Ra1;
34.R7d6+ Ke7; 35.Rd7+ Ke8; 36.Rd8+ Ke7; 37.R8d7+ Ke8; 38.Rd8+
Ke7; 39.R8d7+ Ke6; 40.R7d6+ Ke7; 41.Rd7+ Ke8. Drawn. Southam–
Rositsan, Toronto 1992) 15...Nxe3; 16.fxe3 Qd7; 17.Rad1 Nxd5;
18.Bxd5 Bf6; 19.e4 Be6; 20.Nf3 Rad8; 21.Rd2 Qc7; 22.Bxe6 Rxd2;
23.Bxf7+ Qxf7; 24.Qxf7+ Kxf7; 25.Nxd2 Ke6; 26.Rb1 Rc8.

This is analysis by Kasparov, who claimed sufficient compensation, but it has now been tested in a serious game. 27.Nf3 g5; 28.e5
Be7. (28...Bxe5; 29.Nxe5 Kxe5 leaves Black fighting for draw, which
he should receive thanks to the active piece positions.) 29.g4 h5;
30.gxh5 g4!; 31.Ne1 Rh8; 32.Nd3 Bg5; 33.Rf1 Rxh5; 34.Nf4+ Bxf4;
35.Rxf4 Rxe5.

This endgame, by contrast with that of the last note, is much
worse for Black. 36.Kf2 Rh5; 37.Kg2 Re5; 38.Kf2 Rh5; 39.Rxg4
Rxh2+; 40.Rg2 Rh5; 41.Rg4 Rc5; 42.Rg6+ Kf5; 43.Rg3 Ke4; 44.Rg7
and White eventually prevailed in Sorensen-S. Larsen, Copenhagen
1991.

B) 14...Be6 is a retreat motivated by the artificial position of the
White queen. It makes some sense and may be worth repeating.

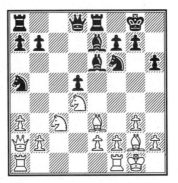

15.Rad1 Nc6; 16.Nc2 Kh8; 17.Nxd5 Qa5; 18.Bf4 Rad8; 19.e4 Rd7; 20.Qa1. An absurd station for her majesty! Hiding out in the water closet? 20...Nxd5; 21.exd5 Bxd5; 22.b4. The point of White's plan is revealed. The pawn at h6 falls. 22...Qd8; 23.Rxd5 Rxd5; 24.Bxd5 Qxd5; 25.Bxh6 Bf6. So what! Black now takes the initiative. 26.Qc1 Ne5; 27.Ne1 Nc4; 28.Bf4 Bb2. Now the pawn is returned with interest. 29.Qc2 Bxa3; 30.Qa4 b5; 31.Qxa7 Bxb4; 32.Ng2 Bc5 and Black is clearly better, Lang–Peterson, Horowitz Memorial 1989.

In any case, we take 12...Be6 as our main line.

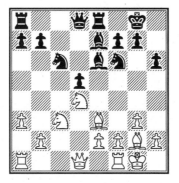

13.Kh1. White is adopting a very quiet strategy, typical of Smyslov but not of much use against Kasparov, who was familiar with the position from his 1983 Candidates' Match against Korchnoi.

13.Qb3 Qd7; 14.Nxe6 fxe6; 15.Rad1 Bd6; 16.Bc1 Kh8; 17.Qa4 Qe7; 18.e3 a6; 19.Qh4 Rac8; 20.e4 d4; 21.Ne2 e5; 22.Bh3 Rc7; 23.Bg5 Kg8; 24.Bxf6 Qxf6; 25.Qxf6 gxf6; 26.Nc1 Na5; 27.Nb3 Nc4; 28.Bf5 a5; 29.Kg2 Kg7; 30.Kh3 Ree7; 31.Nc1 was drawn in a game from the Korchnoi–Kasparov Candidates match in London 1983.

13.Nxe6 fxe6 is better for Black, it seems, at first glance.

A) 14.Kh1 Na5; 15.f4 Nc4; 16.Bg1 Nxb2; 17.Qb3 Nc4; 18.Rad1 Rc8; 19.e4 Qa5; 20.exd5 Ne3! leads to unclear complications, according to Kasparov. Let's try to clarify matters a bit.

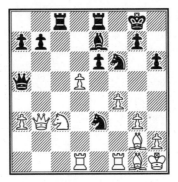

21.d6 is the most logical move, opening up lines toward b7, attacking the bishop, and threatening Qe6+. It is hard to believe that there is a better move for White. 21...Nxd1; 22.Qxe6+ Kh8. Now White is a whole rook down for a pawn, so must capture at d1. But which way? 23.Rxd1 (23.Nxd1 Qa6 pins the d-pawn) 23...Bxd6; 24.Qxd6 Rxc3; 25.Bd4 Rd8!

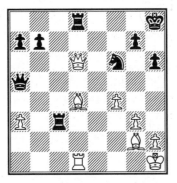

Now things look absolutely hopeless for White. Even the sacrifice at f6 doesn't quite pan out. 26.Qxf6 (26.Qe7 Rcc8) 26...gxf6; 27.Bxf6+ Kg8; 28.Rxd8+ Kf7; 29.Bxc3 Qxd8; 30.Kg1 and Black should be able to win, eventually. (30.h3 Qd3) 30...Qb6+; 31.Kf1 Qa6+ etc.

B) 14.Qa4 is an aggressive try.14...Rc8; 15.Rad1 Kh8; 16.Kh1 a6; 17.f4 Na5; 18.f5?! A bit optimistic. (18.Bd4 would have kept the game in balance.) 18...b5!; 19.Qh4 Ng8!; 20.Qh3 Nc4. Having chased the queen to a useless post on the other side of the board, Black returns to the queenside. 21.Bc1 Bg5; 22.fxe6 Bxc1; 23.Rxc1 Ne3; 24.Nxd5

Nxf1; 25.Rxf1 Rf8; 26.Nf4 Ne7; 27.Qg4? (The final error. With 27.Qh5 White still might have been able to survive.) 27...g5; 28.Qh3 Rf6; 29.Nd3 Rxf1+; 30.Bxf1 Kg7; 31.Qg4 Qd5+; 32.e4 Qd4; 33.h4 Rf8; 34.Be2 Qe3; 35.Kg2 Ng6; 36.h5 Ne7; 37.b4 Kh7; 38.Kh2 Rd8; 39.e5 Rxd3; 40.Bxd3+ Qxd3 and White resigned in the 10th game of the Smyslov–Kasparov Candidates match at Vilnius, 1984.

13...Bg4. 13...Qd7 is not as good. 14.Nxe6 (14.f4 Bh3; 15.Qd3 Rad8; 16.Rad1 Bf8; 17.Bg1 Na5; 18.Qb5 Bxg2+; 19.Kxg2 Nc4; 20.Qb3 Ng4 and Black cleaned up quickly: 21.Nc2 Qc6; 22.Rf3 Na5; 23.Qa2 Rxe2+; 24.Nxe2 Qxc2; 25.Re1 Re8; 26.Kf1 Rxe2; 27.Qxd5 Rxe1+; 28.Kxe1 Qc1+. Masic–Todorovic, Yugoslavia 1992) 14...fxe6; 15.f4 Red8; 16.Bg1 Rac8; 17.Qa4 Kh8; 18.Rad1 Qe8; 19.e4 d4; 20.Ne2 Bc5; 21.Qb5 Bb6; 22.h3 e5; 23.fxe5? (23.Bh2! planning a quick g4 would have given White the advantage.) 23...Nxe5; 24.Qxe8+ Rxe8; 25.Nxd4 Nc4; 26.e5 Rxe5; 27.Bxb7 Rc7; 28.Rc1 Nxb2; 29.Rxc7 Bxc7; 30.Nc6 Re2; 31.Nd4 Re5; 32.Nf5 Bb6; 33.Nxh6 Ra5; 34.Bxb6 axb6; 35.Nf5 Rxa3; 36.Kh2 Nc4; 37.g4 Ra7; 38.Bh1 Ne5; 39.g5 Nh5; 40.Re1 Ra5; 41.Nd6 was agreed drawn in the second game of the Smyslov–Kasparov, Candidates match in Vilnius, 1984.

14.f3.

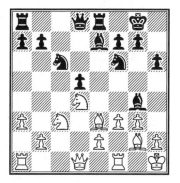

14.Qa4 Ne5; 15.Qb3 Nc4; 16.Nxd5 Nxd5; 17.Qxc4 Nxe3; 18.fxe3 Bf6 gives Black more than enough compensation. 19.Rad1 Rc8; 20.Nc6 Be6; 21.Qxe6 Qxd1; 22.Ne7+ Kf8; 23.Rxd1 fxe6; 24.Nxc8 Rxc8; 25.Bxb7 Rc2 was drawn in Teo–McKenzie, Postal 1991.

14...Bh5; 15.Nxc6.

15.Bg1. The two combatants argued this line a third time: 15...Qd7; 16.Qa4 Bc5; 17.Rad1 Bb6; 18.Rfe1 Bg6; 19.Qb5 Rad8; 20.e3 Qd6; 21.Nce2 Ne5; 22.Qb3 Ba5; 23.Nc3 Nd3; 24.Re2 Nc5 and Black was a little better in the 8th game of the Smyslov–Kasparov 1984 Candidates match in Vilnius.

15...bxc6.

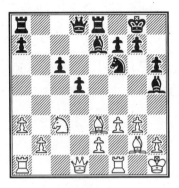

Black has only to reposition the pieces slightly to get a good game, and does so with the following moves. **16.Na4 Qc8; 17.Bd4 Qe6.** 17...Bd6 is also good. **18.Rc1 Nd7; 19.Rc3 Bf6?!** 19...Bg6 would have brought equality, according to Kasparov. **20.e3 Bg6; 21.Kg1.** 21.Bxf6. White misses the opportunity provided by 21...Qxf6; 22.Qd4 Qxd4; 23.exd4 with a small but annoying advantage. The pawn at c6 is a problem. **21...Be7; 22.Qd2 Rab8; 23.Re1.** 23.b4 Nb6; 24.Nb2 might have been worth trying.

23...a5!

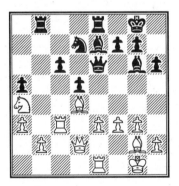

Now Black can claim equality. 24.Bf1 h5; 25.Re c1 Ne5; 26.Bxe5 Qxe5; 27.R xc6 Bf6; 28.R6c5 Qxe3+.

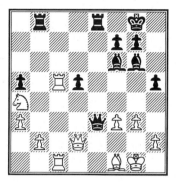

This leads to an endgame which is not winnable by Black, despite a number of small advantages. **29.Qxe3 Rxe3; 30.Rxd5 Rxf3; 31.Be2 Re3; 32.Bxh5 Bxh5; 33.Rxh5 g5; 34.Nc3 Rd8; 35.Rc2 Kg7; 36.Kg2 Kg6; 37.g4 Rd4; 38.h3. Drawn.**

SEIRAWAN VS. KASPAROV
Niksic, 1983

1.d4 d5; 2.c4 e6; 3.Nc3 c5; 4.cxd5 exd5; 5.Nf3 Nc6; 6.g3 Nf6; 7.Bg2 Be7; 8.0–0 0–0; 9.Bg5 cxd4; 10.Nxd4 h6; 11.Bxf6. This quiet line should not pose significant problems for Black.
11...Bxf6.

12.Nb3. 12.Nxc6 bxc6; 13.Rc1. (13.Qc2 Qa5; 14.Rac1 Rb8; 15.Na4 Bf5; 16.Qxf5 Qxa4; 17.b3 Qxa2; 18.Rxc6 Qxe2; 19.Bxd5 Qe5; 20.Qxe5 Bxe5 led to a draw in Geller–Korchnoi, Soviet Championship.) 13...Ba6; 14.Re1 Qa5; 15.Qc2 Rab8; 16.b3 Rfd8; 17.Na4 Bb5; 18.Nc5 Qa3; 19.Nd3 a5 gave Black a promising position in Sterk–Euwe, Budapest 1921.

12...d4. 12...Bg4; 13.Bxd5 Bxc3; 14.bxc3 Qf6; 15.Qc2 Rac8; 16.Qb2 Nb4; 17.Bxb7 Rxc3 didn't turn out any better for Seirawan: 18.e3 Rb8; 19.Be4 Bh3; 20.Rfc1 Nxa2; 21.Rxa2 Rbxb3; 22.Rxa7 Qxf2+; 23.Kxf2 Rxb2+; 24.Kf3 Rxc1 and White resigned in Seirawan–Lobron, Amsterdam 1983.

13.Ne4 Be7; 14.Rc1 Qb6; 15.Nec5 Rd8; 16.Rc4 Bxc5; 17.Nxc5 Qxb2; 18.Qc2 Qxc2; 19.Rxc2.

White does not have sufficient compensation for the pawn.

19...Rb8; 20.Rb2 Rd6; 21.Rd1 b6; 22.Nb3 Bb7; 23.Rbd2 Rbd8; 24.Kf1 Ba6; 25.Bxc6 Rxc6; 26.Nxd4 Rc5; 27.Nb3 Rxd2; 28.Rxd2.

Black's queenside majority is more dangerous than White's e-pawn.

28...Rc7; 29.Rd8+ Kh7; 30.Ke1 Bc4; 31.Kd2 g6; 32.Nc1 Kg7; 33.a3 Kf6; 34.e3 Ke7; 35.Rd4 Rd7; 36.Kc3 Rxd4; 37.Kxd4 b5.

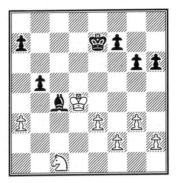

This position clearly illustrates the advantage of a good bishop over a poor knight. Kasparov now foresees a won pawn ending after **38.Nd3 Bxd3; 39.Kxd3 Kd6; 40.e4 g5; 41.f4 gxf4; 42.gxf4 Kc5; 43.Ke3 a5; 44.Kd3 h5; 45.h4 b4; 46.a4 f6; 47.f5 Kc6; 48.Kc4 Kc7!; 49.Kd3 Kd7; 50.Ke3 Kc6; 51.Kd3 Kc5; 52.Ke3 b3; 53.Kd3 Kb4; 54.e5 Ka3. Black won.**

White plays 9.dxc5

1.d4 d5; 2.c4 e6; 3.Nc3 c5; 4.cxd5 exd5; 5.Nf3 Nc6; 6.g3 Nf6; 7.Bg2 Be7; 8.0–0 0–0; 9.dxc5 Bxc5.

This is the major alternative to 9.Bg5. White immediately isolates the Black d-pawn, not allowing ...c4, which would leave it backward, but not as vulnerable. As we noted earlier, the capture at c5 can take place at many different points in the opening. Therefore the position in the diagram is often reached by transposition.

White's basic plan is to win the weak d-pawn. If this could be accomplished easily, then the Tarrasch Defense would be unplayable. As it turns out, Black has plenty of counterplay.

White usually continues with **10.Bg5**, pinning the knight at f6 and thus undermining the support of d5. For 10.Na4, see Schussler–Petursson in the Heroes chapter. Black must now advance the pawn in order to save it, so **10...d4; 11.Bxf6** (11.Ne4 Be7 is nothing. Similarly, 11.Na4 Be7 was fine for Black. See Wunnink–Schiller for details.) **11...Qxf6** is normal, and now the Timman Variation, **12.Nd5 Qc8; 13.Nd2!** is considered best. Black obtains counterplay by using ...Re8 and ...Bg4 to target the White e-pawn.

SHIROV VS. ILLESCAS CORDOBA
Buenos Aires, 1993

1.d4 d5; 2.c4 e6; 3.Nc3 c5; 4.cxd5 exd5; 5.Nf3 Nc6; 6.g3 Nf6; 7.Bg2 Be7; 8.0–0 0–0; 9.dxc5 Bxc5; 10.Bg5 d4; 11.Bxf6 Qxf6; 12.Nd5 Qd8; 13.Nd2 Re8; 14.Rc1.

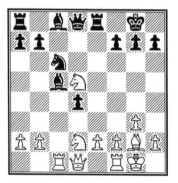

This is the normal continuation. The rook belongs on this square and can move there with gain of tempo.
   14...Bb6; 15.Nf4.
   15.Nxb6 Qxb6; 16.Nb3 Bg4 is comfortable for Black. 15.Re1 is discussed in the game Lerner–Nenashev.
   15...Bg4. Black can capture the pawn at a2, though it is risky. See King–Chandler in the heroes chapter for discussion. **16.Re1 Rc8; 17.Nc4 Bc7.** Here it is worth preserving the dark-squared bishop.
   18.Nd3 Qg5; 19.Bf3.

A surprising move that indicates that something may have gone wrong with White's play.

19...h5; 20.Qb3 Rb8; 21.h4 Qf5; 22.Nd2 Bd6; 23.Bxg4 hxg4.
Black controls a lot more space.

24.Nc4 Bc7; 25.Na3 Ba5; 26.Red1 Bb6; 27.Rc2 Ne5; 28.Nxe5 Rxe5; 29.Qd3. White needs to escape to an ending to avoid an inferior position.

29...Rbe8; 30.Qxf5 Rxf5; 31.Nc4 Bc5; 32.Rd3 b5; 33.Na5 Bb6; 34.Nc6 Re4; 35.Kg2 g5; 36.f3! gxf3+; 37.exf3 Re8; 38.g4 Rd5; 39.Nb4.

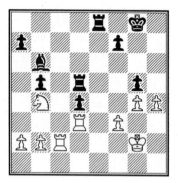

Neither side can make much progress. **39...Rde5; 40.hxg5 Rxg5; 41.Rcd2. Drawn.**

In the next game, we examine the natural move 14.Re1, defending the pawn at e2.

LERNER VS. NENASHEV
Soviet Union, 1991

1.Nf3 Nf6; 2.c4 c5; 3.Nc3 e6; 4.g3 d5; 5.cxd5 exd5; 6.d4 Nc6; 7.Bg2 Be7; 8.0–0 0–0; 9.dxc5 Bxc5; 10.Bg5 d4; 11.Bxf6 Qxf6; 12.Nd5 Qd8; 13.Nd2 Re8; 14.Re1.

Tony Miles has used 14.Re1 as an effective weapon against the Tarrasch. Despite his success, there has not been a large following for the move. However, since play usually transposes to the main lines after 14...Bg4; 15.Rc1 Bb6, it is not really important which rook moves first.

14...Bg4; 15.Rc1.

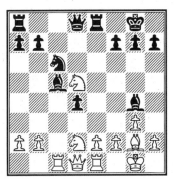

On well established alternative line runs 15.Nb3 Bb6; 16.Qd2 Be6; 17.Nxb6 axb6; 18.Bxc6 bxc6; 19.Qxd4 and White has a superior pawn structure but Black has a bishop.

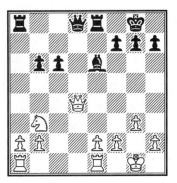

Black can give up the bishop for the knight and obtain a better endgame, or try for more with ...c5. Here are examples of each approach. I prefer the safer plan of capturing at b3.

A) 19...Bxb3!; 20.Qxd8 Raxd8; 21.axb3 Rd2; 22.Ra6 Rb8; 23.Ra2 g6. (23...Rc2; 24.Kf1 Rd8; 25.Rea1 Kf8; 26.Ra8 Rxa8; 27.Rxa8+ Ke7; 28.Ra2 g5 with a decent position for in Kotenko–Lutovinov, Soviet Union 1984.) 24.Kf1 c5; 25.Rc1 Re8; 26.e3 Re6; 27.Ke1 Red6; 28.h4 h5; 29.e4 Kg7; 30.e5 R6d5; 31.Rc3 R2d4; 32.Re3 Rd3; 33.Rxd3 Rxd3. Drawn. Vaiser–Groszpeter, Trnava 1983.

B) 19...c5; 20.Qc3 (20.Qxd8 Rexd8; 21.Red1 Rxd1+; 22.Rxd1 Kf8; 23.Rd6 Rxa2; 24.Rxb6 Bh3; 25.f3 Rxb2; 26.Rb8+ Ke7; 27.Rb7+ Kf6; 28.Nxc5 Rxe2; 29.Ne4+ Kg6; 30.Rb1 Rg2+; 31.Kh1 f5; 32.Rb6+ Kh5; 33.g4+ fxg4; 34.Ng3+ Kh4 was eventually drawn in Poecksteiner–Klinger, Austrian Championship) 20...h5; 21.a3 Qd5; 22.Nd2 h4; 23.Nf3 hxg3; 24.hxg3 Qh5; 25.e4 Bc8; 26.Nh4.

This kind of position, off the beaten track, is Miles' cup of tea. 26...Qg4; 27.Rad1 Bb7; 28.Qf3 Qxf3; 29.Nxf3 Bxe4; 30.Ng5 Bc6; 31.f3 Rxe1+; 32.Rxe1 f6; 33.Re6! Black would have easy equality after any other White move. Black would have easy equality after any other White move. 33...Rc8; 34.Ne4 Bxe4; 35.Rxe4 Kf7; 36.Kf2 Rh8; 37.Re2 Rh2+; 38.Ke3 Rxe2+; 39.Kxe2.

White has a clear advantage as he will create an outside passed pawn. 39...Ke6; 40.Kd3 Kd5; 41.b3 g5; 42.Kc3 f5; 43.Kd3 b5; 44.g4 fxg4; 45.fxg4 Ke5; 46.a4 c4+; 47.Kc3. White won. Miles–Klinger, Biel 1986.

15.Nf4 is also possible, but not dangerous: 15...Bb6; 16.Nc4 Rc8; 17.a3 Bf5; 18.Rc1 Be4; 19.Bxe4 Rxe4; 20.Qd3 Re8; 21.Qf3 Rc7; 22.Nxb6 axb6; 23.Nd3 Rce7; 24.Rc2 Re6; 25.Rec1 Qg5; 26.h4 Qb5; 27.Nf4 Re4. Drawn. Santos–Frois, Lisbon Masters 1996.

15...Bb6. 15...Bf8!?; 16.Nb3 Rc8; 17.Nxd4 Nxd4; 18.Qxd4 Bxe2; 19.Qxa7 Ba6 is a serious alternative.

A) 20.Qd4 Rc2; 21.Rcd1 (21.Bf1 Bxf1; 22.Rxf1 Ree2; 23.Rxc2 Rxc2; 24.Qe5. Drawn. Hjartarson–Petursson, Reykjavik 1984) 21...Rxe1+; 22.Rxe1 Qa5; 23.b4 Qxa2; 24.Bf1 Qa4; 25.Ne7+ Bxe7; 26.Rxe7 Rc8; 27.Qd5 Rf8; 28.b5. White won. Garakian–Bangiev, Postal 1986.

B) 20.b4 Rc2; 21.h4 Ree2; 22.Rxc2 Rxe1+; 23.Kh2 Rb1; 24.Qe3 Rd1 with counterplay for Black, Julian–Sala, Postal 1992.

16.Nc4.

16.Nb3 Qd6; 17.Nf4 Rad8; 18.Nd3 Re7 is solid for Black. For example, 19.Ndc5 Bc8; 20.Qd2 Ne5; 21.Nd3 Nxd3; 22.exd3 Rde8; 23.Rxe7 Qxe7; 24.Qf4 h6; 25.a3 Rd8; 26.Nd2 Be6; 27.Ne4 Bd5; 28.h4 Bc6; 29.Re1 Qd7; 30.Kh2 Re8; 31.Rc1 Bc7; 32.Qd2 Qe7. Drawn. Pedersen–Gokhale Jayant, Singapore 1990.

16...Ba5; 17.Nxa5 Qxa5.

18.b4 is the most aggressive move, attacking the enemy queen. It can be played right away, or after a preliminary advance of the a-pawn.

18.a3 (An unambitious alternative is 18.Nf4 Rad8; 19.h3, for example 19...Bf5; 20.a3 Be4; 21.Nd3 Bxg2; 22.Rc5 Qc7; 23.Kxg2 Qe7; 24.Qd2 Rd6; 25.b4 a6; 26.Qf4 Re6; 27.Rc2 Rf6; 28.Qg4 Rg6; 29.Qf5 Rf6; 30.Qg4 Rg6; 31.Qf5 Rf6; 32.Qg4. Drawn. Trois–Almada Villa Gesell 1985) 18 ...Rad8; 19.b4 Qxa3 and now there is a choice of plans. 20.b5. (20.Ra1 Qb2 21.Rb1 Qa3. Drawn. Rashkovsky–Lputian, Soviet Union 1985.)

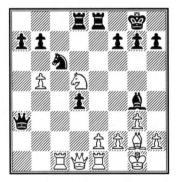

20...Bxe2!; 21.Rxe2 Rxe2; 22.bxc6 bxc6; 23.Rxc6 Qb2; 24.Bf1 Rxf2; 25.Qe1 Rc2; 26.Qe7 Rf8; 27.Qd6? (27.Rxc2 Qxc2; 28.Qxa7 is correct) 27...d3!; 28.Ne7+ Kh8; 29.Ng6+ hxg6; 30.Qxf8+ Kh7; 31.Qd6 Rxc6; 32.Qxc6.

The endgame is winning for Black, but care is required. Black played the careless 32...d2?? (32...Qd4+; 33.Kg2 d2; 34.Be2 d1=Q 35.Bxd1 Qxd1; 36.Qb7 Qc2+; 37.Kh3 Qa2 would have won without difficulty) and after 33.Qa4! Qc1 the game was agreed drawn. Orlov–Leski, Reno 1993.

18...Nxb4! 18...Qxa2; 19.Nc7 d3 isn't good enough for Black.

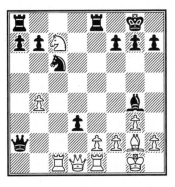

A) 20.Qxd3 Rad8; 21.Bd5 Rxe2; 22.h3. The exchange of rooks now does not solve Black's problems. 22...Rxe1+; 23.Rxe1 Be6; 24.Qe4 Rxd5; 25.Nxd5 Qb2; 26.Nf4 Qxb4; 27.Qxb4 Nxb4; 28.Rd1 Nc6; 29.Nxe6 fxe6; 30.Rd7 b5; 31.Rc7 Nd4; 32.Rxa7 b4; 33.Rb7 b3; 34.Kf1and White's advantage led to victory in Chernin–Georgadze, Soviet Union 1984. On the other hand, the retreat of the bishop is no good either. 22...Bh5?; 23.Bxa2 Rxd3; 24.g4 Nd4; 25.Kf1 Rdd2; 26.Rxe2 Nxe2; 27.Re1. White won. Flear–Martidis, Greece 1984.

B) 20.Ra1! is a little-known game with potentially great significance: 20...dxe2; 21.Qc1 Qb3; 22.Nxa8 Rxa8; 23.h3! Be6; 24.Rxe2 and White has an obvious advantage, Nd4; 25.Rb2 Qd3; 26.Qd1 Qc3; 27.Rd2 Rd8; 28.Rxa7 g6; 29.Kh1 Bb3; 30.Qe1 b5; 31.Ra8 Rxa8;

32.Bxa8 Be6; 33.Qd1 Nb3; 34.Rd8+ Kg7; 35.Qd6 Qe1+; 36.Kg2 Bc4;
37.Qf8+ Kf6; 38.Qh8+ Kf5; 39.g4+ Kg5; 40.f4+! Kxf4; 41.Qf6+ Ke3;
42.Qf3. Checkmate. Colias–Sprenkle, Illinois 1984.

19.Qxd4. 19.Qd2 pins the knight for a moment. 19...Nc6;
20.Qxa5 (20.Qg5 d3; 21.Nf6+ Kf8; 22.Qxa5 Nxa5; 23.Nxe8 d2; 24.Nd6
Be6; 25.Kf1 Rd8; 26.Nxb7 Nxb7; 27.Bxb7 Bxa2; 28.Ra1 dxe1Q+
29.Kxe1 Rb8; 30.Be4 Rb2; 31.Kd1 a5; 32.Bc2 Bc4; 33.Rxa5 Bxe2+.
Drawn. Fominikh–Miljanic, Budapest Sept 1990) 20...Nxa5. White
has tried:

A) 21.f3 d3; 22.Red1 (22.Ra1 Bd7. Drawn. Yusupov–Petursson,
Reykjavik 1985) 22...dxe2; 23.Re1 Rac8; 24.Rc7 Be6; 25.Ne7+ Rxe7;
26.Rxe7 Kf8; 27.Rxe6 fxe6; 28.Rxe2 and Black is better. Dreyev–
Ivanovic, Manila {Interzonal} 1990.

B) 21.Nc7 d3; 22.Rb1 d2; 23.Red1 Bxe2; 24.Rxd2 Rad8; 25.Rbb2
Rxd2; 26.Rxd2 Nc4; 27.Nxe8 Nxd2. Drawn. Spraggett–Leski, San
Francisco 1987.

19...Nxd5; 20.Qxg4 Rad8; 21.Red1.

Black can now solve all problems by retreating the knight and starting to play on the queenside. The game quickly fizzles out to a draw.

21...Nf6; 22.Qc4 b5; 23.Qc2 h6; 24.Bf3 Rxd1+; 25.Rxd1 Rd8; 26.Rxd8+ Qxd8; 27.Qc5 a6; 28.Kg2 Qe8; 29.e3 Qe6; 30.a3 Ne4; 31.Qd4 f5; 32.g4. Drawn.

Now we turn our attention to two games featuring an alternative strategy for White, where instead of targeting the d-pawn, White goes to work right away on the queenside.

WUNNINK VS. SCHILLER
Groningen (GM Open), 1997

1.d4 d5; 2.c4 e6; 3.Nf3 c5; 4.cxd5 exd5; 5.g3 Nc6; 6.Bg2 Nf6; 7.0–0 Be7; 8.Nc3 0–0; 9.dxc5 Bxc5; 10.Bg5 d4; 11.Na4.

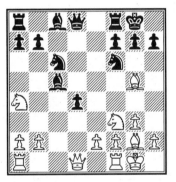

This is the most popular alternative to the capture at f6. The knight can move to e4, adding pressure to the pin, but it dissolves after 11.Ne4 Be7; 12.Bxf6 Bxf6.

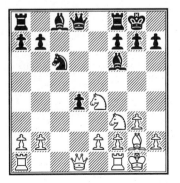

White has been unable to demonstrate any advantage, for example:

A) 13.Nxf6+ Qxf6; 14.b4 Bg4; 15.Qb3 Rad8; 16.Rad1 is Gaspariants–Feys, Cappelle La Grande 1995. 16...b5; 17.a3 Be6; 18.Qb2 Bd5 is fully acceptable for Black.

B) 13.Qd2 Bf5; 14.Nxf6+ Qxf6; 15.Qf4 (15.Rfd1 Rae8; 16.b3 was played in Zakharov-Deev, Russia 1987. 16...d3; 17.exd3 Bg4; 18.Qf4 Qxf4; 19.gxf4 Re2; 20.d4 Rd8; 21.d5 Nb4; 22.Ne5 Bh5 is complicated, but I think Black has enough for the pawn) 15...d3; 16.exd3 Bxd3; 17.Qxf6 gxf6; 18.Rfd1 Rad8, Yuferov-Lputian, Moscow 1979.

C) 13.Rc1 Re8; 14.Ne1 (14.Nc5 Qb6; 15.Nd3 Bg4; 16.Qd2 Rad8 provides equal chances, Valdivia–Boog, Swiss Championship 1993) 14...Be7; 15.Nd3 gives Black two good moves.

C1) 15...Qb6; 16.Qd2 Bg4. (16...h6; 17.Nf4 Rd8; 18.Nd3 Re8 is a good alternative, Chevallier–Tourneur, Paris Championship 1993.) 17.h3 Bf5. Black has achieved equality, Khalifman–S.Arkell, Seville 1993.

C2) 15...Bf8; 16.Qd2 a5; 17.Rfd1 (17.a3 a4; 18.Nec5 Qb6; 19.Qc2 Bf5; 20.Nxb7 Ne5; 21.Nbc5 Ra5; 22.Nxa4 Qb5; 23.b3 Nxd3; 24.exd3 Bxd3; 25.Bc6 Bxc2; 26.Bxb5 Rxb5; 27.Rxc2 Rxb3 is clearly better for Black, Khasin–Malevinsky, Kostroma 1985) 17...Bg4; 18.Ndc5 Bxc5; 19.Rxc5 Qe7; 20.h3 Bxe2; 21.Re1 d3. Black has a very strong position, Nikolic-Kasparov, Niksic 1983.

D) 13.Ne1 Be7; 14.Nd3 Re8; 15.Rc1 Qb6; 16.Re1 (16.a3 Bg4; 17.Re1 Rac8; 18.Nd2 Bg5; 19.Rc5 Be7; 20.Rc1 Bg5; 21.Rc5 Be7; 22.Rc1 was drawn in Schussler–Petursson, Neskaupsstadur 1984) 16...Bf5; 17.Nec5 Rac8; 18.Qa4 Bg5; 19.f4 Bxd3; 20.exd3 Rxe1+. (20 ...Be7 was drawn in Schneider–Petursson, Oslo 1983, but Petursson must have been happy with the result, since 21.Nxb7 Qxb7; 22.Bxc6 Rxc6; 23.Qxc6 Qxc6; 24.Rxc6 Kf8; 25.Rc7 is crushing.) 21.Rxe1 Qxc5; 22.Bxc6 Bxf4; 23.Bxb7 Be3+; 24.Kh1 (24.Rxe3 Qc1+; 25.Kg2 Rc2+; 26.Kh3 Qf1+; 27.Bg2 Qxg2+; 28.Kh4 g5+; 29.Kxg5 Qd5+; 30.Kf4 Rf2+ and Black wins) and Black has good prospects.

E) 13.b4 is an interesting line. 13 ...Nxb4; 14.Nxf6+ Qxf6; 15.Qxd4 Qe7.

Black has not completed development, but the threat of ...Nc2 buys precious time. 16.Qb2 (16.Rab1 Nc6; 17.Qb2 Rb8; 18.Nh4 Ne5; 19.Rfc1 b6 was about equal in Hellsten–Frolik, Mlada Boleslav 1995) 16...Nc6; 17.Rfd1 (17.Rab1 Rb8; 18.Nh4 Ne5; 19.Rfd1 b6; 20.Rd5 f6; 21.Rd4 Be6; 22.Rbd1 is Hellsten–Leito, Hallsdall 1996. Black moved a rook to c8, but the equalizer is 22...Rfd8; 23.e3 Nc4; 24.Qb1 Rxd4; 25.exd4 Rd8) 17...Bg4; 18.h3 was played in Kushch–Ponomarjov, Yalta 1995. Black should have captured the knight at f3.

Let's get back to the game, where White has just played 11.Na4.

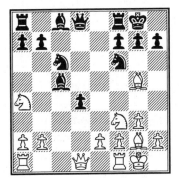

11 ...Be7; 12.Rc1. 12.Qd2 Ne4; 13.Bxe7 Qxe7; 14.Qd3 Rd8 was very comfortable for Black in Werth-Liegel, Postal 1984.

12 ...Bg4; 12 ...h6; 13.Bxf6 Bxf6; 14.Qb3 Qe7; 15.Nc5 b6; 16.Nd3 Bb7 is a reasonable alternative for Black, Mednis–Lputian, Palma de Mallorca 1989.

13.h3 Be6; 14.a3 Rc8; 15.b4 h6; 16.Bxf6 Bxf6; 17.Nc5 Qe7;

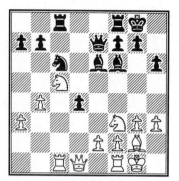

White has succeeded in securing the c5-square, but Black's pieces are well positioned to defend the d-pawn. If White now captures at e6, then there is hardly any way to make use of the c5-square.

18.Ne1. The knight heads to d3 to support its comrade. **18...Rfd8; 19.Ned3 Bd5; 20.Bxd5 Rxd5.** As is often the case when White weakens the kingside by advancing the h-pawn, Black can aim at the newly created targets.

21.Qa4 b6; 22.Na6 Qb7. Perhaps this is a bit ambitious. Settling for equality with 22...b5 did not appeal to me. **23.b5 Ne7; 24.Nab4 Rd6.** I suddenly lost confidence in the kingside attack, perhaps prematurely. 24...Rxc1; 25.Rxc1 Rh5; 26.Nc6 Nd5; 27.Qxa7 Qxa7; 28.Nxa7 Rxh3; 29.Rc6 is too strong for White. 24...Rh5; 25.Rxc8+ Nxc8; 26.Nf4 Rf5 was my original plan, and it would have been better than the move I actually played.

25.Rxc8+ Nxc8. 25...Qxc8; 26.Qxa7 Qxh3; 27.Qb8+ Nc8; 28.Rc1 Rd8; 29.Rc7 is clearly better for White. **26.Rc1 Ne7; 27.Nc6 Rd7; 28.Rc4.** The obvious move, piling on the pawn at d4. **28...Nd5.** Black takes advantage of some tactical resources involving sticking the knight at c3 and forking all sorts of things.

29.Nxd4 Bxd4; 30.Rxd4 Nc3; 31.Rxd7 Qxd7; 32.Qc4 Nxb5.

This is the endgame I was aiming for. I had considered Black's winning chances to be quite good, and saw no possible danger to me.

33.a4 Nc7; 34.Ne5 Qd1+; 35.Kh2 Ne6; 36.Qe4 Qd4; 37.Qf5. Exchanging queens is a bad idea, because Black has a big advantage on the queenside. White's move takes advantage of the vulnerablity of the f7-square.

37...Nd8. My opponent, in time pressure, now allows the exchange of queens. Although the knight endgame is a little tricky, he should have instinctively refrained from going into such a difficult ending, even at the cost of another pawn.

38.Qf4 Qxf4; 39.gxf4 Kf8; 40.Kg3 Ke7; 41.e4 Kd6; 42.Nd3.

White had counted on this move to keep the Black king out. The endgame strategy is not simple. If the Black king tries to infiltrate the queenside prematurely, White will be able to advance the central pawns, or somehow break down the defensive pawn barrier. In a book devoted to an opening repertoire, there is no space for a detailed analysis of the endgame, but strategically there are several stages. First, Black makes a passed pawn on the queenside. Next, the pawn is advanced to tie down the White knight. Third, the kingside pawn formation is clarified. Finally, the Black knight embarks on a remarkable journey to take up a defensive post, after which Black can safely win the White knight. **42...Ne6; 43.Kf3 b5.** This is the most direct way of creating the passed pawn.

44.axb5 Nd4+; 45.Ke3 Nxb5. Stage one accomplished. **46.f5.** I didn't think this move was as good as retreating the knight so that the Black pawn cannot advance so quickly. 46.Nb2 g6; 47.f3 is correct. Note that the Black a-pawn cannot go to a5 because of Nc4+.

46...a5!; 47.f4 a4; 48.Kd2 a3; 49.Nc1.

Stage two achieved, the pawn is advanced and the White knight must be very careful not to allow it to reach a2. Black cannot maneuver a knight to b4 to assist. **49...Kc5.** The king must play an active role, threatening to advance toward the White pawns.

50.Kd3 Nd6; 51.Na2 h5. This pawn wants to advance to h4, so that it will eventually be closer to the promotion square after Black maneuvers the knight to capture the pawn at h3.

52.h4 f6; 53.Nc1. White just moves the knight back and forth. Black must somehow try to entice White to advance the pawn from e4 to e5, where it will be weaker. Then the knight will need to move to e7 to make sure the pawns cannot advance, even with the help of the White king. Under those circumstances, Black will be able to use the king effectively on the queenside.

53...Nc4; 54.Na2 Nb2+; 55.Kc3 Nd1+; 56.Kd3 Nf2+; 57.Ke3 Ng4+. This is a useful post for the knight. Black threatens to play ...Kc4, so White's king must stay somewhere near the center.

58.Kd3 Nh2; 59.Ke3 Kc4; 60.e5.

This move is forced, but another goal has been achieved. Any other plan by White is too slow, as the Black king is ready to take out the enemy knight. **60...Ng4+; 61.Ke4 Nh6!** This move will make sense when you see the continuation.

62.Nc1 Ng8; 63.Na2 Ne7.

White is now lost. There are no White threats on the kingside, so the Black knight can be hunted down. **64.Nc1 Kc3; 65.Na2+ Kb2; 66.Nb4 a2; 67.Nxa2 Kxa2; 68.Kd4 Kb3.** 68...Nxf5+; 69.Kd5 Nxh4; 70.exf6 gxf6; 71.Ke6 Ng2 would have been a more efficient end to the game.

69.Kc5 Nxf5; 70.exf6 gxf6; 71.Kd5 Nxh4; 72.Ke6 Ng2. White resigned, because the king cannot catch the h-pawn. 73.f5 Ne3; 74.Kxf6 h4; 75.Kg5 Nxf5; 76.Kg4 Kc2 is a simple win.

RADULOV– SPASSOV
Slanchev Breag, 1974

1.d4 d5; 2.c4 e6; 3.Nc3 c5; 4.cxd5 exd5; 5.Nf3 Nc6; 6.g3 Nf6; 7.Bg2 Be7; 8.0–0 0–0; 9.dxc5 Bxc5; 10.Na4.

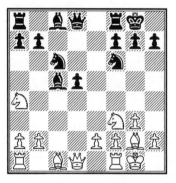

This is often played by those who are not familiar with the main lines of the Timman Variation. Black should retreat to e7, as the knight does not sit well at a4 and will likely retreat to c3 at some point. There are some other minor alternatives.

A) 10.Ne1 d4; 11.Ne4 Be7; 12.Nxf6+ Bxf6; 13.Nd3 Bf5; 14.Qb3 Na5; 15.Qb5 Bd7; 16.Qh5 g6; 17.Qh6 Bg7 and Black has a fine game, Porreca–Molenbroek, Postal 1971.

B) 10.e3 Bb6; 11.Qa4 Bf5; 12.Rd1 Re8; 13.Nh4 Be6; 14.e4? is an invitation to disaster. 14...d4; 15.Be3 Bd7; 16.Bg5 dxc3; 17.Bh3 cxb2; 18.Rab1 Nd4 and now 19.Bxd7 Qxd7; 20.Qc4 Rac8; 21.Qd3 Nxe4; 22.Be3 Nc3; 23.Bxd4 Qxd4; 24.Rxb2 Nxd1; 25.Qxd4 Bxd4 was an easy win for Black in Baeyertz–Sarapu, New Zealand Championship 1964.

C) 10.Qb3 a6; 11.Bg5 d4; 12.Ne4 Be7; 13.Nxf6+ Bxf6; 14.Bxf6 Qxf6 gives Black no problems. The rest of the game is interesting: 15.Rfd1 Re8; 16.Rd2 Rb8; 17.Rad1 Bg4; 18.Qb6 d3; 19.Rxd3 Rxe2; 20.Rb3 Rbe8; 21.h3 Be6; 22.Rc3 Bxa2; 23.Qxb7 Ne5; 24.Rc8 Ng6; 25.Rdc1 h6; 26.Rxe8+ Rxe8; 27.Nd2 Re2; 28.Ne4 Qxb2; 29.Rc8+ Kh7; 30.Qxa6 Be6; 31.Rc5 Qb1+; 32.Kh2 Rxe4; 33.Bxe4 Qxe4; 34.Qf1 Bd5; 35.Rc3 Ne5; 36.Re3 Nf3+; 37.Kh1 Nd2+; 38.Rxe4 Nxf1; 39.Kg1 Bxe4; 40.Kxf1 f5; 41.Ke2 g5; 42.Ke3 and White resigned, Herstein–Bengtsson, Buenos Aires Olympiad 1978.

10...Be7; 11.Be3 Bg4. Black can use many other moves, but this is the most consistent with our overall strategy.

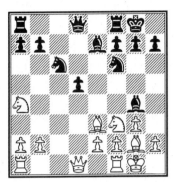

12.Nd4.

Black need not be concerned about this move, but none of the alternatives offer White anything either.

A) 12.Bc5 (12.Rc1 Re8; 13.Bc5 transposes) 12...Re8; 13.Rc1 (13.h3 Bh5; 14.Rc1 Bxc5; 15.Nxc5 Qe7; 16.Re1 Rad8; 17.Nd4 Nxd4; 18.Qxd4 Bg6. Black has a good game, Freisler–Pisk, Usti 1994) 13...Ne4; 14.Bxe7 Qxe7; 15.h3 Bxf3; 16.Bxf3 Rad8; 17.Bg2 Rd6. (17...h5; 18.h4 g6; 19.Nc3 Qe5. Black has a solid position, Anikaev–Lein, Grozny 1968.) 18.Nc5 Nxc5; 19.Rxc5 d4; 20.Rc2 h5. Black is better, and went on to win: 21.Rd2 h4; 22.g4 Red8; 23.Qa4 R8d7; 24.Rc1 Qg5; 25.Rcd1 b5; 26.Qa3 Ne5; 27.b3 Nxg4; 28.hxg4 Qxg4; 29.Kh2 Qf4+; 30.Kh1 Qxf2; 31.b4 h3; 32.Bxh3 d3; 33.Rxd3 Rxd3; 34.exd3 Qf3+; 35.Kh2 Qe2+; 36.Kg3 Re7 and White resigned, Schussler–Petursson, Gausdal 1985.

B) 12.h3 is harmless. 12...Bf5; 13.Rc1 Qd7; 14.Kh2 Rfe8; 15.Nc5 Bxc5; 16.Bxc5 Be4; 17.Bd4 Qf5; 18.e3 h6; 19.Bc3 Rac8; 20.Kg1 a6 was agreed drawn in Szekely–Nunn, Lublin 1978.

12...Ne5. 12...Qd7 is a good alternative.

13.Rc1 (13.Nxc6 bxc6; 14.Rc1 Bh3; 15.Bd4 Bxg2; 16.Kxg2 Rfe8; 17.f3 Qb7; 18.Qd2 Nd7; 19.Rc2 Bf8; 20.b3 Re6; 21.Qc3 Rae8; 22.Rf2 h5 and White is tied down, Tatai–Rajkovic, Italy 1972) 13...Rfe8; 14.Nxc6 bxc6; 15.f3 (15.Qc2 Rac8; 16.Bd4 c5; 17.Nxc5 Bxc5; 18.Bxc5 Rxe2; 19.Qb3 d4; 20.h3 Be6; 21.Qa3 d3; 22.Rcd1 Bxh3; 23.Rxd3 Qf5; 24.Rf3 was drawn in Novikov–Ehlvest, Volgodonsk 1983.) 15...Qe6; 16.Bd4 Bf5; 17.Qd2 Bf8; 18.Rfe1 Nd7; 19.Qc3 Rab8; 20.a3 c5; 21.Nxc5 Nxc5; 22.Bxc5 Bxc5+; 23.Qxc5 Rxb2; 24.Bf1 was agreed drawn in Eliskases–Garcia, Mar del Plata 1966.

13.h3 Bd7.

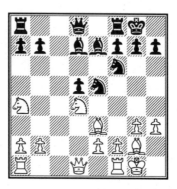

The lack of pressure at d5 makes Black's life easier. **14.Nc3.** 14.Rc1 Qa5; 15.Nc3 Nc4; 16.Nb3 Nxe3; 17.Nxa5 Nxd1; 18.Rfxd1 Bb4; 19.Nb3 Bxc3; 20.Rxc3 Bc6; 21.Nd4 Rfe8; 22.e3 Rac8 proved defensible in Pfeiffer–Burkhardt, Hauenstein 1991.

14...Nc4; 15.Bc1 Rc8; 16.Kh2 Bb4; 17.Nb1 Ne4; 18.b3 Ncd6; 19.Bb2 Qf6; 20.Qd3 Rfe8.

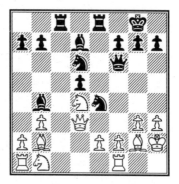

Black has control of almost all of the center and considerable pressure on the c– and e–files. There are also weaknesses in White's kingside pawn structure which can be exploited quickly. White senses the power of the Black knight, and takes measures to evict it, but new and dangerous weaknesses result.

21.f3! White has two alternatives. The first is a mistake. The second deserves further study.

A) 21.Na3 Bc3!; 22.Bxc3 Rxc3; 23.Qd1 Nxf2; 24.Qe1 Qxd4; 25.Qxf2 Qxf2; 26.Rxf2 Ne4; 27.Rf3 Rxf3; 28.Bxf3 Ng5 and Black wins the endgame without difficulty.

B) 21.e3 Nf5; 22.Nxf5 Qxb2; 23.Qd4 Qc2; 24.Nh4 is interesting but not 24.g4?! Bxf5; 25.gxf5 Nxf2 and Black is better.

21...Nxg3!

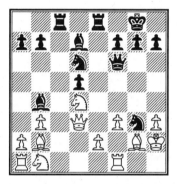

This piece sacrifice gives Black a tremendous attack. **22.Kxg3 Ne4+; 23.Kh2.** 23.fxe4 Bd6+ is brutal: 24.e5 Bxe5+; 25.Rf4 Qxf4. Checkmate. **23...Qf4+; 24.Kg1 Ng5; 25.e4.** 25.Nc3 Re3; 26.Qd2 Bxc3. **25...Bd6; 26.Rf2.** 26.Re1 Qh2+; 27.Kf1 Nxh3; 28.Ke2 Qxg2+; 29.Ke3 (29.Kd1 Nf2+) 29...Bf4. Checkmate.

26...Qh2+; 27.Kf1 Nxh3; 28.Bxh3 Bxh3+; 29.Ke2.

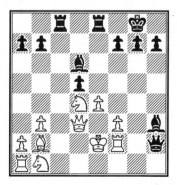

Black is not going to retreat when there are more lines to be opened! **29...dxe4!; 30.fxe4.** 30.Rxh2 exd3+; 31.Kxd3 Bxh2 and Black wins. **30...Bf1+!!; 31.Kxf1 Qh1+; 32.Ke2 Rxe4+; 33.Qxe4 Qxe4+** and Black had no problem finishing up. **34.Kd1 Qe3; 35.Re2 Qg1+; 36.Re1 Qg4+; 37.Ne2 Bb4; 38.Nd2 Rd8.** Black won. Radulov–Spassov, Slanchev Breag 1974.

White Plays 9.b3

1.d4 d5; 2.c4 e6; 3.Nc3 c5; 4.cxd5 exd5; 5.Nf3 Nc6; 6.g3 Nf6; 7.Bg2 Be7; 8.0-0 0-0; 9.b3.

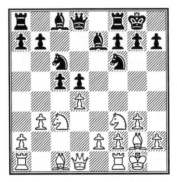

The fianchetto of the bishop is intended to add to the control of the dark squares d4 and e5 in the center, as well as to discourage the advance of Black's c-pawn. Bent Larsen was one of the vigorous proponents of the plan.

The bishop sits more comfortably at b2 than on the kingside, where it can be attacked by enemy pawns at pieces. At the same time, however, Black has less difficulty supporting the d5 square, and the knight at f6 can move to e4 with pressure at c3 and f2.

The b3 system is now seen more often by transposition from flank openings, often when White is not particularly familiar with the opening. In the normal Classical Tarrasch it suffers from a poor reputation, and it is not unusual to see White struggling to draw.

LARSEN VS. KASPAROV
Niksic, 1983

1.c4 e6; 2.Nc3 d5; 3.d4 c5; 4.cxd5 exd5; 5.Nf3 Nc6; 6.g3 Nf6; 7.Bg2 Be7; 8.0-0 0-0; 9.b3 Ne4.

The reorganization with knight at e4 and bishop at f6 is the standard recipe. It was developed by Tarrasch himself. 9...Re8 often transposes, but see Meins–Schiller, below, for some interesting alternatives for Black. **10.Bb2 Bf6; 11.Na4.** This is the only move which even aspires to an advantage.

   11...Re8;12.Rc1 b6; 13.dxc5 Bxb2; 14.Nxb2 bxc5.

   15.Na4. 15.Nd2 is a significant option. 15...Ba6!; 16.Nxe4 dxe4; 17.Rxc5 Qf6; 18.Nc4 Rad8 is the normal continuation.

   The White queen is under attack so there is no time to capture at c6. For the moment, White has an extra pawn. White can either retreat the queen or interpose the rook at d5.

   A) 19.Qc1 Nd4; 20.Re1 (20.Qe3 Nc2; 21.Qf4 Qxf4; 22.gxf4 f5 limits the scope of the White bishop, Strutinskaya–Gurieli, Soviet Union 1989) 20...Rd7; 21.Bh3 Rde7; 22.Bf1 h6; 23.Ne3 Rd7; 24.Nd5 Qd6; 25.Nc7 Ree7; 26.Nxa6 Qxa6; 27.Qb2 f5; 28.Rec1 e3; 29.f4 Qb7; 30.Bg2 Qa6.

Here White should have settled for a draw with Bf1. 31.R1c4? and now Black unleashed a combinational firestorm. 31...Nxe2+; 32.Qxe2 Rd2; 33.Qe1 Qxa2; 34.Bf3 Rf2; 35.Bd5+ Kh7; 36.Rc1 Re2; 37.Qf1 Rd2; 38.Qf3 Qb2; 39.Rc8 Re8; 40.R8c4 Rxd5; 41.Qxd5 Qf2+; 42.Kh1 e2; 43.Qxf5+ Kh8. Black won. Peev–Miljanic, Primorsko 1988.

B) 19.Qb1 Nd4; 20.Re1 e3; 21.fxe3 Bxc4; 22.bxc4 Rxe3; 23.Kh1 Rxe2 was drawn in Szymczak–Netusil, Prague 1989.

C) 19.Rd5 Qe6; 20.Rxd8 Rxd8; 21.Qb1 Nd4 and peace broke out in Fahnenschmidt–Wockenfuss, Germany 1984.

White can also try to reposition the knights, but this is a slow plan. 15.Nd3 Ba6; 16.Nf4 Nb4; 17.Nd2 Nxa2; 18.Nxe4 Nxc1; 19.Nc3 d4. (19...g5; 20.Qxc1 gxf4; 21.Bxd5 Qg5; 22.Bxa8 Rxa8; 23.Rd1 Re8; 24.Rd5 Re5; 25.Ne4 Qe7; 26.Rd7 Rxe4; 27.Rxe7 Rxe7; 28.Qxf4 Bxe2; 29.Kg2 a6; 30.Qg5+ Kf8; 31.Qxc5 f6; 32.f3 Bb5; 33.g4 Kf7; 34.Kg3 Re5; 35.Qc7+ Re7; 36.Qc3 Rd7; 37.h4 Rd3; 38.Qc7+ Rd7; 39.Qc5 Rd1; 40.h5 Rd8; 41.h6 Rg8; 42.Qd5+ Kf8; 43.Qb7 Bd3. White won. Arencibia–Bueno Perez, Cienfuegos 1984.) 20.Qxc1 dxc3; 21.Bxa8 Qxa8; 22.Qxc3 Qc6 and Black was a little better in Kinsman–Ziegler, Germany 1994.

15...Ba6; 16.Re1 c4.

This is now considered virtually forced. The tension at c4 is characteristic of the entire line now. White has a variety of possible continuations. In this game we will explore the most popular ones.

17.Nh4.

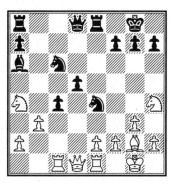

This was Larsen's attempt to find an advantage for White, but Kasparov squashed it flat.

17.Nd2 is most commonly seen, but not necessarily best, because it weakens f2. (17.Nd4 is not troublesome. 17...Rc8; 18.Nxc6 Rxc6; 19.Qd4 Bb5; 20.Nc3 Nxc3; 21.Rxc3 cxb3; 22.Rxc6 Bxc6; 23.axb3 Qb6; 24.Qxb6 axb6 led to a draw in Semkov–Miljanic, Vrnjacka Banja 1987.)

17...Qf6. This is an aggressive line which gives Black good counterplay.

A) 18.Bxe4 dxe4; 19.Nxc4 Rad8; 20.Qc2 Nd4 is a typical line. Then we might have 21.Qb1 Rd5; 22.Nc3 (22.Ne3 Nxe2+) 22...Rf5; 23.Nxe4 Qh6; 24.Ncd6 Rh5; 25.Nxe8 Rxh2; 26.N4f6+ Kf8. (26...Kh8; 27.Qxh7+ Qxh7; 28.Nxh7 Rxh7; 29.Rcd1 Nxe2+; 30.Rxe2 Bxe2; 31.Rd8 g6; 32.Nf6+wins.) 27.Qxh7 Rh1+; 28.Kg2 Rh2+; 29.Kg1 Rh1+; 30.Kg2 with a draw.

B) 18.Nxe4 dxe4; 19.bxc4 (19.Nc3 Rad8; 20.Nd5 Qb2; 21.Rc2 Qe5; 22.bxc4 Nd4; 23.Rd2 Bxc4; 24.Rxd4 Rxd5; 25.Rxd5 Bxd5 was slightly better for Black in Bonsch–Jelen, Portoroz 1987) 19...Rad8; 20.Qb3.

Black now uses one of the tactical weapons. The e-pawn is sacrificed to open up the position. 20...e3; 21.fxe3 Qh6; 22.Rc3 Ne5; 23.Nc5 Bxc4!

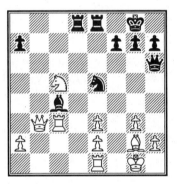

Black tosses in his "extra piece" from the queenside in order to achieve means on the other side of the board. 24.Qa4 (24.Rxc4 Nxc4; 25.Qxc4 Qxe3+; 26.Kh1 Rc8; 27.Rc1 Re5; 28.Bd5 Rxd5–+) 24...Ng4; 25.h3 Qf6; 26.Rcc1 Qf2+; 27.Kh1 Nxe3; 28.Rg1 Bxe2; 29.Ne4 Rxe4; 30.Qxe4 (30.Bxe4 Bf3+; 31.Bxf3 Qxf3+; 32.Kh2 Rd2+ and Black wins) 30...Nxg2. White resigned, Cherepkov–Novik, Leningrad 1991.

17...Qa5.

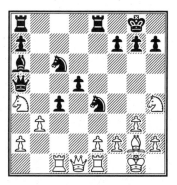

This protects the pawn from the flank, allowing a rook to support it if needed. In addition it eyes the important dark squares on the a5–e1 diagonal. **18.Nf5 g6; 19.Nd4.** White achieves the classical blockade, but Black still has counterplay. **19...Rac8; 20.h4!** 20.Bh3 is shut down by 20...f5. On 20.Nxc6 Rxc6; 21.Qd4 Rec8, Black has a slight initiative, but White has nothing to worry about. 22.Bxe4 dxe4; 23.Qxe4 Bb5; 24.Qe5 c3; 25.Rc2 Qb4; 26.Rec1 Bxa4; 27.bxa4 Qxa4; 28.Rxc3 Rxc3; 29.Rxc3 Rxc3; 30.Qxc3 Qxa2; 31.Qc8+ Kg7; 32.Qc3+ is a draw.

20...Ne5; 21.Bh3 Rc7; 22.Nc2 cxb3. Black has two interesting alternatives. 22...Bc8; 23.Bxc8 Rexc8; 24.Ne3 cxb3; 25.Rxc7 Rxc7; 26.axb3 d4 gives Black a strong initiative. Black can also try 22...c3; 23.Ne3 d4; 24.Qxd4 Bxe2; 25.Bg2 Nd2 with a threat of ...Nf3+.

23.axb3.

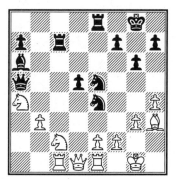

Black has a weak pawn, but the more useful pieces. **23...Bc8; 24.Bg2 Ng4; 25.Rf1 Bd7; 26.Ra1 Bxa4; 27.Rxa4 Qc3; 28.Bxe4 dxe4; 29.e3 Qxb3; 30.Rxe4 Rxe4; 31.Qd8+ Kg7; 32.Qxc7 Rc4; 33.Nd4**

Rxc7; 34.Nxb3 Rc2; 35.Nd4 Ra2; 36.e4 Rd2. 36...a5; 37.f3 Ne5; 38.Rf2 Rxf2; 39.Kxf2 a4 is better for Black.

37.Nc6 a6; 38.e5. 38.f3 Ne3; 39.Rf2 Rd1+; 40.Kh2 Rc1 makes White's defensive task difficult indeed.

38...Re2; 39.Ra1 Rxf2; 40.Rxa6 Rc2; 41.h5 Kh6; 42.hxg6 hxg6; 43.Ra4 Kg5.

White is very tied down Although one might expect endgames with this material to be drawn, Kasparov manages to press on and increase the positional advantage. He already has the White king pinned down and stronger pawns. Now the king takes an active role. **44.Nd4 Rc3; 45.e6.** White wants to get rid of the remaining pawns. **45...Rxg3+; 46.Kh1?** The king winds up in a mating net here. Also unpleasant is 46.Kf1 f5; 47.e7 Re3; 48.Nc6 f4; 49.Ra8 Nf6; 50.Kf2 Kh4.

46...f5; 47.e7 Re3; 48.Nc6 f4.

49.Ra5+! A draw was still possible, according to analysis by Timman. 49.Nd4! Rxe7. (49...Nf6; 50.Ra6 Rxe7; 51.Ne6+ Kf5; 52.Nxf4 Kxf4; 53.Rxf6+ Kg5; 54.Rf2 is a draw with best play.) 50.Nf3+ Kf5; 51.Nh4+ Kf6; 52.Rxf4+ Kg5; 53.Nxg6!! and White draws! 49.Ra8 is rather tricky. 49...Re1+; 50.Kg2 Re2+!; 51.Kf1 (51.Kf3 Re3+; 52.Kg2 f3+; 53.Kf1 Re2 transposes) 51...f3; 52.Rf8 (52.e8Q? Nh2+; 53.Kg1 f2+; 54.Kxh2 f1Q+; 55.Kg3 Qg2. Checkmate) 52...Ne3+; 53.Kg1 f2+; 54.Rxf2 Re1+; 55.Kh2 Ng4+; 56.Kg3 Nxf2; 57.Kxf2 Re6; 58.Kf3 Kf6. Black wins.**49...Kh4!** Black brings the king in to create a mating net!
50.Ra8 Nf6.

51.Kg2. 51.Rf8 Kg3! and the king gets mated. Notice that this is a result of the retreat to h1 at move 46. **51...f3+; 52.Kf1 Kg3; 53.Nd4 Ng4; 54.Nxf3.** 54.e8Q Nh2+; 55.Kg1 f2+; 56.Kh1 f1Q. Checkmate. **54...Rxf3+; 55.Kg1 Nh2; 56.Rf8 Rc3. Black won.**

MEINS VS. SCHILLER
Groningen, 1996

Now we see another approach by Black, one which led to a brilliant game on my part, which was unfortunately ruined by a time-pressure blunder.

1.d4 d5; 2.c4 e6; 3.Nf3 c5; 4.cxd5 exd5; 5.g3 Nf6; 6.Bg2 Be7; 7.0–0 0–0; 8.Nc3 Nc6; 9.b3 Re8.

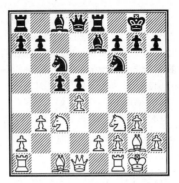

I find this to be a worthy alternative to the normal 9...Ne4. The move ...Re8 is usually part of Black's plan, and White has adopted a slow line with few threats. The advantage of this move order is that Black can decide later whether or not to bring the knight to e4. In some circumstances it can find better grazing elsewhere.

10.Bb2 cxd4. 10...Bg4 leads to well-explored lines, but I wanted to try something a bit different. 11.dxc5 Bxc5; 12.Rc1 Bb6; 13.Na4.

Black can choose from a number of good plans.

A) 13...Qe7! is probably best.

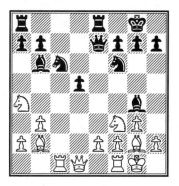

A1) 14.h3 Bf5; 15.e3 Nb4 gives Black good counterplay. 16.Ba3 Bd8; 17.Nd4 Be4; 18.Nc3 a5; 19.Nxe4 dxe4; 20.Qe2 Bb6; 21.Rfd1 Bc5; 22.Qb5 b6; 23.Nc6 Qf8; 24.Rc4 Nd3; 25.Bxc5 bxc5; 26.Rd2 Qd6; 27.Rc3 a4; 28.Bxe4 axb3; 29.Rcxd3 Qe6; 30.Ne7+ Kf8; 31.Qxb3 Nxe4; 32.Nd5 Qxh3; 33.Nf4 Qf5; 34.Rd5 Qf6; 35.a4 g5; 36.Nd3 Nxd2; 37.Qc3 Qe6?? (37...Qxc3 and White would surely have resigned. I suppose there was a time scramble.) 38.Rxc5 Ne4; 39.Qh8+ and White won in Vaulin–Obukhov, Cheliabinsk 1989.

A2) 14.e3 is likely to be transpositional, leading to variation A1. 14...Ne4; 15.h3 reaches the same position as that of the game, but at move 16 rather than 15. 15...Bxf3? misses the point, as we shall see in the main game. 16.Qxf3 Nd2; 17.Qg4 Ne5; 18.Bxe5 Qxe5; 19.Rfd1 Ne4; 20.Bxe4 dxe4; 21.Rd7 and White eventually won, Uhlmann–Espig, East Germany 1976.

B) 13...Qd6 is also not bad. 14.Nxb6 axb6; 15.a3 Rad8; 16.Qd3 d4; 17.Qb5 Re4; 18.Rfd1 h6; 19.Qxb6 Rxe2; 20.Ba1 Re7; 21.h3 Bxf3; 22.Bxf3 Ne5; 23.Qxd6 Nxf3+; 24.Kg2 Rxd6; 25.Kxf3 Ne4; 26.Rc2 d3; 27.Rc4 Ng5+; 28.Kg2 Red7 and Black had no problems in Reshevsky–Hjorth, New York 1984.

C) 13...d4 is interesting. On 14.Nxb6 Qxb6; 15.h3 Black has nothing better than exchanging bishop for knight with 15...Bxf3; 16.Bxf3.

White has the bishop pair and pressure in the center. 16...Rad8; 17.Qd2 Qa6; 18.Ba1 h6; 19.Rfd1 Ne4; 20.Qd3 Qxd3; 21.Rxd3 Ng5; 22.Bxc6 bxc6; 23.h4 Ne6; 24.Rxc6 with better prospects for White, Osmanbegovic–Jelen, Maribor 1994. Although we have seen that Black can play ...Bg4, the capture at d4 is appropriately timed on the tenth move. We choose it as our main line.

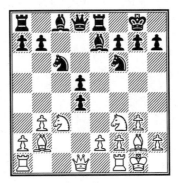

11.Nxd4 Bc5; 12.Nf3. The capture on c6 also comes into consideration, though it is nothing special. **12...Bg4; 13.Rc1 Bb6; 14.Na4.**

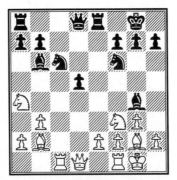

14...Qe7. I thought this was my original idea, but the game transposes to a known position a little later on. The plan is to offer the d-pawn as a sacrifice for rapid development.

15.e3. If 15.Nxb6 axb6. White has pawns hanging at e2 and a2.

15...Ne4. This is a real sacrifice, since White can actually consider taking the pawn at d5, after which Black has a choice between 16...Rad8 and 16...Nb4. I believe that practical chances justify the investment, but the complications need to be worked out by objective analysis. What follows are just some preliminary post–game thoughts.

16.h3. This looks like a strong move, since if the bishop retreats, the power of the pin is lessened. Black, however, has other plans.

When I first had an opportunity to study this game at home, I failed to notice a transposition, and later discovered, using the chess software tool Bookup, that 16.h3 had been played before, but Black failed to find the hidden resource in that game. 16.Qxd5 must be taken into consideration, of course.

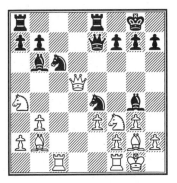

How does Black justify the sacrifice of the pawn. 16...Nb4 looked good to me during the game, but maybe it fails to a maniacally tactical line. 17.Qe5 Qxe5; 18.Nxe5 Bf5; 19.Bxe4 Bxe4; 20.Rc4 Nd3; 21.Rxe4 Nxb2; 22.Nxb2 f5; 23.Rf4 Rxe5; 24.Nc4 Rd5; 25.Nxb6 axb6; 26.a4 b5; 27.Rb4 and White is clearly better.

Therefore Black must try 16...Rad8. White must contemplate sacrificing the queen, but the initiative soon will drift back to Black. 17.Nxb6 forces 17...Rxd5; 18.Nxd5 Qd8; 19.Rfd1 Qa5; 20.a3 Qb5. Black not only threatens the pawn at b3, but also a deadly invasion at e2. 21.Bxg7 Qe2. (21...Kxg7; 22.Nc7 Qe2; 23.Nxe8+ Kf8; 24.Rf1 Bxf3; 25.Rce1 Qb5; 26.Bxf3 Nd2; 27.Bxc6 Qxc6; 28.Rc1 Qxe8 and Black comes out ahead.) 22.Nf6+ Kxg7; 23.Nxg4 h5 and the weakness of f2 is again critical. We can reject the queen sacrifice and concentrate on the retreat of the queen to c4. 17.Qc4.

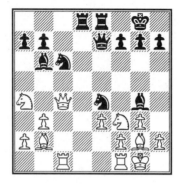

Black has two strategies to consider. The dark squared bishop can move out of the scope of the knight at a4, or the light squared bishop can capture at f3, with a subsequent fork at d2.

A) 17...Ba5 is the more cautious plan. 18.Nd4 Nxd4; 19.Bxd4. Black gets to attack with 19...Nd2! and has a good game.

B) 17...Bxf3; 18.Bxf3 Nd2; 19.Qg4 is probably better for White. After 19...Nxf3+; 20.Qxf3 Ba5 and Black has a lot of activity, but White has a pawn.

16...Nxf2.

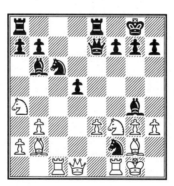

A very strong sacrifice, which gives Black a definite advantage. 16...Bxf3; 17.Qxf3 Nd2; 18.Qg4! and the threat of mate saves the exchange, as we saw above in the discussion of Uhlmann–Espig.

17.Rxf2 Bxf3. The only correct continuation, since 17...Qxe3 fails to 18.Nxb6! and 17...Bxe3; 18.hxg4 is too much of an investment for Black. 17...Qxe3 fails, 18.Nxb6! and 17...Bxe3; 18.hxg4 is too much of an investment for Black. **18.Bxf3 Bxe3; 19.Nc3 Qg5.** There is no need to capture either rook when the bishop is so strong.

20.Kg2 d4; 21.Nd5 Rad8.

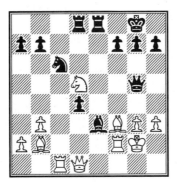

At this point I thought the game was simply winning, but White found a strong reply. **22.Rc5 Bxf2; 23.Kxf2 Ne5.** It took me far too long to work out the complications, and I caught up to my opponent on time. Each of us was down to 12 minutes.

23...Re3 occupied my attention for a while. Far too long, actually. The ensuing time pressure would prove very costly indeed. 24.h4 Qe5; 25.Kg2 and I just could not find anything convincing for Black. 25...Rxf3; 26.Qxf3 Nb4; 27.Qf5 Qe2+; 28.Kh3 Nd3; 29.Rc8 was one line I looked at, but my brain couldn't go any further than capturing the knight if Black checks at f2. 29...Nf2+; 30.Qxf2 Qe6+; 31.g4 Rxc8; 32.Qxd4 and now I am glad I didn't go into this line!

24.Qxd4.

What a picture! White has veiled threats against g7 and the move Ne7+ must always be attended to. Black does not seem to have much of an attack, but in fact the attack continues.

24...Nxf3. This undermines the knight at d5 and exposes the

White king. Each of us is down to 8 minutes here. This undermines the knight at d5 and exposes the White king. **25.Kxf3 Qf5+.** Wrong check. I missed the fact that the White knight is lost after ...a6 and ...b6, so that White cannot afford to exchange queens.

25...Qh5+; 26.Qg4 Qxg4+; 27.hxg4 b6; 28.Rb5 a6; 29.Rxb6 Rxd5; 30.Rxa6 Rd3+; 31.Kf4 Rd2. Black wins. I must admit that I missed the entire line with ...b6 and ...a6. This would have been a much more efficient line, but my move should also win.

26.Nf4 Rxd4; 27.Rxf5. Still, the position is completely winning for Black. **27...Rd2; 28.Bc3 Rxa2; 29.Nh5 f6.** Now 30.Bxf6 fails to 30...g6!

30.Rb5. Ten moves to go and only 2 minutes left, so I try to keep it simple. **30...Rd8; 31.Nf4 Rc2; 32.Be1 b6; 33.h4 Rd1.** This rook should have stayed home, but I didn't see any possible threat to my king.

34.Bb4 Rf1+; 35.Kg4 g6; 36.h5.

All I had to do is play 36...Rb1, but with both flags hanging I thought I saw a mating net. **36...Kg7; 37.hxg6 hxg6; 38.Rd5.** Now things are tougher, because the simple 38...Rc7 fails to 39.Ne6+. Checking at f5 was necessary. **38...Kh6.** Now White forces mate, a pattern I have never encountered. I just never saw it coming.

39.Bf8+ Kh7; 40.Rd7+ Kg8.

41.Nxg6. At first I thought I had won on time here, but I had forgotten to notate the exchange at g6. Then I thought that the position was not winning for me. Finally, it dawned on me that it was mate at g7! So I had to resign. A tragedy but certainly an entertaining and theoretically important game!

White plays 9.Bf4

1.d4 d5; 2.c4 e6; 3.Nc3 c5; 4.cxd5 exd5; 5.Nf3 Nc6; 6.g3 Nf6; 7.Bg2 Be7; 8.0–0 0–0; 9.Bf4.

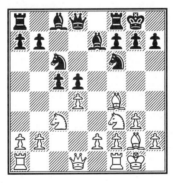

The bishop rarely performs effectively from this square in the Tarrasch Defense. Coverage of c7 is not much of a benefit, and the bishop can be challenged by ...Bd6 whenever Black feels that it is appropriate. We will adopt the central exchange strategy here too, even though 9...cxd4 is not the most ambitious system for Black. I prefer to advance the c-pawn and follow up with ...Qb6. But it is important to keep in mind that we want our repertoire to be harmonious, and try to apply the same logic in all similar positions.

So we adopt the central capture strategy seen in most of the main lines. This approach is still good enough to approach equality, and your results will benefit from your familiarity with the similar configurations in the other lines.

SCHIENMANN VS. SCHWAGLI
Zurich, 1991

1.d4 d5; 2.c4 e6; 3.Nc3 c5; 4.cxd5 exd5; 5.Nf3 Nc6; 6.g3 Nf6; 7.Bg2 Be7; 8.0–0 0–0; 9.Bf4 cxd4.

9...Bf5 is a compromise, because it can lead to typical Tarrasch positions if White captures at c5, for example 10.Rc1 Rc8; 11.dxc5 Bxc5 and now:

A) 12.Ne5 allows Black to equalize: 12...Re8!; 13.Nxc6 bxc6; 14.Na4 (14.Nxd5?? cxd5 and Black wins) 14...Bf8; 15.Nc5 Qb6 and Black is fine.

B) 12.Bg5 was suggested by Shamkovich and Schiller in 1983, but our only line started with 12...d4, and there is no need for that.

C) 12.Nxd5? allows a strong reply: 12...Bxf2+; 13.Rxf2 Qxd5; 14.Qxd5 Nxd5; 15.Ne5 Nxf4; 16.Nxc6 Rxc6; 17.Rxc6 bxc6; 18.Rxf4 Bd7 leads to a drawish endgame.

10.Nxd4.

Black has two interesting plans here. The traditional idea of ...Bg4 is playable, but ...Qb6 is more interesting. **10...Qb6.** 10...Bg4; 11.h3 Be6; 12.Ncb5 Nxd4; 13.Qxd4 Rc8; 14.Rfc1 a6; 15.Rxc8 Qxc8; 16.Rc1 Qd7; 17.Rc7 Qd8; 18.Na7 Ne4! gives Black good attacking chances.

A) 19.Bxe4 dxe4; 20.Qxe4 Bd6; 21.Bxd6 Qxd6; 22.Rxb7 Qd1+. (22...Bxh3; 23.Nc6 Qd1+; 24.Kh2 Be6 or 22...Bd5; 23.Qe7!) 23.Kh2 Qf1!; 24.Nc6 Qxh3+; 25.Kg1 Bxa2; 26.Nb4 Rd8! threatens a back rank mate. After 27.Nd3 Black can play 27...Qc8; 28.Ra7 Be6 with no danger of losing.

B) 19.Rxb7 allows Black to get to the weak f2 square. 19...Bc5; 20.Qa4 Bxf2+; 21.Kh2 Nc5; 22.Qc6 Nxb7; 23.Qxb7 Qd7; 24.Qxd7 Bxd7; 25.e3 g5. Black won. Bukal–Kostic, Mendrisio 1989.

11.Nxc6 bxc6.

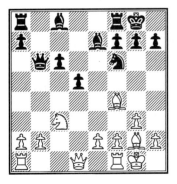

12.Qc2. 12.b3 is an interesting alternative. 12...Re8; 13.Qc2 Bd7; 14.e4 Rac8; 15.e5 Nh5; 16.Na4 Qa5; 17.Bd2 Qc7; 18.Rae1 g6; 19.h3 Ng7 gave Black a seemingly solid position, but the game opened up quickly: 20.Qc3 c5!? (20...Ne6 was the more conservative choice.) 21.Bxd5 Bxh3; 22.Bg2 Bxg2; 23.Kxg2 c4!? 24.Re4 (24.bxc4?? Qc6+! or 24.Qxc4? Qxc4; 25.bxc4 Rxc4 and Black is certainly no worse) 24...Qb7; 25.f3 cxb3; 26.Qxb3 Qxb3; 27.axb3 Rc2; 28.Rf2 Rec8 and Black had nothing to complain about in Knezevic–Dabetic, Yugoslavia Championship 1992.

12...Bg4!? 12...Be6; 13.Be3 Qa5; 14.Qa4 Qxa4; 15.Nxa4 Nd7; 16.Rfd1 Rfc8 is playable for Black, Petrosian–Keres, Amsterdam Candidates 1956. **13.Rac1 Rac8; 14.Be5 Rfd8; 15.e3 Qa6.** This is a useful post for the queen, which keeps an eye on a2 and e2 among other important squares. **16.h3 Be6; 17.g4 Nd7; 18.Bg3 Bf6.** This is a typical redeployment in the Tarrasch.

19.Rfd1 Nb6.

20.f4. Perhaps this is over–ambitious, underestimating the weakness at e3 which Black exploits directly. **20...d4!** This breaks open the game. **21.Ne4.** 21.exd4 Rxd4; 22.f5 Bd5; 23.Nxd5 cxd5; 24.Qb1 Rxc1; 25.Rxc1 Rd2 is clearly better for Black.

21...dxe3; 22.Nxf6+ gxf6; 23.Qc3.

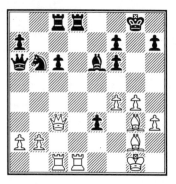

White seems to have made some gains, especially on the kingside!

23...Rxd1+!; 24.Rxd1 Bd5! 25.Qxf6. 25.Bxd5 Nxd5 holds all the weak pawns! **25...Qe2; 26.Rxd5.** White had no choice but to part with some material. 26.Qg5+ Kf8; 27.Qh6+ Ke8; 28.Rxd5 cxd5 and the invasion of the seventh rank will soon be complete.

26...Nxd5; 27.Qg5+ Kf8; 28.f5. 28.Qh6+ Ke7; 29.Bh4+ would have been a much tougher line to handle. 29...f6. (29...Kd7; 30.Qxh7 Qd1+; 31.Kh2 and the weak pawn at f7 is a problem.) 30.Bxd5 cxd5; 31.Qxf6+ Kd7 but Black will have a hard time hiding from the checks. 32.Qe7+ Kc6; 33.Qe6+ Kb7; 34.Qxd5+ Rc6; 35.Qd7+ etc.

28...f6!; 29.Qh6+ Kg8; 30.g5.

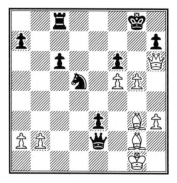

A last gasp, cut short by **30...Nf4!; 31.Bf1.** 31.Bxf4 Qf2+; 32.Kh1 e2; 33.Bd2 Re8! wins despite White's potential mating attack. But

Black must play accurately. 34.gxf6 e1=Q+; 35.Bxe1 Rxe1+! On the queen capture, Black would have difficulty finding a way to win given the threat at g7. 36.Kh2 Qg1+; 37.Kg3 Re3+; 38.Kh4 (38.Kf4 Qf2+; 39.Kg5 Rg3+; 40.Kh5 Qxf5+) 38...Qf2+; 39.Kh5 Qxf5+; 40.Qg5+ Qxg5+; 41.Kxg5 Rg3+ etc. **31...Qf3; 32.Bxf4 Qf2+. Black won.**

White plays 9.Be3 and others

1.d4 d5; 2.c4 e6; 3.Nc3 c5; 4.cxd5 exd5; 5.Nf3 Nc6; 6.g3 Nf6; 7.Bg2 Be7; 8.0–0 0–0.

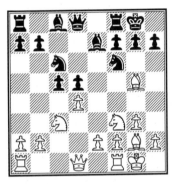

Here we examine the remaining options for White. In general, Black has nothing to fear from irrelevant moves. You can usually just continue development. If White plays exceedingly slowly, then the advance of the c-pawn to c4 comes strongly into consideration, followed by its friends, the a- and b-pawns. Black can play ...Qa5 to support such adventures.

Less ambitious, but also good, is the plan of simple development with ...Re8 and ...Bg4, ...Bf5, or ...Be6. As long as White is not putting direct or indirect pressure at d5, Black is free to make any move which does not weaken the position. Players of the White pieces usually adopt the plans in this section only when they are caught unprepared. The Tarrasch is a vigorous defense and passive play by White can be punished in spectacular fashion. Just don't assume that an offbeat move by White will necessarily give you a superior position. Usually it just concedes a comfortable equality.

We will concentrate on the development of the bishop at e3, the most common alternatives to the main lines. There are a few other moves to be considered, but they don't deserve special attention.

White plays 9.Be3

9.Rb1? is just a stupid waste of time. After 9...Bf5 White has nothing better than 10.Ra1 h6; 11.Nh4 Bh7; 12.dxc5 Ne4; 13.Nf3 Nxc3; 14.bxc3 Bxc5; 15.Qb3 Na5; 16.Qb5 Qb6; 17.Qxb6 Bxb6 presented no problems for Black, Melson–Heinig, Postal 1987.

9.a3 cannot bring White an advantage, weakening as it does the b3 square. 9...Be6; 10.dxc5 Bxc5; 11.b4 Be7; 12.Bb2 Rc8; 13.Nd4 Nxd4; 14.Qxd4 a5; 15.b5 Qd7; 16.Rfd1 Rfd8; 17.Rac1. Here in Rubinstein–Teichmann, San Sebastian 1911, Black played the inferior 17...Qe8 but Black can equalize with 17...Bc5!.

9.h3 c4; 10.Ne5 Be6; 11.Kh2 Qb6; 12.a3 Rad8 equalized in Esposito–Schiller, Chicago 1982. 9...Re8 and 9...h6 are reasonable alternatives.

9.e3 c4!; 10.b3 Qa5; 11.Bb2 Bb4 gave Black a strong queenside initiative in Silva–Schiller, Hastings Challengers 1980/81.

GUREVICH VS. WILDER
USA Championship, 1984

1.d4 d5; 2.c4 e6; 3.Nf3 c5; 4.cxd5 exd5; 5.Nc3 Nc6; 6.g3 Nf6; 7.Bg2 Be7; 8.0–0 0–0; 9.Be3.

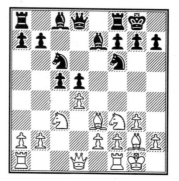

9...Ng4. This is the best reply. A few successes by White against inaccurate defense has created a poor reputation for the line, but it is really quite strong!

10.Bf4 Be6.

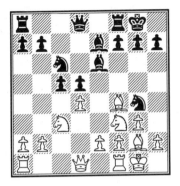

11.dxc5. 11.Rc1 g5!? This leads to interesting complications. 12.Bd2 is forced. 12...Nxd4; 13.Nxd4 cxd4; 14.Nb5 Qb6!; 15.Nc7 Rad8.

16.Qa4 (16.Nxe6 fxe6! and Black has a better position) 16...Bd7; 17.Qa5 Bc6; 18.Qxb6 axb6. Black has an extra pawn, but the structural weaknesses cannot be ignored. 19.Na6 (19.a4 is an interesting alternative, e.g., 19...Rd7; 20.Nb5 Ra8; 21.b3 Bxb5; 22.axb5 Ra2; 23.Rfd1 d3; 24.exd3 Bc5; 25.Be1 Nxf2; 26.Bxf2 Bxf2+; 27.Kh1 and the bishops of opposite color should secure the half–point, eventually) 19...Ne5; 20.Bb4 Rfe8; 21.Bxe7 Rxe7; 22.Nb4 Bb5; 23.Nxd5 and now 23...Rxd5!?; 24.Bxd5 Bxe2; 25.Rc8+ Kg7; 26.Ra1 d3; 27.Rd8 d2; 28.f4.

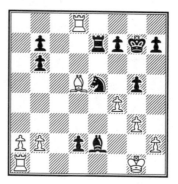

28...d1=Q+; 29.Rxd1 Bxd1; 30.fxe5 Rxe5; 31.Bxb7 Bg4; 32.Rd5 was equal in Lombardy–Emma, Mar del Plata 1958.

11...Bxc5.

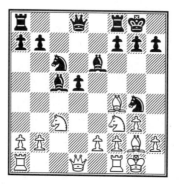

12.Ng5. The most interesting move. Black equalizes without difficulty against others.

A) 12.e3 h6; 13.h3 Nf6; 14.Rc1 (14.g4 Nh7) 14...Bb6; 15.g4 Qe7; 16.Qa4 Rfd8; 17.Rfd1 Rac8! Black threatens ...b4 with equality. 18.a3 Qe8! Black has a solid position and no worries.

B) 12.h3 Nf6; 13.Na4 Be7; 14.Be3 Ne4; 15.Nd4 Nxd4; 16.Bxd4 Qa5; 17.Nc3 Rac8; 18.Kh2 (18.Nxe4? dxe4; 19.Bxe4 Bxh3; 20.Re1 Rfd8; 21.e3 Bf6 Black is much better) 18...f5; 19.e3 Rc4; 20.Qh5. This position was reached in Lazarev–Kopylov, Soviet Union 1963. 20...b5! 21.a4 b4; 22.Nxe4 g6!, a good game for Black, Shamkovich & Schiller (1984).

C) 12.Ne1 Bd4; 13.Nd3 (13.Nc2!? Bxc3; 14.bxc3 Qa5 is unclear, according to Euwe & van der Sterren) 13...Nf6; 14.Rc1 h6; 15.Na4 Ne4 brought equality in Flohr–Lasker, Moscow 1935.

D) 12.Qc2 h6; 13.Rad1 Rc8; 14.Qb1 (Larsen–Sarapu, Sousse Interzonal 1967) 14...a6! is equal, Shamkovich & Schiller (1984).

E) 12.Re1 h6; 13.Na4 Bb6; 14.a3 Rc8 gives Black no problems Csom–Hernandez, Kecskemet 1975.

F) 12.Na4 Be7; 13.Nd4 Nxd4; 14.Qxd4 Qa5 has been seen.

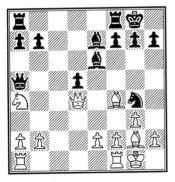

F1) 15.h3 Bf6; 16.Qd1 Ne5; 17.Bd2 Qb5; 18.Bc3?! (18.b3=) 18...d4; 19.Bxd4 Rad8; 20.Nc3 Qc4; 21.e3 Nc63 and Black had the better prospects in Andersson–Pfleger, Manila 1974.

F2) 15.Rac1 Rac8. (15...Bf6; 16.Qd1 Rac8 is also good.) 16.b3 (16.Nc3 Bc5; 17.Qd2 Qb6; 18.e3 d4; 19.exd4 Bxd4 with an equal position. Agdestein–Petursson, Gausdal 1985) 16...Ba3; 17.Bd2 Qa6; 18.Bc3 Nf6; 19.Bb2 Bxb2; 20.Qxb2 b6 is equal. Bergwasser–Minev, Leipzig Olympad 1960.

G) 12.Rc1 a6; 13.Qd3 h6; 14.h3 Nf6; 15.Ne5 Ba7; 16.Na4 Qa5; 17.b3 Rac8; 18.Nxc6 Rxc6; 19.Rxc6 bxc6; 20.Rc1 Rc8 was solid for Black. Tal–Chandler, Yurmala 1984.

The departure of the knight in our main line game weakens the defense of the king, and Black can take advantage quickly.

12...Nxf2!

12...Bxf2+; 13.Rxf2 Qb6; 14.Nh3 Nxf2; 15.Nxf2 Qxb2; 16.Rc1 Rfd8; 17.Nd3 Qa3 was better for White in Miles–Borik, Bad Woerishofen 1985.

13.Rxf2 Bxf2+; 14.Kxf2 Qb6+; 15.Kf1 Qxb2.

16.Qb1. 16.Qc1 Qxc1+; 17.Rxc1 h6; 18.Nxe6 fxe6 is unclear. I think the chances are roughly level.

16...Qxb1+; 17.Rxb1.

Black has a material advantage of rook and two pawns for bishop and knight. White has active pieces which provide enough compensation. **17...d4?!** 17...h6!? is stronger, resolving the situation at e6.

18.Nd5 Rad8; 19.Nc7 Bxa2; 20.Rxb7 h6.

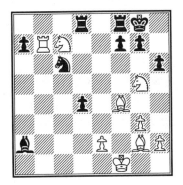

The position has become unhinged. White now obtains a material advantage. **21.Bxc6 hxg5; 22.Bxg5 Rb8; 23.Rxa7 Rb1+; 24.Kf2 Rb2; 25.Bb5.** 25.Nb5!? might have been stronger. 25...d3; 26.Nc3 Be6; 27.Ba4! Rc8; 28.Bc1! Rb4; 29.Bd2 Rb2; 30.Ke1 and White is consolidating.

25...Bb1; 26.Bc1 Rc2; 27.Bf4 Rd8; 28.Ke1 Rc5.

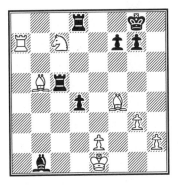

Here White blunders. **29.Kd2?!** 29.h4!? is correct, and Black is still in trouble. **29...g5!** The bishop is trapped. **30.Bxg5 Rxg5; 31.Bc4 Bg6.** White has no real hopes of saving this game. **32.Ra4 Rc5; 33.Nb5 Kg7; 34.h4 Rdc8; 35.Na3 Rb8; 36.g4 Rb2+; 37.Kd1 Be4; 38.Ra7 Bd5; 39.Bd3 Be6; 40.g5 Ra2; 41.g6 Bb3+; 42.Ke1 Rc1+; 43.Kf2 Rca1; 44.h5 Rxa3; 45.Rb7 Bd5; 46.Rb6 Rh1. Black won.**

This concludes our examination of the Classical Variation. More examples may be found in the Heroes chapter.

ASYMMETRICAL TARRASCH

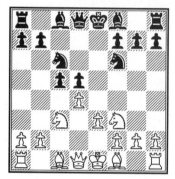

1.d4	d5
2.c4	e6
3.Nc3	c5
4.cxd5	exd5
5.Nf3	Nc6
6.e3	Nf6

The essential characteristic of the Assymetrical variation is the exchange of White's c-pawn for Black's pawn at d5, with a recapture by the Black e-pawn, and no fianchetto by White. This is known as the Asymmetrical Variation because White breaks the pattern by capturing on d5. Black cannot restore the symmetry by force since if Black captures at d4, White can recapture with the knight from f3. If Black then exchanges knights at d4, White recaptures with the queen. The isolated pawn at d5 is very weak and as more minor pieces depart the center may well fall.

For this reason Black usually refrains from ...cxd4. White can still isolate the pawn by playing dxc5, but this brings the bishop into the game from f8 and Black may be able to quickly advance the d-pawn to d4 and get rid of the weakness once and for all.

In many games, neither side makes a move in the center for a while. Instead, development is completed and confrontation is postponed until the middlegame. Generally speaking, Black has little to fear at d5 because the enemy bishop is not at g2, bearing down from the flank, as it does in the Classical lines.

'There are a great many transpositional paths leading to the Asymmetrical Tarrasch. In addition to the featured games presented below, you will find more example in the chapter on the Symmetrical Tarrasch, because sooner or later any symmetry must break down.

EVANS VS. LARSEN
Dallas, 1957

1.d4 d5; 2.c4 e6; 3.Nc3 c5; 4.e3 Nf6. This game starts out as a Symmetrical Variation, but the symmetry is unbalanced when White captures at d5. **5.Nf3 Nc6.** 5...cxd4 6.exd4 Bb4 is a transposition to the Panov Attack of the Caro Kann or Nimzoindian Defense. This is a perfectly good defense, if you happen to know it.
6.cxd5 exd5.

7.Bb5. The pin threatens Ne5 and gives White time to castle. As in the Spanish Game, Black can break the pin immediately by advancing the a-pawn.

For 7.dxc5 see Kurschner–Tarrasch in the Heroes chapter. There are, however, other moves to be considered.

A) 7.a3 is often seen, planning a capture at c5 followed by b4. That would be good for White. Black can advance the c-pawn, but let's stick to our standard strategy and capture in the center. 7...cxd4 allows either recapture 8.Nxd4 (8.exd4 Be7; 9.Bb5 Bd7; 10.0-0 0-0; 11.Re1 Re8; 12.h3 h6 is solid for Black, Schultheis–Stegmann Postal 1982) 8...Be7; 9.Be2 0-0; 10.0-0 a6; 11.b4 Qd6 gives Balck a good game, for example 12.Bf3 Ne5; 13.Nce2 Nxf3+; 14.Nxf3 Ne4; 15.Bb2 Bg4; 16.Be5 Qd7; 17.Nf4 Rfd8; 18.Rc1 Rac8; 19.Rxc8 Qxc8; 20.Nxd5 Bf8; 21.Qd4 Bxf3; 22.gxf3 Ng5; 23.Qd1 Qh3; 24.Bg3 Qf5; 25.e4 Nxf3+; 26.Kg2 Qxe4; 27.Nf6+ gxf6; 28.Qxf3 Qxf3+; 29.Kxf3 Rd3+; 30.Ke4 Rxa3; 31.Bh4 Be7; 32.Rg1+ Kf8; 33.Kf5 Rf3+; 34.Ke4 Rb3. Black won. De Brouwer–De Jong, Wijk aan Zee 1989.

B) 7.Bd3 is another reasonable line. 7...a6 makes a home for the bishop at a7. 8.dxc5 Bxc5; 9.0-0 0-0; 10.Bd2 Re8; 11.Rc1 Ba7; 12.Ne2 Bg4; 13.Bc3 Ne4; 14.Ng3.

The weakness of f2, f3 and e3 now combine to destroy White. 14...Nxf2; 15.Rxf2 Rxe3; 16.Nf5 Rxf3; 17.gxf3 Bxf5; 18.Bxf5 Qg5+; 19.Bg4 h5; 20.Qd2 Be3. Black won. Burn–Lasker, Hastings 1895.

C) 7.g3 Bd6 (both 7 ...Bg4 and 7 ...Ne4 are worth considering). 8.Bg2 0-0; 9.0-0 Re8; 10.dxc5 Bxc5; 11.Nd4 Bb6; 12.b3 Bg4; 13.Nxc6 bxc6 is a typical Tarrasch position. Black made effective use of the d-pawn in the following game. 14.Qc2 Qd7; 15.Bb2 Bh3; 16.Na4 Bxg2; 17.Kxg2 Ne4; 18.Nxb6 axb6; 19.f4 Nd6; 20.Rfe1 Nf5; 21.Qc3 Rxe3; 22.Rxe3 d4; 23.Qd3 Nxe3+; 24.Kg1 Qh3; 25.Qe2 f5; 26.a4 Re8; 27.Rd1 Re6; 28.Qf3 h5; 29.Re1 Ng4; 30.Re2 Rxe2; 31.Qxe2 d3. Black won. Verbundete–Teichmann, Zurich 1916.

D) 7.b3 cxd4; 8.Nxd4 Bb4; 9.Bd2 Nxd4; 10.exd4 0-0. Black has a promising game on the queenside, for example 11.Be2 Qa5; 12.Rc1 Bf5; 13.a3 Bxc3; 14.Bxc3 Qxa3; 15.0-0 Rac8; 16.Ra1 Qd6; 17.Bb2 Bc2; 18.Qd2 Qb6; 19.Ba3 Rfe8; 20.Bc5 Qxb3; 21.Ra3 Ne4; 22.Qc1 Nxc5; 23.Rxb3 Nxb3. Black won. Peterson–Morgado, Postal 1979.

E) 7.Ne5 Bd6; 8.Bb5 Qc7; 9.Qa4 0-0; 10.Nxc6 bxc6; 11.Bxc6 (11.dxc5 cxb5; 12.cxd6 Qxc3+. Black won. Voloshin–Forarasi Hungary 1988) is not as strong as it looks.

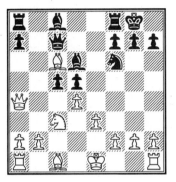

Black can play boldly with 11...cxd4!; 12.Bxa8 dxc3 and Black has many threats. After 13.Qc6 Qxc6; 14.Bxc6, for example, Black can play 14...Be5! White's failure to castle becomes a major factor. 15.Rb1 Bf5! leaves White with nothing better than 16.f4 Bxf4; 17.exf4 Bxf1; 18.bxc3, where 18...Rc8! brings Black an extra pawn.

7...a6; 8.Bxc6+ bxc6; 9.0–0 Bd6; 10.dxc5 Bxc5; 11.e4!

Creating the famous isolated d-pawn. **11...0–0.** 11...Nxe4?; 12.Nxe4 dxe4; 13.Qxd8+ Kxd8; 14.Ng5 is a trick only a beginner would fall for. **12.Bg5 Be7?** Black misses the chance to advance the d-pawn to d4, denying that square to the White knight.

13.Nd4 Qd6; 14.e5? This is a much too clever method of isolating the pawn. The straightforward 14.exd5 cxd5; 15.Re1 would have brought White a significant advantage.

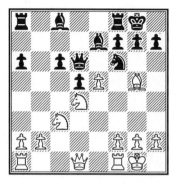

14...Qxe5; 15.Nxc6 Qxg5; 16.Nxe7+ Kh8. Perhaps Evans was counting on capturing at d5, but then 17...Rd8 would cause trouble, so instead he eliminates Black's bishop. **17.Nxc8 Raxc8; 18.Qd3.** This position is not easy to evaluate objectively. If Black plays passively then White will dominate the e-file and go to work on the weak isolated pawn. But Larsen realizes that by giving up some material, he can get the e & c files.

18...Rfd8!! Black's plan is clear — give up the a-pawn and allow White to enjoy two connected passed pawns, but in return Black is going to take all of the files in the center and advance his own pawn.

19.Qxa6 d4; 20.Ne2 Rc2!

A typical infiltration of the seventh rank. **21.Rad1** White is of course prepared to give up his b-pawn for the powerful pawn at d4, but Larsen does not oblige.

21...Qe5!

A powerful centralizing move which brings Black full compensation for his pawn since he now has kingside attacking chances in addition to the files. **22.Ng3.** 22.Nc1 Ng4!; 23.g3 Qh5; 24.h4 Nxf2!!; 25.Rxd4 Nh3+; 26.Kh1 Rdc8 is a piece of fine analysis by Brondum. **22...h5!** Black has achieved complete control of the center of the board, and the laws of chess say that when you have the center, and the enemy forces (in this case the queen) are offside, a flank attack is in order.

23.Rfe1 Qd5; 24.Re2 d3! 25.Re3. And now we must look at the potential fork of f2 and e3 via Ng4. When we see this tactical idea, then Black's next move is obvious! **25...Rxf2!; 26.Ne4.** Of course not 26.Kxf2 because then 26...Ng4+ picks up the stray rook with multiple threats.

26...Nxe4; 27.Rexd3. 27.Rdxd3 might have maintained equality. For example: 27...Qg5. (27...Rxb2; 28.Rxd5 Rb1+; 29.Qf1 Rxf1+; 30.Kxf1 Rxd5; 31.Rxe4 Ra5 and Black is no worse.) 28.Rxd8+ Kh7; 29.Rh8+!! Kxh8; 30.Qa8+ Kh7; 31.Qxe4+ f5; 32.h4! Rxg2+; 33.Qxg2 Qxe3 and White is better.

27...Rf1+!!; 28.Rxf1. 28.Kxf1 Qf5+; 29.Kg1 (29.Rf3 Rxd1+; 30.Ke2 Nc3+!) 29...Qc5+. This is what Larsen had in his mind... 30.Kh1 Nf2+; 31.Kg1 Nh3+; 32.Kh1 Qg1+; 33.Rxg1 Nf2 checkmate and the knowledge of the familiar motif pays off. **28...Qc5+.** Evans resigned, because 29.Kh1 is met by Nf2+ and either the smothered mate or a backrank mate follows. **Black won.**

The plan with an early ...a6 is not considered best, but it is serviceable. The more popular approach is to develop the bishop to d6 and castle. This continuation is much better known and there is a lot of theory on the line. If you want to play for a win, the added effort in studying the following games will be repaid at the chessboard.

VAISSER VS. ILLESCAS CORDOBA
Spain, 1996

1.d4 d5; 2.c4 e6; 3.Nc3 c5; 4.e3 Nf6; 5.Nf3 Nc6; 6.cxd5 exd5; 7.Bb5 Bd6.

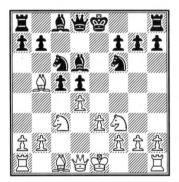

White can take immediate action to maintain an initiative or postpone that until castling.. **8.Ne5.** For 8.dxc5 see Sunye Neto-Kasparov in the chapter on the Symmetrical Tarrasch. White often transposes from the symmetrical lines, as seen in the present game.

8.0-0 (8.Qa4 Bd7 presents no particular difficulty to Black) 8...0-0; 9.h3 is another line (for the capture at c5, again see Sunye Neto-Kasparov). 9...Re8; 10.a3 a6; 11.Bxc6 bxc6; 12.dxc5 Bxc5; 13.Qc2 Bd6; 14.Re1 c5; 15.e4 dxe4; 16.Nxe4 Nxe4; 17.Rxe4 Bb7; 18.Rxe8+ Qxe8; 19.Be3 Bxf3; 20.gxf3 Qe5 and Black is clearly better, Perdomo-Arencibia, San Spiritus 1989. Also good is 9...Bf5; 10.dxc5 Bxc5; 11.b3 Qa5; 12.Bb2 Rfd8; 13.Bxc6 bxc6; 14.Nd4 Bd7; 15.Qf3 Bxd4; 16.exd4 Re8; 17.Rfe1 Rxe1+; 18.Rxe1 where 18...Ne4! brought equality in Karpov–Polugayevsky, Reggio Emilia 1991.

Black must now do something about the situation at c6. **8...Qc7.** 8...Bd7; 9.Nxd7 Qxd7; 10.dxc5 Bxc5 is a reasonable alternative. **9.Qa4.**

9.Nxc6 bxc6; 10.dxc5 Bxc5 is already better for Black. 11.Be2 (11.Ba4 0-0; 12.Qd3 a5; 13.Ne2 Ba6; 14.Qd1 Bd6; 15.Nd4 Bb4+; 16.Bd2 c5; 17.Nc2 Ne4; 18.Bxb4 axb4; 19.f3 Nf6; 20.Kf2 Be2; 21.Qxe2 Rxa4; 22.b3 Ra5; 23.g3 Rfa8; 24.Ne1 c4; 25.Qb2 Qa7; 26.bxc4 Rxa2; 27.Rxa2 Qxa2; 28.Qe2 Qxe2+; 29.Kxe2 dxc4; 30.Kd2 Ra2+; 31.Kc1 Nd5. Black won. Lonne–Segebarth, Postal 1988) 11...Bd6; 12.h3 Qe7; 13.b3 0-0; 14.Bb2 Bf5; 15.Bd3 Bd7; 16.Bc2 Rfd8; 17.Qd3 Rac8; 18.g4 g6; 19.0-0-0 Ba3; 20.f4 Bxb2+; 21.Kxb2 Re8; 22.Rhe1 Rcd8; 23.Qa6 and White later exploited his chances in Ribli–Adorjan, Budapest 1979.

9...0-0 Black sacrifices a pawn at c6 for rapid development. Twice!

10.Nxc6 bxc6; 11.Bxc6 cxd4; 12.Nxd5 Nxd5; 13.Bxd5 Rb8; 14.Qxd4 Ba6.

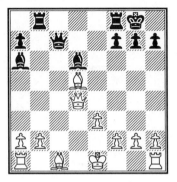

White cannot get the king to safety, and the pawns do not matter. **15.Bd2 Be5; 16.Qa4 Qd6!** Black moves every piece into ideal attacking position. None of White's pieces seem to be able to defend the king except the one bishop at d2.

17.e4 Rxb2; 18.Rd1 Rc8! Black grabs every open file and diagonal! **19.g3.** White hopes that f4 will gain some breathing room, but Black is ready to strike.

19...Rxd2!!; 20.Rxd2.

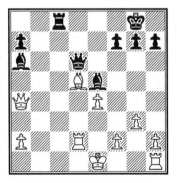

20...Rc1+; 21.Qd1 Qa3! Black is in no hurry. The end is near, and well planned. **22.Bc4 Rxd1+; 23.Kxd1 Qf3+; 24.Kc2 Qc3+; 25.Kd1 Qa1+!** White resigned. 26.Kc2 Qb2+; 27.Kd3 Bxc4+ is hopeless for White.

White plays 6.Bg5

1.d4 d5; 2.c4 e6; 3.Nc3 c5; 4.cxd5 exd5; 5.Nf3 Nc6; 6.Bg5.

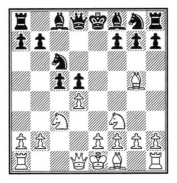

The Burn Variation is not a common line. It tends to be played by those who simply want to avoid the bulk of theory in the Tarrasch. Black should be prepared to meet it by following the suggested lines given in this section.

White invites an exchange of dark–squared bishops, and Black really should oblige, since alternatives can lead to serious trouble. This limits Black's ability to mount a kingside attack and the game takes on a quite different character. Black must keep a close eye on the center. White has two very different plans here. The defense of the center with e3 is the normal line, but sometimes White captures on c5.

BURN VS. ZNOSKO BOROVSKY
Ostende, 1906

1.d4 d5; 2.c4 e6; 3.Nc3 c5; 4.cxd5 exd5; 5.Nf3 Nc6; 6.Bg5 Be7.
6...f6; 7.Bf4 leaves Black's position looking very artificial.
7.Bxe7 Ngxe7.

8.e3. 8.dxc5 gives Black typical Tarrasch counterplay after 8...d4! 9.Ne4 0–0; 10.g3 (10.Ned2 Qa5; 11.Qc1 b6; 12.cxb6 axb6; 13.g3 Ba6; 14.Bg2 Rfe8; 15.a3 Rac8; 16.0-0 Bxe2; 17.Re1 d3 gave Black a lot of space in Lputian–Arkhipov Sochi 1985) 10...Bf5; 11.Nfd2 Qa5; 12.Bg2 Bxe4; 13.Bxe4 Qxc5; 14.0-0 Rad8 and Black has a solid position, Nimzowitsch-Spielmann, Carlsbad 1907.

8...cxd4; 9.Nxd4 Qb6.

Black takes advantage of the opportunity to place maximal pressure on d4 while also attacking b2. White has many plans here, but none will be certain of obtaining an advantage, as long as Black doesn't get carried away.

10.Nb3.

10.Bb5 is Mikhail Tseitlin's attack, but his success with it has been due mostly to overambitious play by Black. The best defense is to castle and then capture at d4. Then do not rush to play ...Nf5, which often lets White get a small advantage. Instead, concentrate on getting rooks to the open files. Then the worst that can happen is a position with slightly bad bishop against knight, but given the symmetrical pawn structures those are easy to defend. 10...0-0; 11.0-0 (11.Qd2 Nxd4; 12.exd4 a6 allows Black to equalize without difficulty) 11...Nxd4. (11...Rd8; 12.Rc1 Nxd4; 13.exd4 Bd7; 14.Bxd7 Rxd7 is another path to equality.) 12.Qxd4 Qxd4; 13.exd4 Be6.

This position has been reached many times and White has not demonstrated any advantage. 14.Ba4 (14.Rfe1 Nf5; 15.Rad1 h6; 16.Ba4 Rac8; 17.Bc2 Nd6; 18.Bb3 Nc4; 19.Bxc4 Rxc4 is an endgame where White's knight is better than Black's bishop, but there are no real winning chances and Simagin–Minev, Moscow 1960 was eventually drawn. 14.Rac1 Rac8; 15.a3 a6; 16.Bd3 Nc6; 17.Ne2 Na5 gave Black a fine game in Hurme–Asomaki, Postal 1990) 14...Rac8; 15.Rfd1 Rfd8; 16.Rac1 Rc4; 17.Bb3 Rb4; 18.Ne2 Nc6; 19.Rc5 Rd6 was passive but very solid for Black in Gruenberg–Brunner, Berlin (Lasker Memorial) 1989.

10.Qd2 is another popular line. Black has three replies.

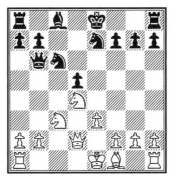

A) 10...0-0 allows 11.Nxc6 Qxc6. (11...bxc6 transposes to the 10.Nxc6 line, and is better than the capture with the queen.) 12.Bb5 Qb6; 13.0-0 Rd8; 14.Rfd1 Bg4; 15.Be2 Bxe2; 16.Qxe2 and Black was left with a weak pawn in Soppe–Izquierdo, Villa Gesell 1985.

B) 10...a5; 11.Na4 Qb4!? is an untested suggestion of mine.

C) 10...Nxd4; 11.exd4 0-0; 12.Be2 Bd7; 13.0-0 Rac8; 14.Rac1 Rfe8 is equal.

10.Nxc6 bxc6; 11.Qd2 a5!

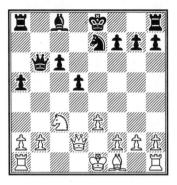

Black prepares to develop the bishop at a6 and will be able to defend the weak pawn at c6 with all of the pieces, if necessary. The a-pawn can also advance to a4, taking that square away from the enemy knight.

A) 12.Na4 Qb4; 13.b3 (13.Qxb4 axb4 would make Black very happy, with an open a-file and control of c3) 13...0-0; 14.Be2 Ba6. (14...Bf5 looks stronger, so that the rook at a8 can defend the c-pawn from c8.) 15.Bxa6 Rxa6; 16.Rc1 Ng6; 17.Qxb4 axb4; 18.Ke2 and the passive position of the rook at a6 made Black uncomfortable in Karpov–Bakus, St Martin 1992.

B) 12.Be2 Ba6?! Black should castle before undertaking active operations. 13.0-0 Bxe2; 14.Qxe2 a4; 15.Qc2 Qa6; 16.Rad1 0-0; 17.Rd4 a3; 18.Ra4 Qb7; 19.b3 and White was clearly better in Andruet–Salaun, France 1989.

A final alternative,10.Qb3 is handled by 10...Qc5! Exchanging queens would bring equality, but White can try for more. 11.Rd1 0-0; 12.Be2 Rd8; 13.0-0 Nxd4; 14.Rxd4 and now Black can sacrifice the b-pawn with 14...Be6; 15.Qxb7 Nf5 since after 16.Qb4 Qc7 the tactical trick 17.Rxd5 Bxd5; 18.e4 fails to 18...Rab8 and on 19.Qa3 Black has 19...Bxe4!; 20.Nxe4 Qc2; 21.Bf3 Nd4; 22.Qxa7 Nxf3+; 23.gxf3 Qxb2; 24.a4 Ra8; 25.Qc7 Qb3; 26.Qg3 Qxa4 and Black is clearly better, Eisele–Koenig, Germany 1991.

10...Be6.

Again White has many choices for the bishop. **11.Bd3.**

A) 11.Bb5 0-0; 12.0-0 Rfd8; 13.Qe2 a6; 14.Bd3 lets Black play actively with 14...d4; 15.Na4 Qb4; 16.Nbc5 dxe3; 17.Nxe6 fxe6; 18.Nc3 Qd6! 19.Rad1 exf2+; 20.Qxf2 Qe5 and 21.Qf7+ is only a minor annoyance after 21...Kh8 since 22.Ne4 loses to 22...Rxd3; 23.Rxd3 Qxe4 and Black won without difficulty in Ljungstrom–Friker, Volvgograd 1996.

B) 11.Be2 0-0; 12.0-0 Rfd8. (12...a6 is probably better, so that the queen can retreat to a7 if needed.) 13.Na4 Qc7; 14.Rc1 Qe5; 15.Nd4 Bc8; 16.Nc5 b6; 17.Nd3 Qf6; 18.Nxc6 Nxc6; 19.Qa4 gives White some pressure. It is instructive to observe how White increases the advantage: 19...Bb7; 20.Qf4 Qxf4; 21.Nxf4 d4; 22.Bf3 Na5; 23.b4 Bxf3; 24.gxf3 Nb7; 25.e4 Rd7; 26.Rfd1 Nd8; 27.Rc4 Ne6; 28.Nxe6 fxe6; 29.Rcxd4 with a substantial endgame advantage in Nielsen–E.Larsen, Alborg 1979.

C) 11.Qd2 0-0; 12.Be2 Rfd8; 13.Rd1 Rac8; 14.0-0 a6 shows the most solid defensive formation for Black. White cannot put enough pressure on the d-file to achieve anything.

15.Bf3 Ne5; 16.Nd4 Nc4; 17.Na4 Qd6; 18.Qe2 b5; 19.Nc3 Qb4; 20.Rb1 Ng6; 21.Rfd1 Nge5 with an active game for Black, Van Drie-De Jong, Postal 1989.

11...0-0; 12.0-0 Rfd8.

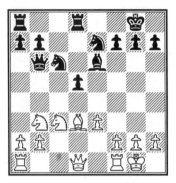

Again I would consider ...a6 to keep the queen on the a7-g1 diagonal. **13.Na4!**

A) 13.Nb5 Ne5; 14.N5d4 N7c6; 15.h3 Rac8; 16.Qe2 a5; 17.Rad1 a4; 18.Nxe6 fxe6; 19.Nd4 Nxd3; 20.Qxd3 Nxd4; 21.Qxd4 Qxd4; 22.Rxd4 Rc4; 23.Rfd1 Rdc8 and Black has a fine game, Dive-Alexander, New Zealand Championship 1987.

B) 13.Qe2 allows 13...d4! 14.Nxd4 Nxd4; 15.exd4 Qxd4 with boring equality in Aronson–Polugayevsky, Soviet Union 1957.

13...Qc7; 14.Rc1 Qe5; 15.Qe2 Rac8.

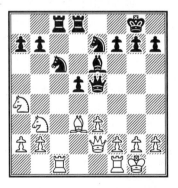

Black's position is fine, except for the somewhat exposed queen at e5. If White plays slowly an advantage can be achieved, but the move chosen by Burn leads to disaster.

16.f4?! 16.Nac5 b6; 17.Nxe6 fxe6; 18.e4 is the best plan for White. 18...Nb4; 19.Bb1 Rxc1; 20.Rxc1 Rc8; 21.Rxc8+ Nxc8; 22.a3 Nc6;

23.Qc2 Qxe4!; 24.Qxe4 dxe4; 25.Bxe4 Ne5; 26.Nd2 Nd6 should not present any problems for Black.**16...Qf6; 17.f5.** This sacrifice must be declined, as otherwise there would be too many open lines.

   17...Bd7!; 18.Nac5 b6; 19.Nxd7 Rxd7.

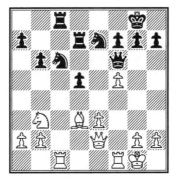

   Here White should have tried 20.Bb5, but Burn is fixated on a kingside attack. **20.g4? Rcd8; 21.Kh1 Rd6; 22.Rg1 Qg5; 23.Rcf1.** White continues to try to build a flank attack, but Black correctly counters in the center. **23...d4!; 24.e4.** 24.exd4 Nxd4; 25.Nxd4 Rxd4; 26.Bb1 Rd2 and it is the White king who must start worrying.

   24...Ne5; 25.Rg3 N7c6; 26.Nd2. This weakens the control of d3. The knight would have been better placed at c1. **26...Nxd3; 27.Rxd3 Ne5!** This is why White should have had the knight cover d3. Black's initiative grows steadily. **28.Rg3 d3!; 29.Qg2 Rc6!** Black controls more space and open lines, and has a large advantage. The rook will infiltrate at c2 or c1.

   30.Nf3 Nxf3; 31.Qxf3 Rc1!

   32.Rgg1 Rxf1; 33.Rxf1 Qd2! The queen uses this square as a temporary home. It will move out of the way, but still close to d2 and d1, so that the pawn can advance. **34.Rb1 Qe2; 35.Qg2 Qe3; 36.Rd1 d2!** White is lost. **37.h3 Qe1+; 38.Qg1 Qe2; 39.e5 Rd3. Black won.**

White plays 6.Bf4

1.d4 d5; 2.c4 e6; 3.Nc3 c5; 4.cxd5 exd5; 5.Nf3 Nc6; 6.Bf4.

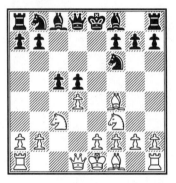

This is a harmless continuation. Black can follow the usual Tarrasch Defense strategies. Our choice is the central exchange. As a twist, we will develop our dark squared bishop at b4. White's problem is that the b8-h2 diagonal is not of particular significance. The e5-square is not a great point of contention in the Tarrasch. At g5, the bishop puts indirect pressure on the pawn at d5, since the defending knight at f6 can be removed. At e3, the bishop puts direct pressure on the pawn at c5. But, at f4, it just stares blankly into space.

PERLIS VS. RETI
Vienna, 1910

1.d4 d5; 2.Nf3 e6; 3.c4 c5; 4.Nc3 Nf6; 5.cxd5 exd5; 6.Bf4 Nc6; 7.e3 cxd4; 8.Nxd4.

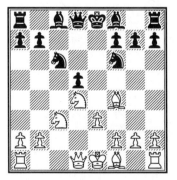

8... Bb4! Normally the bishop is initially more modest, sitting at e7 or d6. The position of the White bishop at f4, instead of g5, makes ...Ne4 available.

9.Bb5. We must consider a lot of alternatives. None of them give us any cause for concern, but it is best to be prepared.

A) 9.Nxc6 bxc6; 10.Qa4 is an aggressive line. 10...Qb6 is safest reply. 11.Bd3 0-0; 12.0-0 d4!; 13.Ne2 Nd5; 14.a3 Nxf4; 15.exf4 Be7 and the bishop pair compensates for the weak pawns, Hort–Espig, Tallinn 1975. If instead 10.Bd3, as in Rubinstein–Nimzowitsch, Carlsbad 1907, Black can play 10...0-0; 11.0-0 Bd6; 12.Bg3 Bxg3; 13.hxg3 c5 with a good game.

B) 9.Be2 allows Black to exploit the pin on the knight at c3 with 9...Ne4!

White must react to the pressure at c3.

B1) 10.Rc1 0-0; 11.0-0 Bxc3; 12.bxc3 is the most logical continuation. Now Black must try to keep the initiative going. 12...Qa5; 13.c4! reaches a critical position.

13...Nc3! This is my suggested improvement for Black. (13...dxc4?!; 14.Bxc4 Nxd4; 15.Qxd4 Nd2; 16.Bd6 Bh3; 17.Rfd1 Nxc4; 18.Bxf8 Rxf8; 19.Rxc4 Qg5; 20.Qe4 and Black resigned in Speelman-Illescas Cordoba, Barcelona 1989.) 14.Qd2 Nxe2+; 15.Qxe2 Nxd4; 16.exd4 dxc4 is an easy endgame to play for Black. With bishops of opposite colors, White cannot advance the passed d-pawn after ...Be6 and ...Rd8. 17.Bd6 Rd8; 18.Qe7 Bd7 holds everything togther.

B2) 10.Ndb5 0-0; 11.0-0 Bxc3; 12.Nxc3 Nxc3; 13.bxc3 Be6 (was played in Psakhis-Ehlvest, Lvov 1984) is not even marginally better for White because of the bishop pair, but the weak pawn at c3 is an inviting target, and can be blockaded by a knight at f4. If White exchanges the light-squared bishop for this knight, a draw is the probable result in the bishop of opposite color endgame.

C) 9.Ndb5 0-0 is at least equal for Black, though White need not follow the disastrous path of this game: 10.Qc2 Bg4; 11.f3 Bh5; 12.0-0-0 a6; 13.Nc7 Bxc3; 14.Qxc3 Rc8; 15.g4 Bg6; 16.Bd3 Na7 and White gave up in Eisenmann-Laren, Postal 1989.

D) 9.Rc1 0-0; 10.Nxc6 (10.Be2 Ne4 transposes to the 9.Be2 Ne4; 10.Rc1 variation discussed above) 10...bxc6; 11.Be2 Ne4; 12.Qa4 Bxc3+; 13.bxc3 Bd7 is at least equal for Black, who has a very powerful knight at e4.

E) 9.Qa4 Qa5!; 10.Qxa5 Bxa5; 11.Nxc6 bxc6; 12.f3 0-0; 13.Kf2 Re8 is already better for Black. 14.g4 Nd7; 15.Na4 Ne5; 16.Rd1 Rb8; 17.b3 Rb4; 18.Rd4 Rxd4; 19.exd4 Ng6; 20.Be3 f5!; 21.gxf5 Bxf5; 22.Ba6 Bd8! takes aim at the White monarch. 23.Bc1 Bh4+; 24.Kg2 Be1! 25.h3 Nh4+; 26.Kf1 Nxf3; 27.Be2.

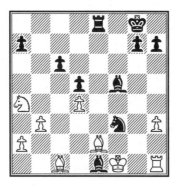

The game comes to a crashing conclusion! 27...Nxd4!; 28.Kxe1 Rxe2+; 29.Kf1 Bd3 and White resigned in Gaertner-Orsag, Prague 1994. We return to the position after 9.Bb5, and the Perlis-Reti game.

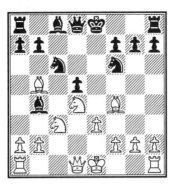

9...Qb6. The position is now rather complex, much to the taste of a true Tarrasch fan! **10.0–0 Bxc3.** This capture is considered necessary, since there was a tactical threat of 11.Qa4, after which 11 ...Bxc3 is too late, with 12.Nxc6! bringing White an advantage. However, given the improvement for White at move 17, it seems that Black should explore another path. I suggest 10...Bd7, for example 11.Qz4 Bxc3 when the intermediate capture at c6 doesn't accomplish anything. The position remains unclear and deserving of further study.

11.bxc3 0–0; 12.Rb1. The White bishop has no effective threat, so the rook at b1 is not dangerous. Black now must meet the threat of a capture at c6, so another central exchange is needed. **12...Nxd4!; 13.cxd4 Ne4!** 13...Qa5; 14.Bd6 Rd8; 15.Be7 picks up the exchange. **14.Bd3.** 14.Qe1! followed by Bd3 was best, according to Golombek.

14...Qa5.

Contrary to published opinion, Black cannot lay claim to equality here. **15.f3.** 15.Bxe4 dxe4; 16.Qc2 Qd5 is a likely draw. **15...Nd2!; 16.Qe1.** Forced, as the only way to prevent the knight from capturing one of the rooks. **16...b6.** Now the queen is defended, and one of the rooks must fall. **17.Bd6?!** At least White will get the rook back! Recent analysis has changed the evaluation of this position. Better is 17.Qh4!, intending to meet 17...h6 with the sacrifice 18.Bxh6 gxh6; 19.Qxh6 f5; 20.Qg6+ Kh8 which was evaluated as a draw by Golombek. John Nunn points out that after 21.Rbc1 Bd7; 22.Rc7 Rad8; 23.Qh6+ White wins with 23...Kg8; 24.Qg5+ Kh8; 25.Qh4+ Kg8; 26.Bxf5! **17...Nxf1; 18.Qh4.** White's attack is insufficient.

18...h6; 19.Bxf8 Ba6!

Black secures a material or positional advantage. **20.Bxa6.** 20.Bxf1 Rxf8; 21.Bxa6 Qxa6; 22.Qf2 Rc8 is a bit better for Black, who has the more active pieces. White can initiate mass destruction and settle for a half point. 20.Bxg7 Kxg7; 21.Bxa6 Qxa6; 22.Rxf1 Qxa2; 23.Qg4+ and White can draw by checking the Black king, which cannot run into the center because it would be too vulnerable there.

20...Nxe3. White is going to have to give back one of the bishops. **21.Qf2.** 21.Bxg7 now fails to 21...Qxa2 with the threat of mate at g2. **21...Kxf8; 22.Bd3.** 22.Qxe3 Qxa6 and Black has an extra pawn.

22...Re8; 23.Re1 Qc3!

A surprising resource that demolishes White's position. **24.Bb5.** 24.Rxe3 Qc1+ and the White rook falls. **24...Re7.** White cannot defend the pawn at d4!

25.Qg3 Kg8. Black eliminates the sting of b8+. **26.h4 Qxd4; 27.Kh1 Kh7; 28.Qh3.** White seems to be hanging on, but the position holds hidden dangers!

28...Ng4!; 29.Qg3.

29.Rxe7 Nf2+; 30.Kh2 Nxh3; 31.Kxh3 Qf6; 32.Rxa7 Qf5+; 33.Kh2 d4 leaves White in a very difficult position. **29...Nf2+.** White resigned. There is no defense to **30.Kh2 Rxe1** and ...Rh1+ follows. **Black won.**

Gruenfeld Gambit (Tarrasch Gambit Deferred)
1.d4 d5; 2.Nf3 c5; 3.c4 e6; 4.cxd5 exd5; 5.Nc3 Nc6; 6.dxc5.

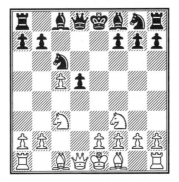

This is a rather dangerous line for Black, and is not all that easy to meet. Black must react vigorously, or else suffer a position with a missing pawn and no real compensation. There is no consensus on the best approach for Black. It is possible to play in gambit style as in the 4.dxc5 variation, or concede the bishop pair early in the game.

Passive defense of the weakling at e6 leads to an inferior position, but one which is surprisingly hard to crack. Since the choice may depend to some extent on tournament situation, we'll take a look at each of the plans.

In any case, Black need not fear falling into a losing position as long as the variation is played accurately. The variation is credited to Gruenfeld, who played it against Tarrasch at the great tournament in Teplitz Schonau, 1922. That game is cited in the note to White's ninth move in Alekhine–Rubinstein, below.

ALEKHINE VS. RUBINSTEIN
Hastings, 1922

1.d4 d5; 2.Nf3 c5; 3.c4 e6; 4.cxd5 exd5; 5.Nc3 Nc6; 6.dxc5 d4. This is the typical Tarrasch approach, and is certainly better than the defense of the pawn.

7.Na4.

The knight is better placed on the rim. This is a bit surprising, but it turns out that the knight cannot stay on e4 for very long.

The alternative is 7.Ne4 Bf5.

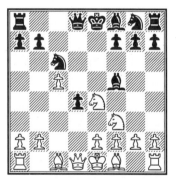

Now the knight must abandon the defense of the c-pawn.

A) 8.Nd6+ Bxd6; 9.cxd6 Qxd6; 10.Qb3? is easily repelled by (10.g3 was relatively best. 10...Nf6; 11.Bg2 0-0; 12.0-0 Rfe8; 13.Bf4 Qd7 is, I think, a bit more promising for Black, since White is very tied down.) 10...Nf6! 11.Qxb7 0-0 and Black is already winning! 12.Bf4 (12.e3 Rab8; 13.Qa6 Qb4+; 14.Bd2 Qxb2; 15.Rd1 Rb6; 16.Qe2 d3 would have been very embarrassing!) 12...Qxf4; 13.Qxc6 Rac8; 14.Qa4 Rc1+; 15.Rxc1 Qxc1+; 16.Qd1 Qxb2; 17.Nxd4 wins a pawn, but at a terrible price.

17...Ne4!!; 18.Qc2 (18.Nxf5 Qc3+ wins instantly, 18.e3 Qxf2. Checkmate.18.Nf3 Qc3+; 19.Nd2 Rd8 and Black wins) 18...Qa1+; 19.Qd1 Qc3+; 20.Qd2 Qxd2. Checkmate. Schneider–Walther, Postal 1962.

B) 8.Ng3 Bg4! 9.e3 Bxc5 is already better for Black, whose bishops place a lot of pressure on the White congregation. 10.Ne4 Bb4+; 11.Bd2 Qe7; 12.Bd3 dxe3; 13.fxe3 0-0-0; 14.Qc2 Bxf3; 15.gxf3 f5; 16.Bxb4. The knight cannot retreat because the e-pawn falls. 16...Qxb4+; 17.Nd2 Qh4+!; 18.Ke2 g6. White's king is vulnerable, and there is no compensating counterplay on the queenside. 19.Rac1 Nf6; 20.Qb3 Rd6; 21.Rc4 Qh3! 22.Rhc1 Nd5; 23.Nf1 (23.Rxc6+ achieves nothing after 23...Rxc6; 24.Rxc6+ bxc6; 25.Ba6+ Kd7; 26.Qb7+ Nc7; 27.Qxa7 Qxh2+; 28.Kd1 Ra8 forces 29.Qd4+ Qd6; 30.Qxd6+ Kxd6 with an easy win for Black) 23...Qg2+ 24.Ke1 Qxf3 and Black went on to win in Huma–Morgado, Postal 1979.

C) 8.Nfd2 is probably White's best. 8...Nf6; 9.Nxf6+ Qxf6; 10.g3 Bxc5; 11.Bg2 Qg6; 12.Qa4 0-0; 13.0-0 Rfe8.

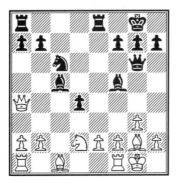

Black has typical Tarrasch pressure here. 14.Qb5 Bb6; 15.Nc4 d3; 16.e3 Rad8 forces White to defend. 17.Bd2 Be4! Black plans a strong pawn sacrifice. 18.f3 Bd5; 19.Nxb6 axb6; 20.Qxb6 Qd6; 21.b3 (21.Qxb7?? Nd4 and the lady is in distress) 21...Qe5; 22.Rab1. White prevents Black's infiltration at b2, and prepares to expand in the center. 22...Ne7; 23.e4 Bc6; 24.f4 Qb8.

Black's pieces are driven back, but the retreats will soon be re-placed by an initiative. 25.Rfe1 Nc8!; 26.Qf2 Nd6! White now must do something about the weak pawn at e4. 27.e5 Nb5; 28.Bxc6 bxc6; 29.Re4 Qb7; 30.Rbe1 Qd7. Black needs to control d4 for the knight. 31.Kg2? (I think that 31.Qc5 Nd4; 32.Kf2 would have been stronger. 31.a4 Nd4; 32.b4 Ne2+; 33.Kf1 Qd5!; 34.Qg2 Qa2 and White loses material.) 31...Qd5!; 32.Kg1 Nd4; 33.Qg2 Ra8; 34.Bc3 Nc2! (34...Ne2+ allows 35.R4xe2! dxe2; 36.Qxd5 cxd5; 37.Rxe2 and White has better winning chances.) 35.Rb1 Qc5+; 36.Bd4 Nxd4. Black won. Sae Heng-Imed, Yerevan Olympiad 1996.

7...Bxc5.

By clarifying the situation in the center with the capture at c5, Black counts on the cramping influence of the pawn at d4 to keep White's pieces frustrated. The pawn at e2 will remain a target.

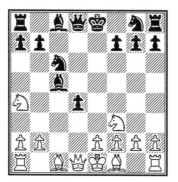

Black wins back the pawn, but parts with the bishop pair, and still has a weak d-pawn. What happens if this pawn falls? One would think that the passed pawn would provide a decisive advantage. Yet it is not so easy to exploit the extra pawn in the endgame. Let's take a little detour to look at the worst-case scenario.

7...Be6 allows White to go after the pawn at d4. 8.e3 Bxc5; 9.Nxc5! Qa5+; 10.Qd2 Qxc5; 11.Nxd4 Nxd4; 12.Qxd4 Qxd4; 13.exd4.

White has an extra pawn, and it is a passed pawn. In addition, White holds the bishop pair. This position was reached in Lindsay–Kahane, US Masters 1996. The player of the White side is a respected Senior Master, and Black is a young Candidate Master and student of mine. I had just introduced him to the Tarrasch a week earlier, and we hadn't analyzed this rare line.

When I saw this position, I was at first appalled. But we had discussed the Tarrasch endgames at length and he felt that even this one could be held. I expected him to go down to defeat quickly, but in fact the game wound up drawn, perhaps with a little help from White's time pressure.

I present the continuation of this game because it shows that even the simplest, and clearly inferior endgames are not easy to win for White. After all, White's strategy, based on the win of the isolated pawn, has succeeded. The bishop pair is tossed in as a bonus! 13...Nf6; 14.Be3 (14.Bd2 Rd8; 15.Bg5 Rxd4; 16.Bxf6 gxf6; 17.Be2 Bd5 is nothing special for White) 14...0-0; 15.Bd3 Nd5; 16.Bd2 Rac8; 17.0-0 Rc7; 18.Rfe1 Rfc8 and the control of the c-file and strong blockade of the pawn gave Black a reliable defense.

Notice that the knight at d5 cannot be chased away and can only be removed if captured by the White bishop. However, the remaining bishops are of opposite color, and such games can rarely be won, even with an extra pawn, provided that Black has not weakened the pawn structure.

As we return to the main line, keep in mind that the worst case is not a lost game. Nevertheless, the endgame holds no prospects of a win for Black, who can at best draw. This is hardly the desired result for our opening!

8.Nxc5. White should certainly capture before Black escapes with
...Bb4+.

8...Qa5+; 9.Qd2.

This move is considered best by most authorities. 9.Bd2 is also
possible 9...Qxc5; 10.e3 dxe3! (10...Bg4 is also interesting, for example: 11.exd4, the tournament book claimed that this would lose a
piece but failed to find Black's reply. 11...Qe7+!; 12.Be2 Bxf3; 13.gxf3
Nf6; 14.Bc3 0-0; 15.Qd2 Rfe8; 16.Kf1 Rad8; 17.Rg1 g6; 18.Rd1 Qe6.
Black's active position and superior pawn structure is worth more
than the bishop pair, Knaak–Lalic, Varna 1985.) 11.Bxe3 Qb4+;
12.Qd2 Qxd2+; 13.Nxd2 Nge7; 14.Bb5 0-0; 15.0-0 (15.Ne4 Nd5;
16.Bc5 Re8 and White loses a piece) 15...Bf5; 16.Nb3 Rfd8; 17.Rfd1
Bc2; 18.Rxd8+ Rxd8; 19.Nc5 b6; 20.Rc1 Rd1+; 21.Rxd1 Bxd1; 22.Ne4
Nb4; 23.Bd2 Nbd5! (23...Nxa2?? would lose to 24.Bc4!) 24.Nd6 Bg4;
25.Bc4 Be6; 26.Nb5 Nc6 and a draw was agreed in Gruenfeld–
Tarrasch, Teplitz Schonau 1922.

9...Qxc5.

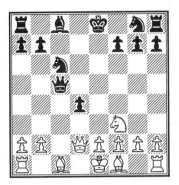

White has a very constricted position if no action is taken to undermine the powerful pawn at d4. **10.e3.** This eases White's position, but leads to a dull endgame. **10...dxe3; 11.Qxe3+ Qxe3+; 12.Bxe3 Nge7.**

12...Be6; 13.Nd4 Nxd4; 14.Bxd4 f6; 15.Be2 Ne7; 16.0–0 Kf7 was a little better for White in Hansen–Bogo, Denmark 1991, but there are no real winning chances as long as Black does not make a serious error, and indeed the game was eventually drawn.

13.Bb5.

A) 13.Nd4 0–0; 14.Bb5 Nxd4; 15.Bxd4 a6; 16.Ba4 b5; 17.Bb3 Nf5; 18.Bd5. White hopes for 18 ...Rb8; 19.Ba7, but there is a much stronger move., which leads to a long forcing variation which does not bring White any advantage.

18...Nxd4!; 19.Bxa8 Bf5; 20.Bb7 Nc2+; 21.Ke2 Re8+; 22.Kf3 Nxa1; 23.Rxa1 a5 with full equality in Shirazi–Gligoric, Lone Pine 1981.

B) 13.Bc4 is interesting. After 13...Be6. (13...Bg4 might be acceptable, for example 14.Ng5 Bh5; 15.g4 Bg6; 16.h4 h6 and I don't see any way for White to secure a meaningful advantage. 17.Nh3 Be4; 18.0-0 Bd5 is one possible continuation.) 14.Bxe6 fxe6; 15.Ng5 Kd7; 16.0-0-0+ Nd5; 17.Rhe1 Ncb4; 18.a3 Rac8+; 19.Kb1 Nc2!; 20.Re2 Ncxe3; 21.Rxe3 Rce8; 22.Re5 Rhf8; 23.f3. White had a small advantage in Knaak–Petursson, Novi Sad Olympiad 1990.

13...0-0; 14.0-0.

14...Be6.

Black has solved all the opening problems, and the bishop pair confers no significant advantage to White.

15.Nd4 Nxd4; 16.Bxd4 Nc6; 17.Bxc6 bxc6.

The tournament book, edited by Watts, puts it best: "It strikes me that no one can reproach the adversaries for having abandoned as drawn a position so sterile and denuded of all interest." **Drawn.**

SYMMETRICAL TARRASCH

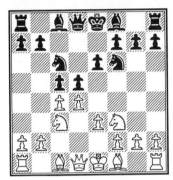

1.d4   d5
2.c4   e6
3.Nc3 c5
4.e3   Nf6
5.Nf3 Nc6

On the one hand, it is always a bit disappointing to see this move because Black will have to be very patient while waiting for a chance to attack. White relies on the advantage of the first move to provide an initiative, but rarely achieves one. Black can only attack after catching up in development. On the other hand, the position is very easy to play for Black and there should not be any difficulties for the second player even with a less than perfect opening play.

In considering a defensive strategy for Black, one has to keep in mind the possibility that the position can arise via several different move orders. In the canonical move order given above, Black doesn't have to play 5...Nc6. Caro-Kann and Nimzo-Indian fans may well prefer 5...cxd4; 6.exd4 Bb4, transposing to the Panov Attack. I have often played 5...a6, just to break the symmetry, intending to capture on c4 and advance with b5. The choice of plans is really just a matter of taste. I tend to select one depending on my mood or on some characteristics of my opponent picked up in pre-game preparation.

SUNYE NETO VS. KASPAROV
Graz, 1981

1.Nf3 Nf6; 2.c4 c5; 3.Nc3 e6; 4.e3 Nc6; 5.d4 d5.

White has an opportunity to transpose to the Asymmetrical Variation. Choosing almost any other path allows Black to determine the contour of the game by capturing at d4 or c4. We will examine some alternatives in the following games.

6.cxd5 exd5; 7.Bb5 Bd6; 8.dxc5 Bxc5.

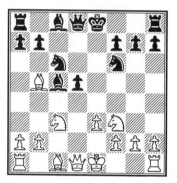

This is a popular variation, and we have seen it once already in the Assymetrical chapter. White has saved a tempo by waiting for Black to develop the dark-squared bishop before capturing at d5.

9.0–0. Surely this is correct, though castling can be postponed for a while. 9.Nd4 Qd6. (9...Bd7; 10.Nxc6 bxc6; 11.Be2 0–0; 12.0–0 Qe7 is solid for Black, Hardicsay–Fernandez, Budapest 1978.) 10.Na4 Bb4+; 11.Bd2 0–0; 12.Bxc6 bxc6; 13.Rc1 Ne4 was at least equal for Black in Böhm–Keilhack, Germany 1991.

9.Ne5 Qd6; 10.Nxc6 (10.Qa4 Qxe5; 11.Bxc6+ Ke7; 12.Bb5 Rd8; 13.0–0 Ng4; 14.Qf4 Qxf4; 15.exf4 Bf5 and Black has the initiative, Hoffmann–Wegemund, West Germany 1988) 10...bxc6 ;11.Be2 Bb6; 12.0–0 Bc7; 13.g3 Bf5; 14.Bf3 0–0; 15.b3 Rfe8; 16.Bb2 Qd7 is very comfortable for Black, Nowak–Luczak, Poland Championship 1981.

9...0–0.

White has tried every reasonable move here, but without much success. **10.b3.**

A) 10.a3 Bb6; 11.b3 (11.b4 a5; 12.bxa5 Bxa5; 13.Na4 Bg4; 14.Nc5 Qb6; 15.Bxc6 Qxc5; 16.Ba4 Ne4 and White had a grim position in Grimm–Danne, Postal 1986) 11...Be6; 12.Bb2 Qe7; 13.Ne2 Rac8; 14.Ned4 Bg4; 15.Be2 Rfd8; 16.b4 Ne4; 17.Qd3 Bc7; 18.Rac1 Bb8; 19.Nxc6 bxc6; 20.Nd4 Qd6; 21.f4 Bd7; 22.Nb3 Qg6 and Black had a good attacking formation, Schmidt–Firmenich, Postal 1968.

B) 10.Ne2 Bg4; 11.Bd2 Ne4; 12.Bc3 Qd6; 13.Bxc6 bxc6; 14.Be5 Qe7; 15.Bf4 f6; 16.Rc1 Rac8 with an active position for Black, Meo–Danner, Caorle 1981.

C) 10.Be2 a6; 11.b3 Qd6; 12.Bb2 Rd8; 13.Rc1 Ba7; 14.Rc2 Bf5; 15.Rd2 Qe6; 16.Nh4 d4!; 17.Bc4 Bg4; 18.Bxe6 Bxd1; 19.Nxd1 fxe6; 20.exd4 Nxd4; 21.Re1 Rd6; 22.Bxd4 Bxd4; 23.Nf3 Rad8; 24.Rxd4 Rxd4; 25.Nxd4 Rxd4; 26.Nc3 Rd3 with a draw in Agzamov–Simic, Belgrade 1982.

The minor damage to the pawn structure does not cause significant problems in the rook and knight endgame, and Black should keep that in mind when considering ...Be6 in a position where it can be captured by White, forcing a recapture with the f-pawn.

D) 10.b4 Re8; 11.Bb2 Bg4; 12.Rc1 Bd6; 13.Na4 Rc8; 14.h3 Bh5; 15.Bxf6 Qxf6; 16.Qxd5 Bxf3 was drawn in Keene–Helmers, Aarhus 1983.

E) 10.h3 a6; 11.Bd3 Ba7; 12.b3 Qd6; 13.Ne2 Ne5; 14.Nxe5 Qxe5; 15.Ba3 Re8; 16.Nd4 Ne4; 17.Nf3 Qf6; 18.Re1 Qg6; 19.Kf1 Qh6; 20.Bxe4 dxe4 and Black has the bishop pair and the attack. Skegina–Miranovic, Novi Sad 1989.

F) 10.Qa4 Qd6; 11.Rd1 Ne5; 12.Qf4 Nxf3+; 13.Qxf3 Bg4; 14.Rxd5 Nxd5; 15.Qxd5 Qxd5; 16.Nxd5 Rfd8 and White had nothing to show for the exchange, Rideau–Caron, Torcy 1991.

The fianchetto plan hopes to create long distance threats on the a1–h8 diagonal.

10...Bg4; 11.Bb2.

11...Rc8.

11...Bd6 is a recent development which has been useful for Black. 12.Ne2 (12.Be2 a6; 13.h3 Bf5; 14.Nd4 Nxd4; 15.Qxd4 Bc7; 16.Rfd1 Qd6; 17.g3 Rad8; 18.Bf3 Bb6; 19.Qh4 Qe6; 20.g4 Be4; 21.Nxe4 Nxe4; 22.Bd4 Bc7; 23.Rac1 Rd7; 24.Rc2 f5; 25.gxf5 Qxf5; 26.Bxe4 dxe4 and Black went on to win in Gyurkovics–Palkovi, Hungary 1994) 12...Bxf3; 13.gxf3 Ne5; 14.Ng3 Rc8; 15.Be2 Re8; 16.f4 Ned7; 17.Bf3 Qa5; 18.Kh1 Rc6; 19.Rg1 Ba3; 20.Bd4 Rec8; 21.Qd3 Rc2; 22.Nh5 Nxh5; 23.Bxh5 g6.

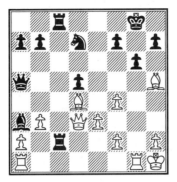

Both sides have lines of attack, giving rise to an exciting battle! 24.Qf5 Rxf2!; 25.Bxg6! fxg6; 26.Qxd7 Rc7; 27.Qe8+ Bf8; 28.Qe6+ Rf7. Black has defended well, and the rook at f7 also helps with the kingside attack! 29.Raf1 Rxf1; 30.Rxf1 Bg7; 31.f5 Qa6!; 32.Qxa6 bxa6; 33.f6 Bh8; 34.Kg2 Kf8; 35.Kg3 Rc7; 36.Kf4 Kf7; 37.Ke5 Rd7 and White could not break through: 38.h4 h6; 39.h5 gxh5; 40.Kf5 Rd6; 41.Rc1. White decides to give up the f-pawn to try to infiltrate on the seventh rank. 41...Bxf6; 42.Rc7+ Be7; 43.Rxa7 h4! This forces the White king back. 44.Bc5 Re6; 45.Kg4 Ke8; 46.Rxe7+ Rxe7; 47.Bxe7 Kxe7; 48.b4 Kd6; 49.a4 Ke5; 50.Kxh4 and a draw was agreed. Ivanov–Abramo, Smolensk 1992.

12.Rc1.
12.Be2 Bd6; 13.Nb5 (13.Nd4 Be6; 14.Ncb5 Bb8; 15.Rc1 Re8; 16.g3 Bh3; 17.Re1 Qe7; 18.Nxc6 bxc6; 19.Nd4 c5; 20.Nf3 Red8 and Black stands well, Wirthensohn–Wilder Lugano 1989) is a prelude to chopping wood with 13...Bb8; 14.Bxf6 Qxf6; 15.Qxd5 Rfd8; 16.Qe4.

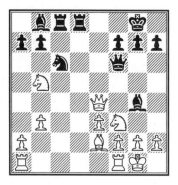

This is an important position. Black must demonstrate some compensation soon. The position resembles a Schara Gambit, treated in *Gambit Opening Repertoire for Black*. 16...h5. (16...Bf5 looks more promising, and 16...Bxf3; 17.Qxf3 Qh4; 18.h3 a6; 19.Nc3 Be5 is also worth investigating.) 17.h3 Re8; 18.Qa4 a6. Some authorities give Black sufficient compensation for the pawn, but I doubt that there is enough. 19.hxg4 axb5; 20.Bxb5 Ne5; 21.Bxe8 Nxf3+; 22.gxf3 Qh4; 23.Bxf7+ Kh8; 24.Rfc1 Rf8; 25.Rc5 g5; 26.Qd4+ Kh7; 27.Qe4+ Kh8; 28.Qe7. White won. Wirthensohn–Scherrer, Lenk 1992.

12...Bd6.

13.Be2. 13.h3 Bh5; 14.Be2 Bb8; 15.Nh4 Qd6; 16.g3 Bg6; 17.Nb5 Qe6; 18.Bxf6 Qxf6; 19.Nxg6 hxg6; 20.Bg4 Rcd8; 21.Nd4 Be5; 22.Nxc6 bxc6 is a little better for White, since Black has no access to important light squares on the c8–h3 diagonal, but with careful play Black should be able to hold, Seirawan–DeFirmian, United States Championship 1994.

13...Bb8. 13...a6!? may be playable. 14.Nd4 is often given with an exclamation mark, but where is the advantage for White? 14...Bxe2; 15.Ncxe2 Nxd4; 16.Qxd4 Rxc1; 17.Rxc1 Re8; 18.Ng3 Be5; 19.Qd2 Bxb2; 20.Qxb2 Qd7; 21.Qd4 Rc8; 22.Rxc8+ Qxc8 was drawn in Makarichev–Balashov, Moscow 1990.

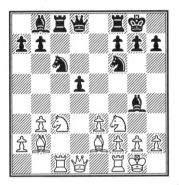

This position has been visited many times! White transfers the knight from c3 to d4 via b5. Black takes control of the e-file with ...Ne4 and ...Re8.

14.Nb5 Ne4; 15.Nbd4.

15...Re8 ; 16.h3.

16.Qd3 would have been more useful. 16...Qd6; 17.g3 h5; 18.Nxc6 bxc6; 19.Nh4 Bh3; 20.Rfd1 Qh6; 21.Bf3 g5; 22.Ng2 h4; 23.Qe2 Bf5; 24.Bd4 hxg3; 25.fxg3 Re6; 26.Rf1 Qh3; 27.Ne1 g4; 28.Bg2.

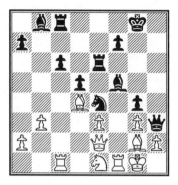

Here Chandler missed a fantastic chance! 28...Nxg3? A time pressure error. (28...Qxh2+!!; 29.Kxh2 Nxg3 and Black wins!) 29.hxg3 Qxg3; 30.Rxf5 Qh4; 31.Bxd5 Rh6; 32.Qg2 Rc7; 33.Nf3 Qh3; 34.Rg5+ Kf8; 35.Bg7+ Ke8; 36.Bxh6 Black resigned, Karpov–Chandler, Bath 1983.

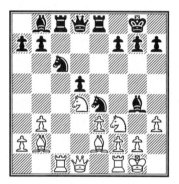

16...Bxf3; 17.Nxf3 Qd6; 18.Qd3 Ng5. 18...a6 was an alternative. **19.Rfd1 Rcd8; 20.Kf1 Ne4; 21.a3 a6; 22.Qc2 Ba7; 23.Bd3 Qe7.** Both sides have reorganized to more aggressive formations.

24.Re1 Rd6; 25.b4 Re6; 26.b5 axb5; 27.Bxb5 h6. Now we have a period of quiet maneuvering as White tries to make progress on the queenside.

28.Rcd1 Rd8; 29.Qb3 Qd6; 30.a4 Bc5; 31.Re2 b6; 32.Kg1 Ne7; 33.Nd4 Rg6; 34.Bd3 Qd7; 35.Kh1 Nf5; 36.Bxe4 dxe4.

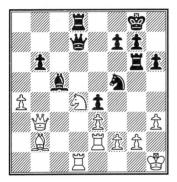

Now the position is more symmetrical, and one would think that it might become drawish. But the rook on g6 insures that Black will have a chance to attack, and White's forces are not posted for defense of the king.

37.Red2 Nh4; 38.Ne6.

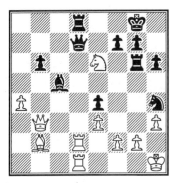

This is an invitation that Kasparov cannot refuse! **38...Qxd2!!; 39.Rxd2 Rxd2; 40.Nf4 Rg5; 41.Kg1 Nf3+!; 42.Kf1.**

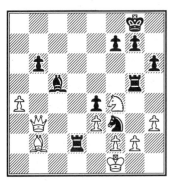

The sacrifices just keep on coming. **42...Bxe3!!; 43.fxe3 Rdxg2.** The queen is no match for the rooks. **44.Qc3 Rh2; 45.Ne2 Kh7; 46.Qc8 Rh1+; 47.Kf2 Nd2; 48.Ng3 Rh2+; 49.Kg1 Nf3+; 50.Kf1 Rxb2. Black won.**

The game we just examined is thrilling and filled with beauty. On any top ten list, however, it ranks well below our next example, justly considered to contain one of the finest combinations ever played.

ROTLEVI VS. RUBINSTEIN
Lodz, 1907

1.d4 d5; 2.Nf3 e6; 3.e3 c5; 4.c4 Nc6; 5.Nc3 Nf6; 6.dxc5 Bxc5.

The exchange of pawns eases Black's development. **7.a3.** White plans to expand with b4. Black's reply seems to carve a new cave for the bishop, but is actually designed just to fight for control of the b5–square. **7 ...a6; 8.b4 Bd6!** with the inclusion of the a-pawn advances, Black has secured this excellent square for the bishop.

9.Bb2 0–0; 10.Qd2?! 10.cxd5 exd5; 11.Be2 would be an asymmetrical approach. **10...Qe7!** This is often a good location for the queen. A rook will come to the d-file to support the d-pawn.

11.Bd3?! White does not comprehend that this bishop belongs on e2. Of course play would then transpose after 11...dxc4, but the point is that White will later return the bishop to d3, which shows that he didn't understand the position. 11.cxd5 exd5; 12.Nxd5 Nxd5; 13.Qxd5 Be6! gives Black more than enough compensation for the pawn, for example 14.Qd1 (14.Qg5 Bxb4+; 15.axb4 Qxb4+ and Black wins) 14...Nxb4!; 15.axb4 Bxb4+; 16.Nd2 Rfd8; 17.Bc1 Rxd2; 18.Bxd2 Rd8; 19.Bxb4 Qxb4+; 20.Ke2 Rxd1; 21.Rxd1 Qc4+; 22.Ke1 Qc3+; 23.Rd2 g6 and White wins without difficulty.

11...dxc4! The timing of central exchanges is of critical importance in the Tarrasch, as in openings in general.

12.Bxc4 b5; 13.Bd3?! As noted, the bishop belongs at e2.

13...Rd8; 14.Qe2.White must get out from under the pin.

14...Bb7; 15.0-0.

Black is in control of the position and has a strong initiative. Rubinstein now increases the pressure. **15...Ne5!; 16.Nxe5 Bxe5; 17.f4.** White recognizes the potential danger in allowing Black to sacrifice the bishop at h2. The immediate tactical threat also involves the knight at d3, which will be under a double attack if Black can play the queen to d6 with check. 17.Rfd1 Qc7; 18.f4 Bxc3; 19.Rac1 was suggested by Kmoch, but 19...Nd5; 20.Be4 Nxf4; 21.exf4 Bxe4; 22.Qxe4 Rxd1+; 23.Rxd1 Rc8 keeps White a pawn up.

17...Bc7; 18.e4 Rac8; 19.e5. 19.Rad1 would have been more sensible, contesting the important b-file.

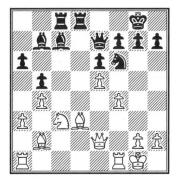

White cannot provide enough support in the center. The attempt to take over the initiative is doomed to failure because White has no position basis for an attack.

19...Bb6+; 20.Kh1 Ng4! The Black minor pieces join together to form a tactical operations force which is the envy of the heavy artillery. Yet all Black pieces will work together to reach the goal in this game. Black threatens to capture at d3, and this threat cannot be ignored. White must also take care open the long diagonal, where the light squares are vulnerable. **21.Be4.** 21.Ne4 Rxd3!; 22.Qxd3 Bxe4!; 23.Qxe4 Qh4 and Black wins: 24.h3 Qg3; 25.hxg4 Qh4. Checkmate!

21...Qh4; 22.g3.

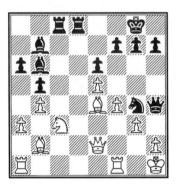

This position should be familiar to all chessplayers. Rubinstein unleashes a combination of striking beauty.

22.h3 Rxc3!! is another form of execution, for example 23.Qxg4 (23.Bxc3 Bxe4; 24.Qxe4 Qg3; 25.hxg4 Qh4. Checkmate) 23...Rxh3+!!; 24.Qxh3 Qxh3+; 25.gxh3 Bxe4+; 26.Kh2 Rd2+; 27.Kg3 Rg2+; 28.Kh4 Bd8+; 29.Kh5 Bg6. Checkmate.

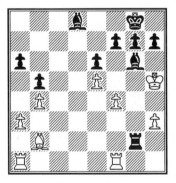

A wonderfully artistic tableau! The continuation of the game is no less impressive.

22...Rxc3!!

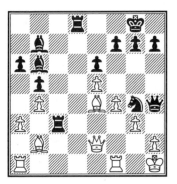

The theme now is played in another key. **23.gxh4.** 23.Bxc3 Bxe4+; 24.Qxe4 Qxh2. Checkmate.

23...Rd2!! Black has given up a queen, but the generosity does not stop there. Now another rook goes, while other pieces remain under enemy fire.

24.Qxd2 Bxe4+; 25.Qg2.

25...Rh3! Mate is inevitable. Black won.

DENGLER VS. NOGLY
Bargteheide, 1988

1.d4 d5; 2.c4 e6; 3.Nc3 c5; 4.Nf3 Nc6; 5.e3 Nf6; 6.Be2.

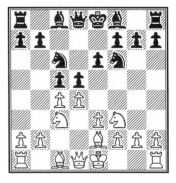

This quiet developing move does not lead to disaster for White, but won't cause Black to sweat, either. Black can continue the boring symmetry, or take off in a new direction. Here are two possibilities.

6...a6.

An interesting option is 6...Bd6; 7.0-0 (7.dxc5 Bxc5; 8.cxd5 exd5; 9.Bb5 0-0; 10.Bxc6 bxc6; 11.0-0 Bg4; 12.Ne2 Bxf3; 13.gxf3 Nh5; 14.Ng3 Qh4 was better for Black in Petit–Caldwell, Buenos Aires Olympiad 1978. Just compare the positions of the minor pieces and potential files for the rooks) 7...0-0 when we can enter the Asymmetrical Variation 8.cxd5 exd5; 9.dxc5 Bxc5. Here are some more examples of typical strategies.

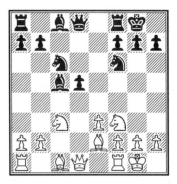

A) 10.b3 Be6; 11.Bb2 Qe7; 12.Nb5 Ne4; 13.Rc1 (13.Nbd4 Rac8; 14.Nxc6 bxc6; 15.Nd4 Bd7; 16.Bd3 f5 is good for Black, Z.Nikolic–Ivanovic Bor 1986) 13...Rfd8; 14.Nbd4 Rac8; 15.Bd3 Bg4; 16.Be2

Ba3; 17.Nxc6 bxc6; 18.Bxa3 Qxa3; 19.Nd4 Bxe2; 20.Qxe2 Qd6; 21.Rc2 c5; 22.Rfc1 Rb8; 23.Nf5 Qf6 brought Black equality in Kaluzny–Kolasinski, Poland Championship 1981.

B) 10.Nb5 Ne4; 11.a3 Be7; 12.Nbd4 Bf6; 13.Qd3 Bg4; 14.Rd1 Re8; 15.Rb1 Rc8; 16.Nb3 Bf5; 17.Qxd5 Qxd5; 18.Rxd5 is too greedy. 18...Be6; 19.Rb5 Nd6; 20.Nbd4 Nxd4; 21.Nxd4 Bxd4; 22.exd4 Nxb5; 23.Bxb5 Bd7 and White resigned in Kolb–Schwicker, Germany 1992.

C) 10.Na4 Bd6; 11.b3 Qe7; 12.Bb2 Rd8; 13.Rc1 Ne4; 14.Nc3 Be6; 15.Nb5 Bb8; 16.Nbd4 Bd7; 17.Bb5 Ne5; 18.Bxd7 Qxd7; 19.Qe2 Bd6; 20.Nxe5 Bxe5; 21.f3 Nd6; 22.Rc5 Bxd4; 23.Bxd4 Nf5; 24.Rd1 b6; 25.Rc3 Rac8 was eventually drawn in Kuzmin–Liavdansky, Tallinn 1965.

7.dxc5 Bxc5; 8.cxd5 exd5; 9.0–0 0–0.

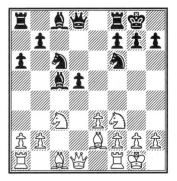

A typical isolated d-pawn position has been reached.

10.a3 Re8.

10...Bd6; 11.b4 Bc7; 12.Bb2 Qd6; 13.g3 Bh3; 14.Re1 Rad8; 15.Rc1 Rfe8; 16.Qc2 d4!; 17.exd4 Bg4; 18.Nb1 Qd5; 19.Ne5 Bxe5; 20.dxe5 Nxe5 is already much better for Black. 21.f4 (21.Bxe5 Qxe5; 22.Bxg4 Qxe1+; 23.Rxe1 Rxe1+; 24.Kg2 Nxg4; 25.Nc3 would not have led to a quick loss.) 21...Bh3!; 22.Bh5 (22.Bd1 Nd3; 23.Rxe8+ Rxe8; 24.Bc3 Nxc1 also wins) 22...Nd3; 23.Rxe8+ Rxe8; 24.Rd1 Qe4; 25.Qe2 Qc6; 26.Be5 Qb6+. Black won. Pospisil–Brecht, Sumperk 1990.

11.b4 Ba7; 12.Qc2 Bg4; 13.Rd1 Rc8; 14.Bb2.

White hopes to continue with Rc1 and Qb1, but Black disrupts his plans.

14...d4!; 15.exd4 Nxd4; 16.Nxd4 Bxd4; 17.Bxg4 Nxg4.

Black is clearly better, with a strong pin on the knight at c3 and a growing kingside attack. **18.Qf5 Qh4!; 19.h3.** White is lost. **19...Bxf2+; 20.Kh1 Ne3; 21.Qf3 Nxd1; 22.Rxd1 Re3; 23.Qf5 Rce8. Black won.**

TARRASCH GAMBIT

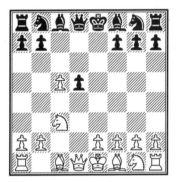

1.d4   d5
2.c4   e6
3.Nc3   c5
4.cxd5   exd5
5.dxc5

The capture of the pawn is an obvious candidate move. Black can fight for equality or play with greater ambition. In either case, 5...d4 is the most promising move. 5...Nf6 is the alternative, but White usually manages to retain some advantage in those lines. This plan differs from the Gruenfeld Gambit in that the knights have not been developed to f3 and f6.

SMAGAR VS. SKUROVICH
Postal, 1980

1.d4 d5; 2.c4 e6; 3.Nc3 c5; 4.cxd5 exd5; 5.dxc5 d4; 6.Na4. 6.Ne4 has made a comeback, but Black is doing well, for example 6...Bf5.

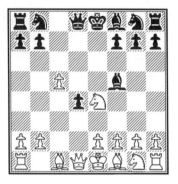

A) 7.Ng3 Be6!; 8.Qa4+ (8.e3 Nc6; 9.Nf3 Bxc5; 10.exd4 Nxd4; 11.Nxd4 Qxd4; 12.Bb5+ Kf8; 13.0-0 Qxd1; 14.Rxd1 Nf6; 15.b3 Ke7; 16.Bb2 Rhd8; 17.Bd3 Rac8; 18.Rac1 Bb4; 19.Rxc8 Rxc8; 20.Bxf6+ gxf6; 21.Bxh7 a5; 22.Kf1 Rh8; 23.Be4 Rxh2; 24.Bxb7 Rh8; 25.Ba6 Rh4; 26.Rd3 Bd6; 27.Rc3 was eventually drawn in Vladimirov–Frois, Cordoba 1990) 8...Qd7. (8...Nc6; 9.b4 a5?!, 9...Nf6 is more accurate, 10.b5 Nb4; 11.e4 dxe3; 12.b6+ Ke7; 13.fxe3 Nc2+; 14.Kf2 Nxa1; 15.Nf3 Bd3; 16.c6 Nc2; 17.Bxd3 Qxd3; 18.Rd1 Qxd1; 19.Nf5+ Kf6; 20.Bb2+ Kxf5; 21.Qf4+ Ke6; 22.Qe5#, Ruygrok–Snijders Netherlands 1988.) 9.Qxd7+ Nxd7; 10.Nf3 Bxc5; 11.Ne4 Bb6; 12.Nd6+ Ke7; 13.Nb5 Ngf6; 14.Bd2 Rhc8; 15.Nbxd4 Ne4; 16.Bb4+ Bc5; 17.Bxc5+ Rxc5; 18.Nxe6 fxe6; 19.Nd4 Rac8; 20.Nb3 Rc2; 21.f3 Nd6; 22.Rb1 Nc4; 23.g3 Nxb2; 24.Bh3 Na4. Black eventually won. Degli Eredi–Petzold, Postal 1990.

B) 7.Qa4+!? Nc6 (7...Qd7; 8.Qxd7+ Nxd7; 9.Nd6+ Bxd6; 10.cxd6 Ngf6; 11.Nf3 and White is better.) 8.Ng3 and now 8...Be6 transposes to the previous note.

C) 7.Nd6+ Bxd6; 8.cxd6 Qxd6; 9.Nf3 Nc6; 10.Bd2 Nf6; 11.g3 0-0; 12.Bg2 d3; 13.e3 Rac8; 14.0-0 Be4; 15.Qb3 Rfd8; 16.Rfd1 Qd7; 17.Bc3 Qe7; 18.Ne1 Bxg2; 19.Kxg2 Qe4+; 20.Kg1 Ng4; 21.Rd2 Rd6; 22.Ng2 Rh6; 23.f3 Qxf3; 24.Rf1 Nce5; 25.Bxe5 Nxe5; 26.Rxf3 Nxf3+; 27.Kf2 Nxd2; 28.Qxd3 Rd6!; 29.Qb5 b6; 30.Nf4 Rcd8; 31.h4 h6; 32.g4 Ne4+; 33.Kf3 Nc5; 34.b4 Ne6; 35.g5 hxg5; 36.Nxe6 g4+; 37.Kxg4 Rxe6; 38.Kf3 Rde8. Black won. Garcia Fernandez–Frois, Candas 1992.

D) 7.Qd3 Qd5; 8.f3 Nc6; 9.Nh3 Bxe4; 10.fxe4 Qxc5; 11.e3 Rd8;

12.Qb3 Qb4+; 13.Bd2 Qxb3; 14.axb3 Bc5; 15.Bb5 Nge7; 16.exd4 Bxd4; 17.Bc3 0–0; 18.Ng5 a6; 19.Be2 Be3; 20.Nf3 Ng6. Black eventually won. Griesbach–Konig, Postal 1985.

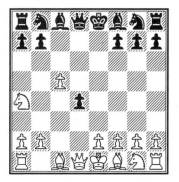

6...b5! This is the most aggressive plan. Black attacks the White knight, forcing an en passant capture at b6. Black then remains down a pawn, but White must do something to extricate the knight from its perilous post at a4.

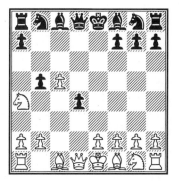

7.cxb6 axb6; 8.b3.

Against 8.Qb3, Black can, and probably should, just play 8...Be6, since 9.Qxb6?? loses to 9...Rxa4. For the adventurous, I offer the following game, where Black manages to keep enough pressure on his opponent to compensate for the pawn. 8...b5; 9.Qxb5+ Bd7; 10.Qe5+ Be7; 11.b3 Bxa4; 12.bxa4 Nc6; 13.Qb5 Bb4+; 14.Bd2 Bxd2+; 15.Kxd2 Nge7; 16.Nf3 Rb8; 17.Qc5 0–0; 18.g3 Qd7; 19.Bg2 Rb2+; 20.Ke1 Rfb8; 21.Ne5 Nxe5; 22.Qxe5 Ng6; 23.Qa5 Qe7; 24.Bf3 Ne5; 25.Bd5 Nd3+. Black won. Plath–Petzold, Postal 1989. White might improve with 13.Qxg7 Bf6; 14.Qg3 Rxa4; 15.a3 so that any advance of the d-pawn can be met by Ra2.

8...Nf6; 9.e3 Bd7; 10.Qxd4 Nc6. Black develops with tempo and there are many weak dark squares on White's queenside.

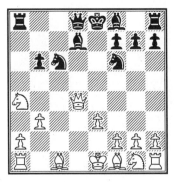

11.Qb2. An awkward post for the queen but retreating to d1 is not going to blunt the initiative. 11.Qd1 Ne4; 12.Nf3 b5! A remarkable little sacrifice. 13.Bxb5 Qa5+; 14.Kf1? This lets the bishop fall with check. 14...Qxb5+; 15.Kg1 Be7; 16.Bb2 Rd8; 17.Nc3 Nxc3; 18.Bxc3 Bg4; 19.Qf1 Qb7; 20.Nd4 Nxd4; 21.Bxd4 0-0. Black has finally completed development! White, on the other hand, still has a rook stuck at h1. 22.f3 Be6; 23.Kf2 Rc8; 24.Qe2 Ba3; 25.Rhd1 Rc6; 26.Bb2 Bxb2; 27.Qxb2 Qc7; 28.Kg1 Rc2. Black won. Kirste–Petzold, Postal 1989. White should play 14.Nd2.

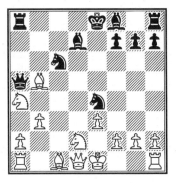

Black's best is now 14...Nxd2!; 15.Bxd2 Qxb5. White has three pawns for a piece, but they are all on open files and therefore vulnerable. Perhaps more critical is the fact that White cannot castle.

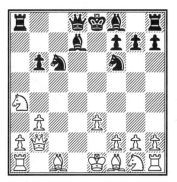

11...Ne4; 12.a3. 12.Nf3 b5; 13.Bd3 f5; 14.Nc3 Ba3 gives Black an initiative: 15.Qe2 Nxc3; 16.Qc2 Qf6; 17.Bd2 Nb4; 18.Qxc3 Qxc3; 19.Bxc3 Nxd3+; 20.Ke2 b4; 21.Kxd3 bxc3; 22.Kxc3 Ke7; 23.Ne5 Rhc8+; 24.Nc4 Be6; 25.Rhd1 Bxc4; 26.bxc4 Ra4; 27.Rd4 Rb8; 28.Kd3 Bb2; 29.Rb1 Rxa2; 30.Rd5 Rb3+; 31.Kc2 Rc3+; 32.Kd1 Rxc4; 33.Rxf5 Bc3; 34.Rc1 Ke6; 35.Rf3 Rc7. Black won. Scriba–Wacker Postal 1946.

12...b5; 13.Bd3 f5; 14.Nc3.

A) 14.Bxe4 fxe4; 15.Nc3 Ne5; 16.Kf1 Nd3; 17.Qd2 Bb4; 18.Bb2 Be7; 19.Rb1 Qc7; 20.Nce2 0-0; 21.Nf4 Nxb2; 22.Qxb2 Bxa3; 23.Qd2 Rf5; 24.Nge2 g5; 25.Nd4 Qd6; 26.Nh3 Rd5; 27.Qe2 g4; 28.Ng1 Bb4; 29.g3 Bc3; 30.h3 h5; 31.hxg4 Bxg4; 32.Qc2 Bxd4; 33.exd4 Rxd4; 34.Nh3 Rc8. Black won. Molo–Skurovich, Postal 1985.

B) 14.f3 Qh4+; 15.Kf1 bxa4; 16.fxe4 fxe4; 17.g3 Qg4; 18.Bc4 Bd6; 19.Qe2 Qg6; 20.Kg2 Bg4; 21.Qe1 Ne5; 22.Bb2 Nxc4; 23.bxc4 0-0; 24.Ne2 Bf3+. Black won. Schaffer–Kuperman , Postal 1986.

14...Ne5. This is a tempting move, but the knights operate more effectively in tandem from posts on the dark squares, bearing down on d4 and d3.

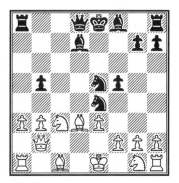

That's why I think that 14...Nc5 is stronger, for example 15.Bc2 b4; 16.Nb5 bxa3; 17.Nxa3 Nb4; 18.Qc3 Nxc2+; 19.Qxc2 Be6; 20.Nh3 Nxb3; 21.0-0 Nxa1; 22.Qc3 Nb3; 23.Nb5 Rc8; 24.Qe5 Qd7; 25.Bb2 Nc5; 26.Nf4 Rg8; 27.Ra1 Be7; 28.Nxe6 Nxe6; 29.Qxf5 g6. Black won. Bostrom–Baumler, Postal 1991.

15.Bc2. 15.Bxe4 fxe4 is not a problem for Black. 16.Qe2 (16.Kf1 Nd3; 17.Qb1 Bc6; 18.Nge2 Qf6; 19.Nd1 Bd6; 20.Nf4 0-0; 21.Ke2 b4. Black won. Erben–Petzold, Postal 1989) 16...Qf6; 17.Nxe4 Nd3+; 18.Qxd3 Qxa1; 19.Ne2 Bxa3; 20.0-0 Be7; 21.Nd6+ Bxd6; 22.Qxd6 Qf6; 23.Ba3 Qxd6; 24.Bxd6 Kf7; 25.Nd4 Ra6; 26.Bc5 Rc8; 27.b4 Ra2; 28.Nf3 Bc6; 29.Ne5+ Ke6; 30.Nxc6 Rxc6; 31.Rd1 Drawn. Thielen–Knorr, Postal 1989.

15...Nc5? 15...Qa5! is best, since White cannot play 16.b4? because of Bxb4. **16.Qb1 Bc6; 17.Kf1 Ncd3; 18.Nf3 Nxf3; 19.Bxd3 Nh4; 20.Rg1 b4; 21.Nb5 Bc5; 22.Bb2 0-0; 23.axb4 f4; 24.bxc5 fxe3; 25.f3 Bxb5; 26.Bxb5 Qd2; 27.Bc4+ Kh8; 28.Be2 Nxf3; 29.Bxg7+ White won.**

MARSHALL GAMBIT

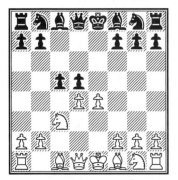

1.d4   d5
2.c4   e6
3.Nc3   c5
4.cxd5   exd5
5.e4

Leave it to Gambiteer General Frank Marshall to find a way to sacrifice a pawn against the Tarrasch. He simply refused to allow Black to take the initiative, and wanted further to annoy Black by using the technique of an advanced d-pawn! There is no reason for Black to decline the offer.

What does White get for the pawn? Not much. The advanced pawn at d5 can be a pain, which is not surprising since this is a method we use ourselves as Black in the Tarrasch. In addition, it is such a rare move that most Tarrasch players can be caught by surprise fairly easily. You should study the responses that are recommended below, and refresh them from time to time (once a decade, perhaps) just in case someone tries to shock you with it.

In general, however, just don't get too greedy and you should be able to survive the opening with a good position. Virtually no one recommends the gambit, so not many players will have any interest in it. Just relax, watch out for tactical threats, and exchange pieces while you have an extra pawn, then clean up in the endgame.

MARSHALL VS. SPIELMANN
Vienna, 1908

1.d4 d5; 2.c4 e6; 3.Nc3 c5; 4.cxd5 exd5; 5.e4 dxe4; 6.d5. The only move you'll find in most books, but there are some interesting alternatives.

A) 6.Bc4 requires careful handling. The safest reply is 6...Nf6, ignoring the pawn at d4. After 7.Qb3, Black can play 7...Be6; 8.Bxe6 fxe6; 9.Qxb7 (9.Qxe6+ Qe7; 10.Qxe7+ Bxe7; 11.Nb5 Na6 does not look too bad for Black) 9...cxd4; 10.Nb5 Bb4+; 11.Kf1 0-0; 12.Qxa8 Qb6; 13.Nxa7 Qa6+ and Black comes out on top.

B) Marshall also tried 6.Bb5+ Nd7. (6...Bd7; 7.dxc5 Bxb5; 8.Qxd8+ Kxd8; 9.Nxb5 Bxc5; 10.Nh3 h6; 11.Be3 Nd7; 12.Rd1 Bb4+; 13.Bd2 Bxd2+; 14.Rxd2 Ngf6; 15.0-0 Ke7; 16.Nd6 Rhb8; 17.Re1 Nc5; 18.b4 Ne6; 19.Nxe4 Nxe4; 20.Rxe4 Rd8 with obvious equality in Marshall–Janowski, Paris 1905, though White did manage to win in the end.) 7.Bf4 Ngf6; 8.d5 g6; 9.f3 Bg7; 10.fxe4 0-0; 11.Nge2 Re8; 12.e5 Nh5; 13.e6 Nxf4; 14.exf7+ Kxf7; 15.0-0 was seen in Williams–Headlong, Wigan 1997, where 15...g5 was necessary.

C) 6.dxc5 Qxd1+; 7.Kxd1 Nf6; 8.Be3 Bg4+ and Black has the initiative, Steinhoff–Morgado, Postal 1979.

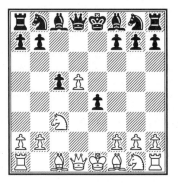

6...f5. 6...Nf6 can be played, but the text is more challenging. **7.Bb5+.** There are three alterntives which have been tried. None of them are any good.

A) 7.Nh3 a6; 8.f3 Nf6; 9.Bg5 Bd6; 10.fxe4 0-0; 11.Bd3 h6; 12.Bxf6 Qxf6; 13.Nf2 was played in Burn–Janowski, Ostende 1905. Here Black should play 13...b5 with a good game.

B) 7.Bf4 is best challenged by 7...Bd6 and now:

B1) 8.Bb5+ Kf7; 9.Nh3 (9.Bxd6 Qxd6; 10.f3 a6; 11.Be2 Nf6; 12.Nh3 Re8; 13.fxe4 fxe4; 14.Ng5+ Kg8; 15.0-0 Qe5 and Black went on to win in Wehmeier–Zolnierowicz, Miedzybrodzie 1991) 9...Nf6 10.Bc4 a6; 11.a4 Re8; 12.Qd2 Qe7. Black has the better prospects, Tolush–Furman, Moscow 1957.

B2) 8.Nh3 leads to some excitement, but in the end Black emerges on top: 8...a6!? 9.f3 Nf6; 10.fxe4 fxe4; 11.Nxe4 Nxe4; 12.Qa4+ Kf7; 13.Qxe4 Re8; 14.Ng5+ Kg8; 15.Ne6 Bxe6; 16.dxe6 Bxf4; 17.Qxf4 Rxe6+; 18.Be2 Qa5+ and eventually Black won. Burn–Tarrasch, Ostende 1905.

C) 7.f3 gives Black a pleasant choice: The development of a knight at f6 and bishop at d6 are the cornerstones of the plan, and they can be played in either order. 7...Bd6; 8.Nh3 Nf6; 9.Bb5+ Nbd7; 10.fxe4 fxe4; 11.Ng5 a6; 12.Ne6 Qe7; 13.0-0 axb5; 14.Nxb5 Ra6; 15.Bg5 h5; 16.Qb3 Nf8; 17.Nxg7+ Qxg7; 18.Bxf6 Bxh2+; 19.Kxh2 Rxf6; 20.Qc3 Nd7; 21.Nd6+ Kd8; 22.Rxf6 Nxf6; 23.Qa5+ Qc7; 24.b4 b6; 25.Qa8 Qxd6+; 26.Kg1 Ng4. Black won. Marshall–Duras, San Sebastian 1911.

7...Bd7.

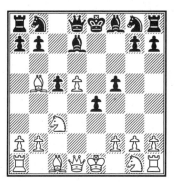

8.Bxd7+. The alternatives also cause no problems for Black. 8.Nh3 (8.a4 is nothing if Black captures at b5) 8...Bxb5; 9.Nxb5 Qa5+; 10.Nc3 Na6; 11.f3 Nf6; 12.0-0 and here 12...Bd6 would have given Black a good game in Oskam–Euwe, Amsterdam 1920.

8...Qxd7. White has nothing to show for the pawn. The attempt to undermine e4, seen in this game, goes nowhere and Black simply exchanges pieces and enters a better endgame with a powerful attacking queen. **9.Nh3 Bd6; 10.Ng5 Na6; 11.0-0 Nf6; 12.f3 0-0; 13.Ne6 Rf7.** Now the pieces come flying off the board.

14.fxe4 Nxe4; 15.Nxe4 fxe4; 16.Be3 Rxf1+; 17.Qxf1 Nc7; 18.Qc4 Re8; 19.Nxc7 Qxc7.

All of Black's pieces are well positioned, while White's are simply defending. Black expands on the queenside and gets both the c-pawn and the e-pawn rolling. **20.g3 a6; 21.a4 Qd7; 22.Rf1 b5; 23.axb5 axb5; 24.Qc2 c4; 25.b3 Qc7; 26.bxc4 Bc5; 27.Bxc5 Qxc5+; 28.Kg2 bxc4; 29.Rd1 e3; 30.Qe2 c3; 31.d6 c2; 32.Rc1 Qd5+; 33.Qf3 Qd2+; 34.Kh3 Rf8; 35.Qh1 e2; 36.Re1 Qh6+; 37.Kg2 Qf6; 38.d7 Qc6+; 39.Kh3 Qxd7+; 40.g4 Qd3+; 41.Kh4 Qd1. Black won.**

ANGLO-INDIAN

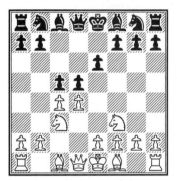

1.d4	d5
2.c4	e6
3.Nc3	c5
4.Nf3	

This move allows a transposition to the Anglo–Indian Variation of the English Opening after 4...cxd4. Of course we can stay within the Tarrasch scheme with 4...Nc6, but why not take advantage of the situation?

The capture at d4 undermines White's center and allows Black to advance the e-pawn to e5 with gain of tempo. Although Black does not develop a piece in the first half–dozen moves, the constant threats prevent White from continuing development.

White is not adopting a hypermodern strategy, or if so, is not doing it correctly. Black will be able to maintain the strong pawn center, and use the space in the center to maneuver freely. This is a very pleasant life for Black, with few complications to worry about.

BERNSTEIN VS. LEONHARDT
San Sebastian, 1911

1.d4 d5; 2.c4 e6; 3.Nc3 c5; 4.Nf3 cxd4; 5.Nxd4 e5. This simple move can get White into serious trouble as the center falls apart quickly.

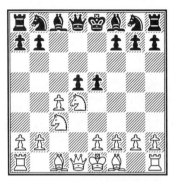

Black has taken over the center and already has the initiative.
6.Ndb5.

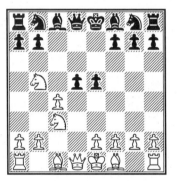

6.Nf3 d4; 7.Nd5 Nc6 is the major alternative.

A) 8.e3 Nge7! challenges the strong knight at d5 right away, without allowing the sort of annoying pins that could be set up if the
knight went to f6. Now if White plays Bg5, Black can usually reply

...f6. 9.exd4 Nxd5; 10.cxd5 Qxd5; 11.dxe5 Qxd1+; 12.Kxd1 leaves Black down a pawn, but that is a temporary condition. 12...Bg4. (12...Bc5 is also acceptable. 13.Bb5 Bxf2; 14.Ke2 Bb6; 15.Be3 0-0; 16.Bxc6 bxc6; 17.Rac1 Ba6+; 18.Kf2 Bxe3+; 19.Kxe3 Bb7 is a little passive, but playable, Otto–Hoffmann, Germany 1994.) 13.Bf4 Bc5; 14.Bb5 0-0-0+; 15.Ke1 Bb4+; 16.Kf1 Bxf3; 17.gxf3 Bd2 and Black has a strong initiative, Roes–Bulthaupt, Baden–Baden 1987. 8...Be6 is too ambitious, as I found out (the hard way) in Lanchava–Schiller, Groningen 1997.

B) 8.e4 is fine for Black provided that development remains priority one. There are two acceptable formations, one with ...Bd6 ...Nge7 and the other with ...Be7 ...Nf6. Both are good, and the choice between them is a matter of taste. 8...Nf6. (8...Bd6; 9.Bd3 Nge7; 10.h3 Ng6; 11.g4 Be6; 12.a3 a5; 13.Bg5 f6; 14.Bd2 0-0. White controls more space, but Black has a protected passed pawn and a very solid position, T.Arnason–Jonasson, Reykjavik 1988.) 9.Bg5 Be7; 10.Bxf6 Bxf6; 11.h3 0-0; 12.Qd2 Be7; 13.g4 Be6; 14.a3 Bd6; 15.Bd3 a5 and Black has a better position on the queenside. If White castles in that direction, hoping for an opposite–wing attacking game, then Black should be very happy. For example: 16.0-0-0 a4!; 17.Kb1 Na5; 18.Rdg1 Re8; 19.Qc2 Rc8; 20.Qe2 Nb3; 21.g5 and now it is time to get rid of the knight: 21...Bxd5; 22.exd5.

Black now opens up the game to great effect. 22...e4!; 23.Bxe4 Nc5; 24.Rg4 d3!; 25.Qe3 b5!; 26.Re1 (26.cxb5 Qa5 and Black's heavy artillery will soon occupy the b- and c-files) 26...bxc4; 27.Qc1 c3!; 28.bxc3 (28.Qxc3 loses a piece to 28...Nxe4; 29.Rgxe4 Rxe4; 30.Rxe4 Rxc3; 31.bxc3 Bxa3 and White cannot survive.) 28...Rb8+; 29.Ka2 Qb6; 30.Nd2 Nb3; 31.Qb2 Qxf2; 32.Rd1 Nc5; 33.Bxh7+ Kxh7; 34.Qc1 Nb3. Black won. Chistiakov–Bronstein, Soviet Union 1945.

6...d4; 7.Nd5.

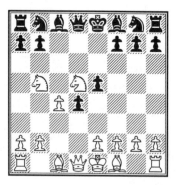

White's knight at d5 looks strong, but it can be undermined. **7...Na6; 8.e3.** The tournament book preferred 8.e4, but that plan fails to put pressure on Black's pressure.

White can try to set up a discovered check with 8.Qa4, but after 8 ...Bd7; 9.e4 dxe3; 10.Bxe3 Nf6; 11.Bg5 Bc5. Black has at least equality. 12.Be2 allows 12...Bxf2+!; 13.Kf1 (13.Kxf2 Ne4+; 14.Ke1 Qxg5 gives Black a tremendous game) 13...Bc5; 14.Rd1.

Black now plays a surprising queen sacrifice: 14...Nxd5!!; 15.Bxd8 Ne3+; 16.Ke1 Rxd8! White cannot castle, having forfeited that privilege by moving the king. Black has only two pieces as compensation, but the many threats, combined with the power of the pin against the knight at b5, provides more than enough compensation.

White tries to limit the damage now by returning a little material. 17.Rxd7 Rxd7; 18.Bf3 0-0; 19.Nc3 Rfd8. Black has one piece, a rook and a pawn for the queen, which is almost enough material. 20.Nd5 Nxd5; 21.Bxd5 Nb4!

This wins another pawn, since White does not dare to move the bishop and let the enemy rooks in. 22.Ke2 Nxd5; 23.cxd5 Rxd5; 24.Rc1 g6; 25.Rc2 Rd4; 26.Rc4 Rd2+! Exchanging rooks would have worked to White's advantage, since it is harder to coordinate a single rook and bishop. 27.Ke1 b5! A nice deflection to get the queen to abandon the d1-square. 28.Qxb5 Rd1+; 29.Ke2 R8d2+; 30.Kf3 Rf2+; 31.Ke4 Rf4+; 32.Kxe5 Bd6. Checkmate. Black won. Heyder–Chasin, Postal 1978. So, we have established that 8.e3 is correct.

8...Nf6.

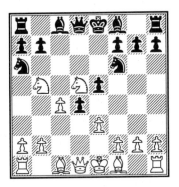

The battle revolves around the d5-square. **9.Nxf6+ Qxf6; 10.exd4.** Rejecting the strong knight is worth temporary custody of a pawn.

10...Bb4+! 10...exd4; 11.Qxd4 Bb4+ is less good, even though there are more open lines. 12.Bd2 Qe7+; 13.Be2 0-0; 14.Nc3 Re8; 15.0-0 Bc5; 16.Qe5 Be6; 17.Ne4 Bb6; 18.Bc3 Bc7; 19.Qg5 Qxg5; 20.Nxg5.and White has an obvious advantage, Cacho–Gonzalez Custodio, Canete 1994.

11.Bd2.

11...exd4; 12.Be2. 12.Bxb4 Nxb4; 13.Nc7+ Kd8; 14.Nxa8 Re8+; 15.Be2 d3 is much better for Black. The move 12.Be2 was recommended by O. Bernstein but this game shows that the idea fails to save White's position. **12...0–0.** 12...d3; 13.Bxd3 0–0; 14.0–0 Rd8 is refuted by 15.Bc3! Bxc3; 16.Nxc3 Be6; 17.Nd5 since 17...Bxd5; 18.cxd5 Rxd5 loses to 19.Bxh7+!

13.Bxb4 Nxb4; 14.0–0. White has managed to get the king to safety, but Black still has a dangerous initiative. **14...d3!; 15.Bf3 Nc2; 16.Rb1 Bf5!; 17.Qd2.** 17.Bxb7 Rab8 gives Black sufficient compensation for the pawn, for example 18.Bf3 Rfc8; 19.Bd5 Nb4! **17...Rad8; 18.c5** White has a hard time finding anything to do, but this move just creates another weakness.

18...b6!

19.b4.

White must defend the pawn, since neither an advance nor an exchange at b6 is of any value. On 19.c6 a6; 20.Nc3 Nd4! and the bishop at f3 is under attack. Capturing at b6 is no better: 19.cxb6 Qxb6; 20.Nc3 Nd4; 21.Qd1 Rfe8 and White has no useful moves. **19...a5!** The queenside pawn structure falls apart.

20.cxb6 axb4; 21.b7. 21.Qf4 Qxb6; 22.Qxf5 g6; 23.Qg5 h6; 24.Qe5 Rfe8 and the knight at b5 cannot be defended by the queen. **21...Qb6; 22.a4!** This is White's best chance, in a bad position. **22...Qa5.** The pawn at b7 is not a problem. **23.Qf4 g6.** Black is in no hurry.

24.Nd6?

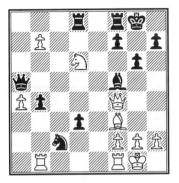

A terrible oversight, but the position was in any case indefensible. 24.Nc7 Nd4! threatens ...Ne2+, and after 25.Kh1 d2; 26.Rbd1 Bd3; 27.Rg1 Ne2. White would not last long.

24...Qc7! This sets up a strong pin. White now puts up only minimal resistance.

25.a5 Qxd6; 26.Qc4 Na3; 27.Qxb4 Nxb1; 28.Qxb1.

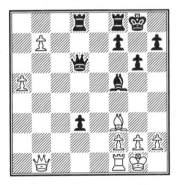

White's advanced passed pawns are of no consequence.

28...d2!; 29.Qb2 d1Q; 30.Bxd1 Qxd1!; 31.a6. 31.Rxd1 Rxd1. Checkmate. **31...Rfe8!; 32.f3 Re1; 33.Qf2 Rxf1+; 34.Qxf1 Qxf1+; 35.Kxf1 Bd3+.** White resigned, as both the a-pawn and b-pawn will be captured.

WHITE PLAYS 3.Nf3

When White plays Nf3 before Nc3 it is usually just a way to avoid the Schara Gambit (3.Nc3 c5; 4.cxd5 cxd4!?), but sometimes White decides to develop the knight at d2 instead. The difference is very important. From d2, the knight covers the c4–square, but does not put any pressure on d5.

That can be a little misleading. Remember that when playing against an isolated d-pawn, the standard strategy is to blockade the pawn with a knight. We see this in the main lines of the Classical variation, when we capture at d4 and White recaptures with the knight. When the knight is developed at d2, however, it can later travel to b3 and then to d4. The other knight remains at f3, where it controls the important e5 square.

The games in this section show how Black can take advantage of this quiet developing plan. We start with a game in which White adopts the typical kingside fianchetto plan.

ROMANISHIN VS. MCCAMBRIDGE
Dortmund, 1982

1.d4 Nf6; 2.Nf3 e6; 3.g3 d5; 4.Bg2 Be7; 5.c4 0–0; 6.0–0 c5; 7.cxd5 exd5; 8.dxc5 Bxc5.

By yet another transposition, from a Catalan Opening, we reach a typical Tarrasch position. This is a fairly popular continuation for White and it can arise via many different transpositional paths. **9.a3.** White plans to chase the bishop from c5. Other plans are unimpressive.

A) 9.Bg5 Nc6. (9...Be7; 10.Nc3 Be6; 11.Bf4 Qd7; 12.Ng5 Nc6; 13.Nxe6 fxe6 reaches, by transposition, Esposito–Schiller, Chicago 1982. Black has a good position.) 10.Qc2 (10.Bxf6 Qxf6; 11.Qxd5 Qxb2 is obviously better for Black. After 12.Qxc5 Qxa1; 13.Nc3 Qb2; 14.Rb1 Qc2 the queen slides out of the net) 10...Bb6 is correct, as given by Euwe and Van der Sterren. Note that 10.Nbd2 is a stupid move. After 9...h6, Black was already better in Schiller-Gersshon, New York Open 1998.

B) 9.b3 Nc6; 10.Bb2 Ne4; 11.Nc3 Nxc3; 12.Bxc3 d4; 13.Bb2 Bg4 gave Black a good game in Bondarevsky–Lilianthal, Soviet Championship 1941.

C) 9.Nbd2 Nc6.

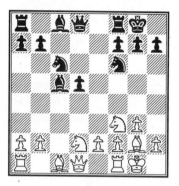

This position is frequently reached via transposition from the Catalan and various flank openings. 10.Nb3 (10.a3 a5; 11.Nb3 Bb6; 12.Nbd4 Re8; 13.Be3 a4; 14.Rc1 Bd7; 15.Qd3 h6; 16.h3 Ne4 gives Black a fine game. White has no active plan. Platonov–Dementiev, Riga 1970. No better is 10.Ne1 Re8; 11.Nd3 Bb6; 12.Nf4 Bf5; 13.h3 Nd4; 14.Nf3 Bc2; 15.Qe1 Nf5 and Black's initiative led to a quick win in Dieks–Nunn, Amsterdam 1975.) 10...Bb6 with:

C1) 11.Bg5 h6; 12.Bf4 Re8; 13.Nbd4 Nxd4; 14.Nxd4 Bg4 with strong pressure for Black, Rapoport–Nor, Israel Championship 1996.

C2) 11.Nfd4 Re8; 12.Re1 Ng4; 13.e3 Qf6; 14.Rf1 Ne7; 15.Bd2 Bd7; 16.Bc3 Qh6; 17.Nf3 Nf5; 18.Bd4 Nxd4; 19.Nbxd4 Rac8 and Black had plenty of counterplay in Euwe–Lundin, Groningen 1946.

C3) 11.Qd3 Re8; 12.Bd2 Bg4; 13.Bc3 d4; 14.Nbxd4 Nxd4; 15.Bxd4 Bxf3; 16.Bxb6 Qxd3; 17.exd3 Bxg2 forced White's resignation in Lida Garcia–Nogues, Buenos Aires 1970.

C4) 11.Nbd4 Ne4.

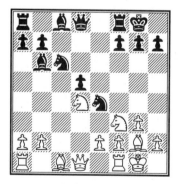

Black has scored well from this position. White has absolutely no pressure at d5. 12.Be3 (12.Bf4 Qf6; 13.Nxc6 bxc6; 14.Be5 Qe7;

15.Rc1 Bb7; 16.Qa4 Nd2; 17.Nxd2 Qxe5; 18.Rc2 Qxe2 with a much better game for Black in Jahn–Dive, Geneva 1996.) 12...Qf6; 13.Rc1 (13.Qd3 Bd7; 14.Rfd1 Rac8; 15.Qb3 Be6; 16.Nxe6 fxe6; 17.Bxb6 axb6; 18.Qxb6 g5; 19.Rd3 g4; 20.Nd2 Qxf2+; 21.Qxf2 Nxf2; 22.Re3 Nd4; 23.Rf1 Rc2; 24.Rxf2 Rxd2; 25.Rxf8+ Kxf8; 26.Kf2 Rxb2 and Black went on to win in Johner–Euwe, Göteborg 1920) 13...Bg4; 14.Nc2 Qxb2; 15.Bxb6 axb6; 16.Rb1 Qxa2; 17.Rxb6 Ra7; 18.Qd3 Nc5; 19.Qe3 Qxc2; 20.Rc1 allows Black to win in spectacular style.

    20...d4; 21.Nxd4 Nxd4; 22.Rxc2 Ra1+; 23.Bf1 Nxc2 and White resigned, Camara–Michel, Buenos Aires 1948.

After 9.a3, White threatens to advance with b4.

9...a6.

    This makes room for the bishop at a7. It is important to keep the bishop on th a7–g1 diagonal in this line.

10.b4 Ba7; 11.Bb2 Nc6; 12.Nbd2 Re8; 13.Nb3.

White will blockade the d-pawn with a knight which will arrive at d4 via b3. Black can't just sit back and let this happen, so it is necessary to apply some pressure. **13...Bg4!; 14.Rc1 Qe7; 15.h3.** This weakens the kingside. As long as there is a bishop at g2, that is not a severe problem but it does force the bishop to stay home.

15...Bxf3!; 16.exf3. 16.Bxf3 Ne4 threatens to capture at g3, and after 17.Kg2, 17...Rad8 gives Black a solid position.

16...Rad8!; 17.Nc5 d4!

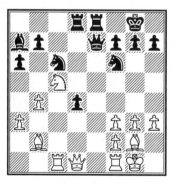

The thematic advance of the d-pawn is possible because the capture at a6 fails tactically. **18.Qd2.** 18.Nxa6? Qe2; 19.Qxe2 Rxe2; 20.Ba1 d3 and the knight at a6, looks silly.

18...Bxc5; 19.bxc5. 19.Rxc5 Qe2; 20.Rc2? d3!; 21.Qxe2 Rxe2; 22.Rxe2 dxe2; 23.Re1 Rd1; 24.Bc3 Nd5 and Black wins. **19...h6.** McCambridge later suggested 19...h5 as an improvement. Time pressure was becoming a factor for both sides.

20.Rfe1 Qd7.

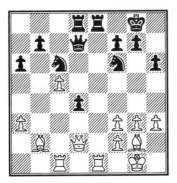

21.Red1? 21.f4 is better. Still, after 21...Rxe1+; 22.Rxe1 Qf5; 23.Bxc6 bxc6; 24.Bxd4 Qd5; 25.Rd1 Ne4 (analysis by Shamkovich and Schiller) Black has a great game. **21...Qf5!?** The simpler ...h5 would have been objectively stronger, but this speculative sacrifice works out well, and White in either case is fighting for equality.
22.f4 d3; 23.g4 Nxg4!; 24.hxg4 Qxg4; 25.f3! The best defense. 25.Re1 is met by 25...Re2. 25.Qc3 Nd4 simultaneously eliminates White's pressure on the long diagonal and brings another piece into the attack. **25...Qf5; 26.Re1!** 26.Bf1 leaves the king defenseless. 26...Re6; 27.Bxd3 Rg6+; 28.Kf2 Qh3!; 29.Bxg6 Rxd2+; 30.Rxd2 fxg6; 31.Rg1 Ne7; 32.Rg2 Nf5!; 33.Rxg6 Qh2+; 34.Rg2 Qxf4 and Black should win.
26...Rxe1+; 27.Rxe1 Qxc5+; 28.Kf1 Na5.

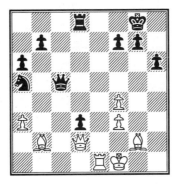

Here White could have kept the game about even, but blunders and allows Black to develop a serious advantage. **29.Re5!** 29.Qc3 Qxc3; 30.Bxc3 Nc4; 31.Kf2 d2!; 32.Rd1 Rd3 leaves the bishop in a quandary. 33.Ba1 (33.Bb4 a5; 34.Bc5 Nb2; 35.Ke2 Nxd1; 36.Kxd1

Rxa3 and Black wins) 33...Nxa3; 34.Ke2 Rd5; 35.Rxd2 Rxd2+; 36.Kxd2 Nc4+; 37.Kd3 b5 and Black's pawns are worth more than the piece. **29...Qxe5; 30.Bxe5.** 30.fxe5 Nc4; 31.Qc1 d2; 32.Qd1 Nxb2; 33.Ke2 Nxd1; 34.Kxd1 is also hopeless.

30...Nc4!

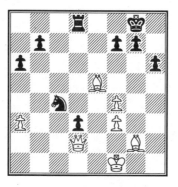

Black has given up the queen, but the d-pawn will soon replace it! **31.Qc1 d2; 32.Qxc4 d1Q+; 33.Kf2 Rd2+; 34.Kg3.** White's material deficit is not the problem. The position of the king is more important. **34...Rc2; 35.Qf1 Qd2.** White is almost in zugzwang. **36.Bb8 h5; 37.Kh2 Rc1.** White resigned, since the queen is trapped. **Black won.**

TISDALL VS. HARDARSON
Reykjavik, 1988

1.Nf3 d5; 2.d4 e6; 3.c4 c5; 4.cxd5 exd5; 5.g3 Nc6; 6.Bg2 Nf6; 7.0-0 Be7.

In this game we examine alternatives to 8.Nc3, which leads to the Classical lines, except for the lines with dxc5 which are covered in Romanishin–McCambridge in the previous game. Many transpositional paths are available, but the single unifying theme is a refusal by White to enter the main lines.

8.Be3. 8.b3 0–0; 9.Bb2 Ne4; 10.Nc3 Bf6 transposes to the Larsen Variation of the Classical Tarrasch. **8...Ng4.** The knight sits well on this square. If White chases it away with an eventual h3, that creates another target on the kingside. Meanwhile, the bishop must relocate from e3.

9.Bf4 0–0; 10.Nc3. This position is the same as the main line with Nc3, and Bf4, except that the Black knight is at g4.

10...Be6; 11.dxc5 Bxc5.

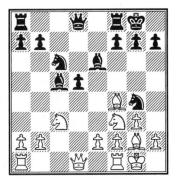

Now White must choose a plan.

12.Qc2. 12.Na4 chases the bishop, and the retreat 12...Be7 is usually seen. I don't see anything wrong with ...Bd6, but it seems not to have found favor in professional chess.

A) 13.Nd4 Nxd4. (13...g5 comes into consideration.) 14.Qxd4 Qa5; 15.Nc3 is solid for Black.

B) 13.Rc1 d4. (13...Qa5; 14.Ng5 Nf6; 15.Nxe6 fxe6; 16.a3 Kh8; 17.Bd2 Qd8; 18.Nc5 Bxc5; 19.Rxc5 Nd7; 20.Rc1 Nde5; 21.e3 Qf6; 22.f4 Nc4; 23.Bc3 gave White the advantage in Cifuentes Parada–S.Arkell, Ostende 1991.)

13...Rc8 looks best to me, but it awaits a practical test. 14.a3 Bd5; 15.Nc5 Re8; 16.b4 b6; 17.Na6 and Black suffered from weaknesses on the dark squares, Smyslov–Blokhuis, London 1989.

12.e3 Nf6; 13.Rc1 Bd6; 14.Bxd6 Qxd6; 15.Nb5 Qe7 should not present Black with any problems.

12.Ng5 h6; 13.Nxe6 fxe6; 14.Bh3 was played in Puri–Demers, Canadian Junior Championship 1987. Black sacrificed at f2, but...h5 is safer.

12...Be7. Black retreats the Bishop to a safer sqare.

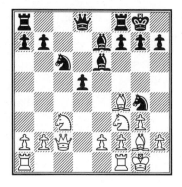

13.Rad1 Qb6; 14.Ng5 Nf6.

Now things get interesting!

15.Nxd5. 15.Nxe6 fxe6; 16.e4 d4 gives Black plenty of counterplay in the center.

15.Bxd5 is best met by 15...Nb4!; 16.Qb1 Nbxd5; 17.Nxd5 Bxd5; 18.Rxd5 and of course Black cannot capture at d5 because of mate at h7. However, after 18...h6! White cannot keep the position together. 19.Be3 Qa6; 20.Re5 Bd6 etc.

15...Bxd5; 16.Bxd5 Nb4. 16...Rad8; 17.e4 would be better for White.

17.Bxf7+. White will make good use of the a2–g8 diagonal. 17...Rxf7; 18.Qc4 Raf8; 19.Nxf7 Rxf7; 20.Bc7.

20.e4 is a sensible alternative. 20...Qc6; 21.Qxc6 Nxc6; 22.e5 Nh5; 23.e6 gives White the initiative.

20...Qc6; 21.Qxc6 Nxc6; 22.Bd6 Bxd6; 23.Rxd6 Re7.

White is certainly a little better here, but I doubt that Black has any reason to worry about losing as long as the defense is precise. After all, Black has three pieces to work with, and by reducing the number of pawns, can look for exchange–down endgames that are drawable by sacrificing a knight for at least two pawns. The present game, though imperfectly played, shows just how complex these endgames can be.

24.e3 Kf7; 25.Kg2 Re5; 26.Rc1 Rb5. Both players try to activate all their pieces. This is the proper strategy.

27.b3 Ke7; 28.Rd2 Re5; 29.Rd3. I think that doubling rooks would have made it more likely for success. Now Black manages to get one pair of rooks off the board easily. In defense of White's choice, it must be said that after ...Ke6 Black could control the d5 square anyway. **29...Ra5; 30.a4 Rd5; 31.Rxd5 Nxd5; 32.e4 Ndb4; 33.Kf3.** A bit artificial. I would have played f4 first. Still, transpositions are likely.

33...Nd3; 34.Rc3 Nde5+; 35.Ke2 Kd6; 36.f4 Nd7; 37.Rd3+ Ke6.

White has made a lot of progress, but what next? It is too early to advance either the e-pawn or f-pawn, as that allows the enemy knights more scope. As for Black, a waiting game is indicated.

38.Kd2 Nc5! Black will try to attack the base of the pawn chain when possible. Since h2 is inaccessible, the invitation is at b3. **39.Re3 Na5; 40.Kc3.** On the last move of time control, Tisdall, probably in time trouble as usual, decides to sacrifice a pawn to tie up the enemy knights.

40.b4 Nc4+; 41.Ke2 Nxe3; 42.Kxe3 Nxa4 and Black wins.

40.Kc2 Nc6; 41.Kc3 a5 would be hard to crack.

40...Ncxb3; 41.g4 Nc5; 42.Kb4 b6.

White's advantage is almost gone. The knight at c5 will stay in place and force White to defend the pawn at a4. The other knight can return to the center to help impede the advance of the pawns.

43.g5 a6; 44.Rh3. White gives up the e-pawn for the h-pawn. Black's position is very good and there is no longer any reason to fear losing. **44...Nc6+; 45.Ka3 Nxe4; 46.Rxh7 Kf7; 47.Rh8.** White wants to circle around and go after the queenside pawns. **47...b5!; 48.axb5 axb5; 49.Rc8 Nd4; 50.h4 Kg6!** The king takes an active role in the defense. Black can draw by exchanging a knight for the kingside pawns, but has too few pawns to play for a win.

51.Rc7 Nf5; 52.Kb4 Ned6. 52...Nxh4; 53.Kxb5 Ng2 looks like a try for a win, but White always has 54.Rxg7+ Kxg7 and two knights cannot defeat a lone king.

53.Kc5 Kh5; 54.Kd5 Kxh4; 55.Ke5 Kg4; 56.Rc1 Nc4+; 57.Ke6 Ncd6. 57...Kxf4; 58.Rf1+ Kxg5; 59.Rxf5+ Kg4; 60.Rxb5 Ne3 is a drawn endgame. **58.Ke5 Nc4+; 59.Ke6 Ncd6. Drawn.**

WHITE AVOIDS THE QUEEN'S GAMBIT

Here we examine openings with 1.d4 d5, where White does not play an early c4. These variations have almost nothing in common with each other, but all are seen frequently in competition, so Black must be prepared for each one. I have tried to present easy to learn lines which do not require a great deal of preparation or memorization.

We will start out by examining the Torre Attack, where White plays Nf3 and Bg5. I can't say much against the opening, as I have written extensively on it and often play it as White. Nevertheless, the Torre is not really so effective when Black does not play ...Nf6, and so we have nothing to worry about.

The London System uses a bishop at f4, which as we have seen is harmless against the Tarrasch formation. As long as Black doesn't fall for any cheap tactics, it is very comfortable to sit at the Black side of the table. Indeed, my own score against the London system is something over 80%, which is just wonderful as Black.

Next up is the Colle System, which is like the Torre except that the bishop sits at home on c1, locked in by a pawn at e3. The Colle is popular among weak players because it is easy to learn, but has no real effect at higher levels of play.

The Veresov Attack uses 2.Nc3, instead of 2.Nf3, in conjunction with Bg5. It was once part of my repertoire as White but I threw it away after I realized just how easy it is for Black to get a decent game.

Finally, the disreputable Blackmar-Diemer Gambit never worries a strong player, as it is possible to defend and take advantage of the extra pawn without much difficulty. After 2.e4 we will capture the pawn and then strike at the center with ...e5, which is known as the Lemberger Countergambit. Not to be confused with Limburger (a stinky cheese), this defense is quite reliable and easy to learn.

Torre Attack 2.Nf3 e6; 3.Bg5

ANDONOV VS. GARCIA PALERMO
Camaguey 1987

1.Nf3 d5; 2.d4 e6; 3.Bg5

White offers an exchange of dark–squared bishops, but accelerates Black's development in the process.

3...Be7; 4.Bxe7 Qxe7; 5.Nbd2. 5.c3 Nd7; 6.e3 Ngf6; 7.Nbd2 (7.Bd3 e5; 8.dxe5 Nxe5; 9.Nxe5 Qxe5; 10.Qa4+ Bd7; 11.Qh4 c5 is very comfortable for Black, Behrmann–Fritze, Germany 1989) 7...e5 8.Be2 e4; 9.Ng1 c6; 10.Nh3 Nf8; 11.Nf4 Ne6 and Black has nothing to worry about, Ravi–Ganesan, India 1988.

5.c4 is recommended in my book on the Torre Attack (Chess Digest 1996). After 5...Qb4+; 6.Qd2 Qxd2+; 7.Nbxd2 Nf6. (7...dxc4 8.Nxc4 Nf6; 9.e3 Ke7; 10.Nce5 Nbd7 comes into consideration. I think that in general all Black has to do is vigorously contest the e5–square and equality will follow. 11.Bd3 Nxe5; 12.Nxe5 Nd7 and Black has no worries.) 8.Rc1 c6; 9.e3 Ke7; 10.Bd3. White enjoyed a slight advantage in Ye Rongguang–Van Riemsdyck, Manila Interzonal 1990.

5...Nf6; 6.e3 Nbd7!

Fight for e5! That is the key to defending against most of the systems with 2.Nf3.

7.Ne5?! 7.Bd3 0-0; 8.0-0 c5; 9.c3 e5; 10.dxe5 Nxe5; 11.Nxe5 Qxe5; 12.Nf3 Qh5 presents no problems. Still, it is better for White than the text.

7...Nxe5; 8.dxe5 Nd7; 9.Qg4. White can at best attack with queen, knight and bishop. Black has enough defense, so castling is good.

9...0-0.

10.f4. 10.Bd3 f5; 11.exf6 Qxf6; 12.0-0 e5 destroys any chance of a White attack. **10...Qb4!** This clever move threatens ...Nxe5. **11.Bd3 f5!; 12.Qh3.** 12.exf6 Nxf6; 13.Qh4 e5! 14.0-0-0 e4; 15.Be2 a5; 16.g4 a4; 17.a3 Qc5. Black's attack is stronger than White's.

12...Nc5; 13.Rb1 b6. Black plans to capture at d3 and then play ...Ba6. 13...Nxd3+ 14.cxd3 b6 would have been more accurate. **14.a3.** 14.Be2 Ne4; 15.c3 would have been wiser.

14...Nxd3+; 15.cxd3 Qb5; 16.d4 Ba6.

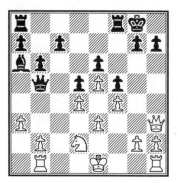

White's weaknesses on the light squares are quickly exploited. **17.Qf3 c5!** Time to open things up! **18.dxc5 Rac8!; 19.Qd1.**

19.cxb6 Rc2; 20.bxa7 Qd3; 21.Rd1 Rxb2; 22.h4 Rc8 and White will not last long.

19...Qxc5; 20.Kf2 d4!; 21.exd4 Qxd4+; 22.Kg3.

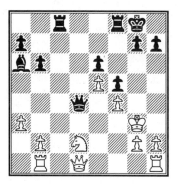

Black continues to open lines and is not done yet! **22...g5!** 22...Rfd8; 23.Nf3 keeps White in the game. **23.fxg5 Rfd8. Black won.**

London System 2.Nf3 e6; 3.Bf4

STESSER VS. KOUWENHOVEN
Rimavska Sobota, 1992

1.d4 d5; 2.Nf3 e6; 3.Bf4

The London System is not a very effective plan at top levels, where defensive technique is strong, but it does present problems for amateurs. The Tarrasch Defense is not the best response, though it is solid enough to be recommendable. If you are sure your opponent is going to play the London, you can try 2...g6 instead, or 2...c6 followed by an early ...Qb6. The problem is that when facing an unknown opponent you do not know the intentions of 2.Nf3. Rather than learn a set of individual defense against the London System, Torre Attack, Colle, etc., it is easier to learn just one basic formation which we use throughout the book.

3...c5; 4.e3 Nc6; 5.c3. 5.c4 Nf6; 6.Nc3 Be7; 7.Bd3 dxc4; 8.Bxc4 cxd4; 9.exd4 is a Tarrasch Defense in reverse, but you should be familiar enough with the isolated pawn position as Black to play effectively as if you were White. The position of the bishop at f4 is artificial, and after you get a knight to d5 you will recover tempo. 9...0-0; 10.0-0 Nb4! This is the knight that belongs on d5. 11.Rc1 a6; 12.a3 Nbd5; 13.Bg3 b5! Black controls the initiative. 14.Bd3 Bb7; 15.Qe2 Rc8; 16.Nxd5 Qxd5; 17.Qe5. White would love to exchange queens and stop worrying about the firepower which is concentrated on the a8–h1 diagonal. 17...Qb3!; 18.Qe2 (Not 18.Rc7? 18...Bxf3; 19.Bxh7+ Nxh7; 20.Rxe7 Bd5. Black won. Steinbeck–Heyne, Bad Worishofen 1988) 18...Bxf3; 19.Qxf3 Qxb2; 20.Rxc8 Rxc8; 21.Be5 Qxa3 is hopeless for White. 22.Bxf6 gxf6. (22...Bxf6??; 23.Bxh7+ Kxh7; 24.Qxa3) 23.Qg4+ Kh8; 24.Qh3 f5; 25.d5 Qc3; 26.dxe6 fxe6;

27.Qe3 Rc6 and the queenside pawns march.

5...Nf6.

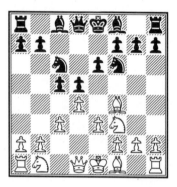

6.Nbd2. 6.Bd3 Be7; 7.Nbd2 b6; 8.Qa4 Bd7; 9.Bb5 Qc8; 10.Ne5 Nxe5; 11.Bxe5 0-0 is comfortable for Black, for example 12.Nf3 Bxb5; 13.Qxb5 Qd7; 14.Qxd7 Nxd7; 15.Bf4 cxd4; 16.exd4 Rac8; 17.Ne5 Nxe5; 18.Bxe5 Rfd8; 19.0-0 Bd6 and Black is certainly no worse, Taiana-Pisani, Postal 1990.

6...Be7.

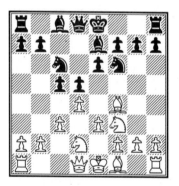

The bishop can also come to d6. **7.Be2.** 7.Bd3 a6; 8.h3 b6; 9.Ne5 Bb7; 10.Qc2 Nd7! is fine for Black, for example:

A) 11.Bxh7 Ndxe5; 12.Bxe5 (12.dxe5 g6; 13.Bxg6 fxg6; 14.Qxg6+ Kd7 and the Black king is perfectly safe) 12...Nxe5; 13.dxe5 g6; 14.Bxg6 fxg6; 15.Qxg6+ Kd7 and Black threatens ...Rg8. After ...Rac8, Black can slide the king to b8. White has some passed pawns, but they are not enough to compensate for the piece.

B) 11.0-0 is more reasonable. 11...Ndxe5; 12.Bxe5 Nxe5; 13.dxe5 Qc7 is a bit better for Black. 7.Ne5 is often recommended. 7...Nxe5!; 8.Bxe5. (8.dxe5 Nd7; 9.Bd3 0-0; 10.h4 f6; 11.Qh5 f5; 12.0-0-0 Rf7 gives Black a solid formation and White cannot achieve anything with an attack on the kingside. Black will soon start operations on the other wing. Porth–Sonntag, Bad Worishofen 1988.) 8...0-0; 9.Bd3.

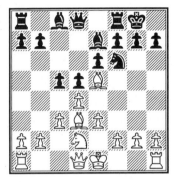

Soltis claims that White has a "freer and more coordinated position." I don't see it, and White's small space advantage does not seem significant. White has only a single real plan, to bring the queen to the h-file and attack with h7 as the target. This is not a fast attack, and Black can defend by ...g6. Meanwhile, b2 is a target. 9...Nd7. (9...c4 10.Bc2 Qb6 comes into consideration.) 10.Bg3 f5! This cuts off the bishop, making it harder for White to attack. 11.0-0 c4; 12.Bc2 (12.Be2 b5 gives Black an initiative on the queenside, while White still has nothing on the kingside) 12...b5; 13.Nf3 b4; 14.Ne5 Nxe5; 15.Bxe5 Qa5; 16.Qd2 Bd7 with strong queenside play for Black, Georgievski–Stamnov, Macedonian Championship 1993.

7...Nh5; 8.Bg3 Nxg3; 9.hxg3.

White counts on using the open h-file for an attack, or to provide breathing room for the king.

9...Rb8. I am by no means convinced that this is the best move in the position, but sooner or later the rook may wish to support the advance of the b-pawn. I'd play the simple 9...Bd7. The important thing is not to castle before White does. In fact, as the game shows, the Black king is safe in the center, the h-file may be useful to Black.

10.Qc2 h6. This pawn is going to continue its forward march, and there was no reason not to station it at h5 right away.**11.dxc5 Bxc5; 12.Nb3 Bd6; 13.Nh4?** A rather pointless move. 13.Rd1 made more sense, with a dynamically balanced game. Castling queenside is also possible, though Black may be able to whip up an attack there.

13...b5; 14.0–0 Be7; 15.Nf3. Black can safely castle here, but chooses to use the kingside as a base of attack, not defense! **15...Bd7; 16.Nbd4 Nxd4; 17.Nxd4?** Poor positional judgment. White should have recaptured with the c-pawn. **17...h5!** Now the attack begins.

18.Qd1? White has no time for such luxuries. A flank attack should be countered by central activity. 18.e4 dxe4; 19.Qxe4 Qc7 would be better for Black, who has the bishop pair, but the advantage is not very large.**18...h4!; 19.Bg4.** 19.gxh4 Bxh4 is playable for White, as no immediate disaster is on the horizon. **19...Bd6; 20.Qf3** Now capturing at h4 would allow Black to recapture using the queen, creating a powerful attack on the h-file.

20...Qg5; 21.gxh4 Rxh4. The queen is already in attacking formation, so this is the correct move, bringing the rook closer. **22.Bh3 Ke7!** The other rook can now join the fun! **23.Ne2 Rbh8; 24.Ng3 Qh6.** Now all the Black pieces except the bishop at d7 are attacking, and White has only queen and two minor pieces to use in defense.

25.Rad1 g5; 26.Rd4. White has succeeded in bringing the rook to a defensive position, but now Black adds a lowly pawn to the attack, and this proves too much for White.

26...f5!; 27.Rxh4 Qxh4.

White is already lost, as the pawn will come to g4. **28.Bxf5.** White resigned before waiting for the ...Qh2 mate. **Black won.**

Colle System 2.Nf3 e6; 3.e3

YASVOYIN VS. KOPAYEV
Leningrad, 1947

1.d4 d5; 2.Nf3 e6; 3.e3 c5

White can adopt the Colle in two ways, with b3 or c3. 4.c4 transposes to Rotlevi–Rubinstein in the chapter on the Symmetrical Tarrasch. Other moves have very little to offer, as we shall see.

4.Bd3. 4.b3 Nf6; 5.Bd3 Nc6; 6.0–0 Be7; 7.Bb2 0–0 does not offer White much, as long as Black keeps an eye on the kingside 8.Ne5 (8.dxc5 Bxc5; 9.Ne5 Nxe5; 10.Bxe5 Bd6 is even) 8...Nxe5!; 9.dxe5 Nd7; 10.c4 b6; 11.f4 dxc4!; 12.Bxc4 Qc7; 13.Nc3 Bb7. White's bishops are useless, but Black's are efficiently placed. The queenside pawn majority gives Black a long–term advantage. 14.Nb5 Qc6; 15.Rf3 Rfd8; 16.Qe2 a6; 17.Nc3 Qc7! 18.Rh3 Nf8! An important defensive move, guarding h7. 19.Rf1 Rd7; 20.Bd3 (20.e4 Rad8; 21.Rd1 Rxd1+; 22.Nxd1 Bxe4! wins a pawn.) 20...g6; 21.Bc2 Rad8; 22.Nb1. The Black rook must not be allowed to get to d2. 22...b5; 23.Bc3 b4; 24.Bb2 Qa5; 25.e4 Qxa2; 26.Bc1 Rd4; 27.Re1 c4; 28.Be3 Bxe4!; 29.Bxd4 Bxc2; 30.Qxc4 Bxb1 and White resigned in Halprin–Marco, Vienna 1898.

4.c3 Nf6; 5.Bd3 Nc6; 6.Nbd2 Bd6. (6...Qc7; 7.0–0 e5; 8.Nxe5 Nxe5; 9.dxe5 Qxe5; 10.e4 dxe4; 11.Nxe4 Bd7; 12.Ng5 Be7; 13.Re1 Qd6; 14.Ne4 Nxe4; 15.Rxe4 0–0–0; 16.Bf4 Qf6; 17.Bg3 Bf5; 18.Rxe7 Rxd3; 19.Rc7+ Kd8; 20.Qb3 Rxg3; 21.Qxb7 Rxg2+; 22.Kh1 Rxh2+; 23.Kxh2 Qe5+; 24.Kg1 Qxc7; 25.Rd1+ Bd7; 26.Qa8+ Qc8; 27.Qxa7 h5; 28.b4 Rh6; 29.b5 Rg6+; 30.Kf1 Ke8. Black won. Goria–Balduzzi,

Lecco 1966.) 7.0–0 0–0; 8.Qe2 Qc7; 9.Re1 e5!

Black's comfortable development enables this freeing maneuver. White is already in trouble.

A) 10.dxe5 Nxe5; 11.Nxe5 Bxe5; 12.Nf3 Bd6; 13.e4 dxe4; 14.Bxe4 Re8; 15.Qc2 (15.Bxh7+ Kxh7; 16.Ng5+ Kg8; 17.Qxe8+ Nxe8; 18.Rxe8+ Bf8 wins for Black) 15...Nxe4; 16.Rxe4 Rxe4; 17.Qxe4 h6 gives Black a small advantage.

B) 10.e4? is bad. After 10...cxd4,

B1) 11.exd5 dxc3; 12.dxc6 (12.bxc3 Nxd5 and the knight aims at both c3 and f4) 12...cxd2; 13.Bxd2 Qxc6; 14.Nxe5 Re8; 15.Bc3 Bxe5; 16.Bxe5 Ng4; 17.Be4 Rxe5; 18.Bxc6 Rxe2; 19.Rxe2 bxc6; 20.Rc1 Bd7; 21.Rd2 Nf6 and Black is better.

B2) 11.cxd4 give Black an initiative after 11...Bg4! For example: 12.dxe5 (12.Nb3? is met by 12...exd4 and faced with the threat of ...Bxh2+ as well as dxe4, White resigned in Larsen–Andersen, Hedehusene 1994) 12...Nxe5; 13.h3 dxe4; 14.Bxe4 (14.hxg4 exd3; 15.Qd1 Nexg4 is winning for Black. 14.Nxe4 Nxf3+; 15.gxf3 Bxh3; 16.Nxf6+ gxf6; 17.Qe4 f5; 18.Qh4) 14...Nxe4; 15.Qxe4 Bxf3; 16.Nxf3

Nxf3+; 17.Qxf3 leads to boring equality. Finally, 4.Bb5+ leads to
4...Bd7; 5.Bxd7+ Nxd7, which eliminates the bad bishop. **4...Nc6;
5.c3 Bd6; 6.Nbd2 Nf6; 7.0–0 0–0** gives Black a solid position with
the e5-square is controlled, there is nothing for Black to worry about.

    **8.dxc5 Bxc5; 9.e4 Qc7; 10.Qe2 Ng4; 11.h3 Nge5; 12.Nxe5 Nxe5;
13.Bc2 d4; 14.cxd4 Bxd4; 15.Bb3 b6; 16.Nf3.**

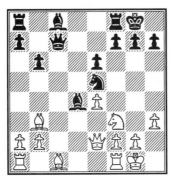

It looks as though White is relatively safe, but Black plays a tremendous move which blows apart the White position. **16...Ba6!!;
17.Qxa6 Nxf3+; 18.gxf3 Qg3+.** Mate is forced. **19.Kh1 Qxf3+; 20.Kg1
Qg3+; 21.Kh1 Qxh3+; 22.Kg1 Be5.** White resigned.

Veresov Attack 2.Nc3
    1.d4 d5; 2.Nc3

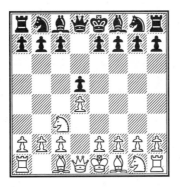

The Veresov Attack is a logical opening. White tries to play an
early e4, and if Black contests the square with ...Nf6, then Bg5 continues the battle. It is somewhat like a left-handed Spanish Game,
but chess is not based on left right symmetry in the opening. The d-
pawn, unlike an e-pawn, is already defended and needs no further

support. So Nc3 doesn't attack anything directly. For our repertoire, we need to consider the balance of effort versus frequency. The Veresov has been rendered ineffective in a number of ways. I should know–I used to play it.

The main lines are all fine for Black. They require a fair bit of preparation, however. The lines with ...Nf6 are well studied and White will be prepared for them. One solid way to fight for the e4–square is 2...Bf5, but that too requires a lot of study. To keep within the confines of our Tarrasch repertoire with 2...e6 allows 3.e4, transposing to the French. Black can try 2...c5, leading to a Chigorin Defense with colors reversed, but White can also try 3.e4 there.

In any case, there is no point in trying to set up a Tarrasch when White is committed to Nc3. I am going to be a less conservative than usual with my recommendation for Black, suggesting an obscure little gambit that at worst leaves Black at a slight positional disadvantage.

If you prefer to study the main lines of the Veresov, by all means do so. But if you just need a little something to avoid being surprised, this can turn the tables on your opponent.

KHACHATUROV VS. SHAVLIUK
Moscow, 1960

1.d4 d5; 2.Nc3 e5!?

This gambit is very rare. I only found 2 games in my million game database, and Black won both of them! The idea is actually in the spirit of the Tarrasch, as Black temporarily gives up a pawn to advance the d-pawn.

3.dxe5 d4.

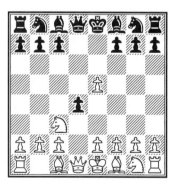

This gain of tempo and the weakness of the pawn at e5 are the compensation for the pawn. White is likely to return the pawn quickly.

4.Nb5.

4.Ne4 Qd5; 5.Ng3 h5. (5...Nc6 is a reasonable alternative.) 6.e4 Qxe5. Black has the pawn back but White has a lead in development 7.Nf3 Qa5+; 8.Bd2 Qb6; 9.Bc4 Nc6; 10.a4 Bg4; 11.Bb5 0-0-0 and Black is catching up in development. 12.Bxc6 Qxc6; 13.h3 Bxf3; 14.Qxf3 h4!; 15.Ne2 Nf6. Black has a fine game. Now White over-reaches. 16.e5 Ne4!; 17.Qd3 Nxd2; 18.Qxd2 Qxg2; 19.Rg1 Qd5; 20.Rg4 Qxe5 and Black won without difficulty, Coll–Sowray, Postal 1989.

4...c5; 5.e3 a6; 6.Nd6+ Bxd6; 7.exd6 Qxd6.

Black would have a great game if it were not for the pin on the e-file. White can arrange for Black to have an isolated d-pawn. Of course as a Tarrasch player that is hardly frightening!

8.c3 Nc6; 9.exd4. 9.Nf3 Bg4; 10.Be2 (10.exd4 cxd4; 11.cxd4 Qb4+; 12.Qd2 Bxf3; 13.gxf3 0-0-0 is good for Black.) 10...Bxf3. This is the only move given by Smith and Hall, but I see no reason to capture at f3 right away. (10...0-0-0; 11.exd4 cxd4; 12.cxd4 Nf6! is much more logical and Black will regain the pawn. For example: 13.Be3 Bxf3; 14.Bxf3 Qb4+; 15.Qd2 Qxd2+; 16.Kxd2 Nxd4; 17.Bxd4 Rxd4+; 18.Kc3 Rhd8 and Black will have no problems in the endgame.) 11.Bxf3 Nge7; 12.exd4 cxd4; 13.0-0 and "White is somewhat better"–Smith and Hall.

9...cxd4; 10.Be3. White wants to win the d-pawn without compromising the pawn structure, but this takes time. **10...Nf6!; 11.Bxd4 0-0; 12.Be2 Re8.** 12...Nxd4!; 13.Qxd4 Qe7; 14.0-0-0 Bf5 gives Black good attacking prospects on the queenside.

13.Be3. White must cover up on the d-file. Black has a lead in development and some pressure for the pawn.

13...Qe7; 14.Nf3 Ng4. 14...Bf5; 15.0-0 Rad8; 16.Nd4 Nxd4; 17.cxd4 Nd5 is also fine for Black.

15.Qc1? 15.Bf4! would have maintained equality, for example 15...Bf5; 16.Bd6 Qe4 with a complicated position where White is tied down. **15...Nxe3.** There was no rush, and 15...Bf5 would have been stronger. **16.Qxe3 Qf8!!** 16...Qxe3; 17.fxe3 Rxe3; 18.Kf2 Re7 is obviously no problem for Black, but is likely to lead to a draw.

17.Qf4 Qc5; 18.Rd1 Bf5.

Black still has compensation for the pawn, since the bishop at e2 is pinned and White cannot castle. Here White should probably try Rd2, although after ...Re4 Black has a strong initiative. **19.g4.** An attempt to gain some space, but the pawn is very weak.

19.Rd2 Re4; 20.Qc7 Re7; 21.Qd6 Qxd6; 22.Rxd6 Rae8; 23.Rd2 allows 23...Bd3; 24.Ng1 Bb1; 25.b3 Bf5 and White still has a difficult time developing.

19...Bg6; 20.Rd2 Re4; 21.Qg5 Qc4; 22.Ne5 Rxe5; 23.Qxe5 Nxe5; 24.Bxc4 Nxc4.

Black has achieved a very favorable endgame, and soon picked up the point.

25.Re2 Bd3; 26.Re7 Kf8; 27.Rd7 Be4; 28.f3 Bxf3; 29.Rf1 Re8+; 30.Kf2 Bc6; 31.Rd4 Nxb2; 32.g5 Na4; 33.Rc4 Bb5; 34.Rc7. **Black won.**

Blackmar–Diemer Gambit 2.e4

1.d4 d5; 2.e4

The Blackmar–Diemer Gambit can be safely declined with 2...e6 and 2...c6, but that requires knowledge of the French or Caro–Kann Defense. There are several good defenses that make it difficult to justify the gambit, but they require a good deal of preparation. Here is a reliable defense which is easy to learn.

VON POPIEL VS. RETI
Vienna, 1915

1.d4 d5; 2.e4 dxe4; 3.Nc3 e5

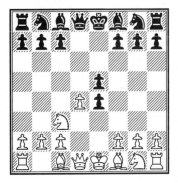

This is the Lemberger Defense. No, this isn't a smelly cheese, but it can leave a sour taste in White's mouth. Black invites an early endgame, which is hardly likely to appeal to those who play the Blackmar–Diemer Gambit.

4.dxe5. There is no shortage of alternatives, but none of them are any good:

A) 4.d5 Bb4; 5.Bd2 Nf6; 6.Bc4 c6; 7.dxc6 Nxc6; 8.Nge2 Bg4 is good for Black. 9.h3 Bxe2; 10.Qxe2 Nd4; 11.Qd1 Qc7; 12.Bb5+ Ke7; 13.Ba4 Qa5; 14.Bb3 Rhd8; 15.a3 Bxc3; 16.Bxc3 Qa6; 17.Bb4+ Ke8; 18.Bd2 Nxb3; 19.cxb3 e3; 20.fxe3 Ne4. Black won. Engman–Markwardt, Postal 1970.

B) 4.Bb5+ Bd7; 5.dxe5 Nc6; 6.f4 exf3; 7.Nxf3 Bc5; 8.Qd5 Qe7; 9.Ne4 Bb6; 10.Bg5 f6; 11.Bd2 0-0-0 12.0-0-0 Be6; 13.exf6 Nxf6. Black won. Diemer–Ducommun Geneva 1956.

C) 4.Nxe4 is best handled by the bold 4...Qxd4!; 5.Bd3 f5; 6.Nf3 (6.Ng3 g6; 7.c3 Qb6 is better for Black, who will continue with ...Bg7 and rapid development) 6...Qd8 7.Bb5+ c6; 8.Qxd8+ Kxd8; 9.Neg5 cxb5; 10.Nxe5 Ke8; 11.Nef7 h6; 12.Nxh8 hxg5; 13.Bxg5 gives Black a small advantage according to Lane.

D) 4.Bc4 Bb4!; 5.Qh5 Qe7; 6.Qxe5 Qxe5; 7.dxe5 Nc6; 8.Bd2 Nxe5; 9.Nxe4 Nxc4; 10.Bxb4 Bf5; 11.Nd2 Nxd2; 12.Kxd2 0-0-0+; 13.Kc1 Nf6 and the position of the White king gives Black a real advantage, for example 14.Ne2 Rhe8; 15.Ng3 Bg6; 16.Bc3 Ng4; 17.Bxg7 Nxf2; 18.Rf1 Ng4; 19.c3 Ne3 and White resigned in Muth–Roos, Postal 1969.

E) 4.Qh5 is a popular line known as the Studier Attack. 4...Nc6! is the best reply.

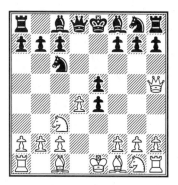

E1) 5.Bb5 is met by 5...exd4 and now White has three tries, none of which are any good:

E1a) 6.Qe5+ Be6; 7.Nxe4 Qd5; 8.Bf4 Nge7; 9.Rd1 Qxe5; 10.Bxe5 0-0-0 and Black is clearly better. Arens-Boehm, Postal 1986.

E1b) 6.Nxe4 Qe7; 7.Qe2 Bd7; 8.Bf4 0-0-0; 9.0-0-0 h6; 10.a3

Nf6; 11.Nxf6 Qxf6 and Black had nothing to show for the pawn in Pohl–Augustin, Postal 1986.

E1c) 6.Bxc6+ bxc6; 7.Nxe4 Qe7; 8.Qe2 Bf5; 9.Ng3 Bxc2 and White is busted.

E2) 5.Bc4 g6 and here:

E2a) 6.Qe2 Nxd4. (6...Bf5; 7.dxe5 Nd4; 8.Qd1 e3; 9.Bd3 exf2+; 10.Kxf2 Bc5; 11.Be3 Bxd3; 12.cxd3 Nh6; 13.Qa4+ c6; 14.Nf3 Ng4+. Black won. Wetherell–Tejler, Postal 1988.) 7.Qxe4 Bg7; 8.Bd3 Bf5 and Black wins the pawn at c2, Morin–Clauser, Postal 1988.

E2b) 6.Qd1 Qxd4; 7.Qe2 Bb4; 8.Bd2 Na5; 9.Bb5+ Bd7; 10.Bxd7+ Qxd7; 11.Qxe4 Nc6; 12.Nf3 0-0-0; 13.0-0-0 f6. Black has nothing for the pawn. Jensen–Purser, Postal 1987.

E3) 5.dxe5 allows Black to take the initiative. 5...Nd4; 6.Qd1 Bg4; 7.Qxg4 Nxc2+; 8.Ke2 Qd3. Checkmate. Won by Diemer as Black against an unknown opponent in West Germany, 1973.

F) 4.Be3 exd4; 5.Bxd4 (5.Qxd4 Qxd4; 6.Bxd4 Nc6; 7.Bb5 Bd7; 8.0-0-0 0-0-0; 9.Nge2 (9.Nxe4? Nxd4 gives Black an extra piece at b5 or d4) 9...f5; 10.Bxc6 Bxc6 and White resigned, Clauser–Muller, Postal 1987.) 5...Nc6; 6.Bb5 Bd7; 7.Nge2 Qh4! Lane assesses this as equal. I prefer Black. 8.Ng3 0-0-0; 9.Bxc6 Bxc6; 10.a4 Nh6; 11.Nce2 e3!; 12.f3 (12.fxe3 Bxg2; 13.Rg1 Qxh2) 12...Bd6; 13.0-0 Rhe8; 14.c3 Re6; 15.Qb3 Nf5. White gave up, Druke–Purser, Postal 1985. Black will transfer the rook to h6 and finish the job.

G) 4.Qe2 Qxd4; 5.Qxe4 Bb4; 6.Bd2 Bxc3!, forced instant resignation in Plath–Pohl, Postal 1988.

H) 4.Nge2 Bb4; 5.Be3 Nc6; 6.dxe5 Bg4!; 7.Qxd8+ Rxd8; 8.a3 Ba5; 9.b4 Bb6; 10.Bxb6 axb6; 11.Nxe4 Nxe5 gave Black equality in Mantila–Finegold, USA 1993.

4...Qxd1+; 5.Nxd1. Capturing with the knight is considered best. 5.Kxd1 Nc6! and Black is marginally better, since castling is still an option. For example, 6.Nxe4 (6.Nd5 Bg4+; 7.f3 0-0-0 8.c4 exf3; 9.gxf3 Be6; 10.f4 Rxd5+. Black won. Chalker–Bernstein, Continental Open 1976) 6...Nxe5 and now:

A) 7.Bd3 Bg4+; 8.f3 Nxd3; 9.cxd3 Be6; 10.Bf4 0-0-0; 11.Kc2 Be7; 12.Rc1 Bxa2; 13.b3 Bf6; 14.Nxf6 Nxf6; 15.Kb2 Nd5; 16.Ne2 Rhe8; 17.Rhe1 Rxe2+; 18.Rxe2 Nxf4; 19.Re3 Nxd3+ and Black won quickly, Rehfeld–Polland, Postal 1986.

B) 7.Be2 Bf5; 8.Nc3 0-0-0+; 9.Bd2 Bc5; 10.Nf3 Ng4; 11.Rf1 N8f6 12.h3 Nxf2+; 13.Kc1 N6e4; 14.Nxe4 Nxe4; 15.Be1 Be3+; 16.Kb1 f6; 17.Ne5 Nd2+; 18.Bxd2 Rxd2; 19.Nd3 Rxe2; 20.Rxf5 Rxg2; 21.Rf1 Rh2. Black won. Tejler–Muller, Postal 1987.

C) 7.Bf4 Bf5; 8.Ng3 0-0-0+; 9.Kc1 Ng4; 10.Nh3 Bg6; 11.f3 N4f6 12.Bc4 Bc5; 13.Re1 Ne7; 14.Be5 Ned5; 15.Bxd5 Nxd5; 16.Bxg7 Rhe8; 17.Rxe8 Rxe8; 18.b3 f6; 19.c3 Nxc3; 20.Bxf6 Re1+; 21.Kb2 Nd1+; 22.Rxd1 Rxd1; 23.Bg5 Bb4; 24.Ne4 Bxe4; 25.fxe4 Rd8. Black won. Joergensen–Rasmussen, Postal 1992.

5...Nc6.

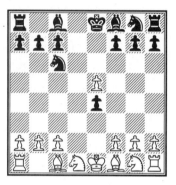

6.Bf4. 6.f4 exf3; 7.Nxf3 Bg4; 8.Bb5 Nge7; 9.0-0 0-0-0; 10.Bg5 Bxf3; 11.Rxf3 Nxe5 and Black is clearly better, Rittenhouse–Morin, Postal 1990.

6...Nge7; 7.Bb5 Bd7; 8.e6?! 8.Nc3 Ng6; 9.Nge2 (9.e6 Bxe6; 10.Bxc7 Bb4 is unclear, but should be fine for Black) 9...Nxf4; 10.Nxf4 Nxe5; 11.Bxd7+ Nxd7; 12.Nxe4 Bc5; 13.0-0-0 (13.Nxc5 Nxc5; 14.0-0-0 0-0; 15.f3 is Lane's preference, but he admits it should just be equal) 13...Bb6; 14.Rhe1 0-0-0. This is ancient analysis by Von Popiel, and Lane evaluates the position as holding chances for both sides. I agree, but the bishop gives Black a slight preference.

8...Bxe6; 9.Bxc7 Nd5; 10.Bxc6+ bxc6; 11.Bg3 Bc5!; 12.Ne2 0-0;

13.0–0 Rad8; 14.a3. After 14.Ndc3 Nxc3; 15.Nxc3 Bd4. Black has a powerful bishop pair and a clear advantage.

14...a5; 15.b3 Rfe8; 16.c4 Nf6; 17.Ndc3 Bg4; 18.Bc7 Rd2; 19.Rfe1.

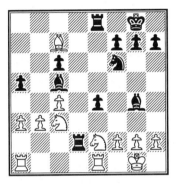

Black's army has shifted into position to deliver the final blows. White's position is quickly reduced to ashes.

19...Bxe2!; 20.Rxe2 e3!; 21.fxe3. 21.Rxd2 exd2; 22.Kf1 Bd4; 23.Bxa5 Ne4 is a brutal exploitation of the pin at c3.

21...Rxe2; 22.Nxe2 Rxe3; 23.Kf1 Rxb3; 24.Bxa5 Ng4. White resigned as more pawns are falling.

Well, you have now explored the entire repertoire and have seen how the game should be played. Now let's turn to the heroes of the Tarrasch Defense for more model play.

HEROES OF THE TARRASCH DEFENSE

THE FOUNDING FATHER

SIEGBERT TARRASCH

Siegbert Tarrasch was born on March 5, 1862 in Breslau (now Wroclaw, Poland). A follower of the classical style, Tarrasch had strong beliefs about the role of the center. During his lifetime opening, theory underwent several revolutions, including the great Hypermodern movement of the late 1920s which saw the focus shift from the Closed Game with 1.d4 d5 to the Indian Defenses with 1.d4 Nf6.

Tarrasch believed that the isolated d-pawn was a powerful weapon, and was very dogmatic on this point. Actually, he was dogmatic on just about all chess matters. His ultra–conservative views are still valued as the basis for sound play, although the door has opened to alternative views.

His chess career started very late, at the age of fifteen, and his frist tournament was in Berlin in 1881. We are lucky he stuck with the game, as his debut was a disaster. Undaunted, he worked hard on his game and played very well in his next tournament, two years later in Nuremberg, which was to become a frequent chess stop for him.

In 1885 he was awarded the title of Master, helped by a second-place finish in Hamburg. After that his career really took off and he won many major international tournaments. Eventually he established himself as a leading contender for the World Championship.

In 1908 he got his chance, but was clobbered by Lasker, 10.5–5.5. His result in the 1916 rematch was even more embarrassing and from then on he only managed middling results.

Though he is remembered for some fine games and tournament results, Tarrasch's real legacy is to be found in the great books and magazine articles he wrote throughout his career. His *Dreihundert Schachpartie, Die Moderne Schachpartie*, and his treatise on the Queen's Gambit remain classics of the literature, and new generations of chessplayers are still weaned on his *The Game of Chess*.

Here is a fine game, which is still of importance to the theory of the opening.

KURSCHNER VS. TARRASCH
Nuremberg, 1887

The father of the Tarrasch Defense won many fine games as Black. In this early example, he demonstrates the tactical resources of his defense. All of the commentaries in quotation marks below are by Tarrasch himself.

1.d4 d5; 2.c4 e6; 3.Nc3 c5. "I instinctively consider this the proper counter to the Queen's Gambit. In recent times it is steadily coming to be recognized as the correct defense." **4.e3 Nf6; 5.Nf3 Nc6;** "I consider this the normal position of the Queen's Gambit. The following isolation of the Queen's pawn gives Black a positional advantage, in my view."

6.cxd5 exd5; 7.dxc5 Bxc5.

This is a key position in the Tarrasch Defense. The isolated pawn at d5 is not attacked from the flank, but it is still a little weak. Tarrasch met this approach early in his career. **8.Be2.** This position is no longer common, because White is a tempo behind by comparison with 7.Be2 Bd6; 8.dxc5 Bxc5. **8...0–0; 9.0–0 Bf5.** Black has a nice free game, while White has to work to develop the dark–squared bishop which has no good square to go to. As we often see, such positions often leads to errors, as in the continuation of this game.

9...Be6 is rather passive. 10.a3 (10.Re1 a6; 11.a3 d4; 12.exd4 Nxd4; 13.Nxd4 Qxd4; 14.Be3 Qxd1; 15.Nxd1 Rac8; 16.Rc1 Bxe3; 17.Nxe3 is obviously even, Fenoglio–Bolbochan, Mar del Plata 1934. 10.b3 Qe7; 11.Bb2 Rad8; 12.Nb5 Ne4; 13.Nbd4 Rc8; 14.Rc1 Bd6; 15.Nxc6 bxc6; 16.Bd3 Bg4; 17.Bxe4 Qxe4; 18.Qd4 Qxd4; 19.Nxd4 c5; 20.Nf3 Rfd8 gave Black no problems in Udovcic–Portisch, Zagreb 1965) 10...Bd6; 11.b4 Ne5; 12.Nb5 Nxf3+; 13.Bxf3 Be5; 14.Nd4 Qd6; 15.h3 Qd7; 16.Nxe6 fxe6; 17.Rb1 Rac8; 18.Bb2 Bb8; 19.e4 Qc7 and Black had a strong attack in Cochrane–Staunton, London 1842!

10.Nd4 Bxd4; 11.exd4 Qb6.

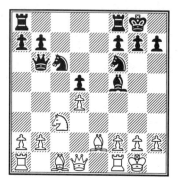

How can White cope with the pressure at d4? Only by radically weakening the kingside pawn structure! **12.g4 Be6; 13.g5 Ne4; 14.f3 Nd6!** The knight pivots to f5.

15.Be3 Nf5; 16.Bf2. White hangs on to the d-pawn, but Black can afford to snatch the b-pawn. **16...Qxb2; 17.Na4 Qa3; 18.Re1 Qd6; 19.Qd2** "The Black queen threatened to go to f4."

19...f6; 20.Nc5 fxg5; 21.Nxb7 Qf4; 22.Red1 Rac8; 23.Nc5.

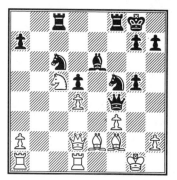

Now a lot of pieces come off the board, leaving a simple endgame. **23...Qxd2; 24.Rxd2 Ncxd4; 25.Nxe6 Nxe6; 26.Rxd5 Nf4.**

"Both knights are well posted." **27.Re5.** 27.Rd2 "was somewhat better, but then ...Rfe8 would have been good." **27...Rc2; 28.Bf1 Nh4; 29.Bxh4 gxh4; 30.Rae1 h6.** "Black does not dare take the a-pawn because of Bc4+."

31.R5e4 g5; 32.Bc4+ Kg7; 33.Re7+ Kg6; 34.Bb3 Rg2+; 35.Kh1 h3; 36.Rd1 Rc8; 37.Rd6+ Kf5.

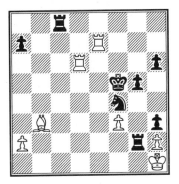

"Naturally not ...h5 because of Bf7+."

38.Rxa7. "White underestimates Black's attack. He had to play defensively with Re1 or Rd1. Now there follows an interesting ending." **38...Rc1+; 39.Bd1.** "On 39.Rd1 there follows 39...Nd3 and mate with ...Nf2 cannot be prevented."

39...Ne2; 40.Ra5+ Kf4; 41.Rf6+ Ke3; 42.Re5+ Kf2; 43.Rxe2+ Kf1.

White resigned. The mate with ...Rg1 can only be delayed for a moment by exchanging rooks.

Tarrasch died on February 13, 1934, while his defense was growing in popularity. He once wrote "The future will decide who has erred in estimating this defense, I or the chess world!" Boris Spassky and Garry Kasparov, among others, have carried the torch for his beloved opening. Now we will meet some of the other heroes of the Tarrasch Defense.

THE STANDARD BEARER

SVETOZAR GLIGORIC

The great Yugoslav Grandmaster Svetozar Gligoric, born in Yugoslavia in 1923, was one of the greatest of the post–war players from chess–addicted Yugoslavia. He dominated the country's chess in the 50s and 60s, and remained a vibrant force into the 90s. He was decorated for bravery for acts he performed fighting against Nazi invaders, his chess shows this underlying courage. The Tarrasch Defense and the Nimzoindian Defense (which have similar structural characteristics including frequent isolated d-pawn positions) were his favorites. He won many tournaments and brilliancy prizes, and has written extensively on chess. As he grew older he became an International Arbiter and has refereed many World Championship events.

Here is one of his endgame contributions to the library of Tarrasch Defense games:

TORAN VS. GLIGORIC
Buenos Aires, 1955

1.d4 Nf6; 2.c4 e6; 3.Nf3 c5; 4.e3 d5; 5.cxd5 exd5; 6.Nc3 Nc6; 7.Be2 Be7; 8.0-0 0-0; 9.dxc5 Bxc5; 10.a3 a6; 11.b4 Bd6; 12.Bb2 Bc7; 13.Rc1 Qd6; 14.Na4 Rd8; 15.Nc5 Ng4; 16.g3 Qh6; 17.Qd2 Be5; 18.h4.

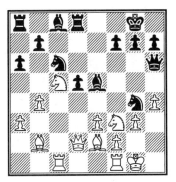

18...d4! Typical Tarrasch play. Black's attack forces a transition into an endgame. **19.exd4 Qxd2; 20.Nxd2 Bxd4; 21.Bxd4 Nxd4; 22.Bd1 Ne5.** Black's pieces are much better positioned, so White decides to eliminate some of them.

23.Nc4 Nxc4; 24.Rxc4 b6; 25.Nb3 Nb5; 26.a4 Be6!; 27.Rc1 Nd4; 28.Nxd4 Rxd4.

The endgame is better for Black, with more active pieces and less vulnerable pawns. But can it be won? With best play by both sides, probably not, but chess is an imperfect game, and Gligoric is a great endgame player.

29.Bf3 Rad8; 30.Rfd1 Kf8; 31.Rxd4 Rxd4; 32.Rb1 Ke7; 33.Kg2 Kd6; 34.a5 b5; 35.Rc1 Bd7; 36.Rb1 Bc6; 37.Bxc6 Kxc6; 38.Rc1+ Kd7; 39.Rb1 h5.

Watch Gligoric use his more active rook to squeeze a win from this position! **40.Kf3 Kd6; 41.Ke3 Kd5; 42.f3 g6; 43.Rb2 Ke5; 44.Rb1 Rc4; 45.Rb3 f6; 46.Kd3 g5; 47.hxg5 fxg5; 48.Rb1 Kf5; 49.Rb2 h4; 50.gxh4 gxh4; 51.Ke3 h3; 52.Kf2 Kf4; 53.Rd2 Rxb4; 54.Rd6 Rb1. White resigned.**

THE RESURRECTOR

BORIS SPASSKY

For a while, Gligoric was one of very few Grandmasters who used the Tarrasch Defense at the highest levels of chess. That changed in 1969, when Boris Spassky used it to successfully challenge Tigran Petrosian for the World Championship. The opening featured prominently in that match, and caused commentators and analysts all over the world to re-evaluate the opening.

Boris Vasilyevich Spassky was born in 1937 in Leningrad, and learned a lot of his chess as a child during the Second World War. He rose to prominence in Russian circles, and afterward received training from Leningrad's finest trainers. He first qualified for the Soviet championship in 1955 and was a participant 11 times. He rose to the top of the Soviet talent pool and after tremendous victories in the 1960s was able to work through the international ranks and qualified for a World Championship bid in 1966, but lost by a point. In 1969 he was better prepared, and armed with new ideas in the Tarrasch he won the title, only to lose it in 1972 to the American phenomenon Bobby Fischer.

Losing the title brought serious consequences for Spassky, who was persecuted by the Soviet regime. Eventually he fled to France, where he still makes his home. The fine French culture cooled his fighting spirit, and his games were more often drawn than not. He nevertheless remains a popular figure, known as "The Gentleman of Chess," quite a contrast to the World Champions who preceded and followed him.

Here is one of the most famous Tarrasch games of the Spassky era.

PETROSIAN VS. SPASSKY
World Championship, 1969

1.c4 e6; 2.d4 d5; 3.Nc3 c5; 4.cxd5 exd5; 5.Nf3 Nc6; 6.g3 Nf6; 7.Bg2 Be7; 8.0-0 0-0; 9.Bg5 cxd4.

Spassky defended the Tarrasch five times in this match, drawing four and winning this game. Ranking the greatest achievement the opening has had–so far! **10.Nxd4 h6; 11.Be3.** This is how all match games began, except for the 16th.

11...Bg4.

This was one of Spassky's prepared novelties. Although we prefer the 11...Re8 lines in our repertoire, it is instructive to examine Spassky's handling as well. **12.Nb3 Be6; 13.Rc1 Re8.** 13...Qd7; 14.Bc5 Rfd8; 15.Bxe7 Qxe7; 16.Nd4 Rac8; 17.e3 Ne5; 18.Nce2 Bg4; 19.Rxc8 Rxc8 gave Black equality in Andersson–Marjanovic, Banja Luka 1979.

14.Re1. 14.Nb5 Qd7; 15.N5d4 Bh3; 16.Nxc6 bxc6; 17.Qd3 Bxg2; 18.Kxg2 a5; 19.Rc2 a4; 20.Nd2 Qb7 was eventually drawn in another game from this match. **14...Qd7; 15.Bc5 Rac8.** 15...Rad8!? comes into consideration. **16.Bxe7 Qxe7; 17.e3.** 17.Nxd5 Nxd5; 18.Bxd5 Rcd8; 19.e4 Bxd5; 20.exd5 Qxe1+; 21.Qxe1 Rxe1+; 22.Rxe1 Rxd5 would have been equal.

17...Red8; 18.Qe2 Bg4; 19.f3?! White weakens the dark squares around her king, never a safe strategy in the Tarrasch. 19.Qf1 would have left Black with a slight initiative, but nothing too dangerous. **19...Bf5.** Black could have settled for equality with 19...Be6, but this is a much more active move. **20.Rcd1 Ne5.** The c-file belongs to Black now.

21.Nd4 Bg6; 22.Bh3 Rc4; 23.g4 Rb4?! Spassky is a little bit over-confident here. The rook has no support on the queenside and cannot accomplish much. The coordination of pieces is one of the hallmarks of the Tarrasch, and isolated forays are rarely rewarded. 23...Rc5; 24.f4 Ned7; 25.f5 Bh7. White must justify the weakening advances on the kingside.

24.b3? White reacts prematurely. A better sense of timing would have produced the preliminary advance of the f-pawn. 24.f4 Nc4; 25.b3 Nd6; 26.f5 is much better for White. Black would have suffered from a misplaced knight at d6 and rook at b4, neither of which could be easily relocated to a more useful post.

24...Nc6; 25.Qd2 Rb6; 26.Nce2. The game is level again. 26.Na4 Ra6! maintains the balance. 27.Bf1 Nxd4; 28.Qxd4 (28.Bxa6?? loses to 28...Nxf3+. 28.exd4 Re6; 29.Nc5 Rxe1; 30.Rxe1 Qc7; 31.Re5 leaves the situation unclear) 28...Rc6 (28...Re6; 29.Qxa7 d4!) 29.Qxa7 h5! and Black has a strong attack.

26...Bh7; 27.Bg2 Re8. The flexible placement of the rooks in the Tarrasch allows Black to take advantage of weaknesses in the White camp.

28.Ng3 Nxd4; 29.exd4!

A natural, but fatal, move. After 29.Qxd4 White would have maintained an equal game, although Black might later exploit the weakness of the kingside. **29...Re6!; 30.Rxe6 Qxe6; 31.Rc1 Bg6!** This introduces a maneuver which is not uncommon in the Tarrasch. **32.Bf1 Nh7!** Black threatens such moves as f7–f5 combined with Nh7–g5. With his next move White prevents this plan, but allows Black to reorganize in another effective manner. **33.Qf4 Nf8; 34.Rc5?** White could have maintained some chances after 34.Qe5! **34...Bb1!; 35.a4 Ng6; 36.Qd2 Qf6; 37.Kf2 Nf4; 38.a5?** A final blunder, but Black was winning anyway. **38...Bd3; 39.Nf5 Qg5; 40.Ne3 Qh4+; 41.Kg1 Bxf1.** White resigned, since he is mated after 42.Nxf1 Re2 while 42.Kxf1 is met by 42...Qh3+ and White must lose at least a piece.

EXPLOSION IN THE 80'S

The 1980s saw the Tarrasch rebound from its loss of popularity after Spassky gave it up, and during the 1970s it was not seen with great frequency. A shift began around 1980, when Armenian, Yugoslav, East German and English Grandmasters revived it. There was no current literature on the opening, and that meant that both original and new ideas could be used without fear that the opponent would be well prepared.

The first major examination of the Tarrasch in English was my book with Grandmaster Leonid Shamkovich, *Play the Tarrasch*, published by Pergamon Press in 1984. Garry Kasparov had received a copy of the manuscript from me long before it was published, and he started to play it at that time. I take no credit for his adding the opening to the repertoire. We were meeting frequently throughout the period of writing the book (he had collaborated with me on *Batsford Chess Openings* and *Fighting Chess*, and I had translated some of his books) and had great respect for the theoretical ideas of my co–author.

In any case, the games below were well known to him from his studies and I think the Tarrasch just fit in well with Kasparov's style of play at the time. He stuck with the Tarrasch until severe defeats at the hands of Anatoly Karpov led him to the Gruenfeld, which, in some lines, is like a Tarrasch reversed, with Black adopting the fianchetto against White's central bastion at d4.

Let's briefly meet some of the heroes of the 1980s...

SMBAT LPUTIAN

The Armenian Grandmaster (born in 1958) rose to prominence in the early and mid–1980s, and played the Tarrasch Defense consistently. The following wild game was seen all over the world.

AZMAIPARASHVILI VS. LPUTIAN
Soviet Union, 1980

1.c4 e6; 2.Nf3 Nf6; 3.g3 d5; 4.Bg2 c5; 5.0–0 Nc6; 6.cxd5 exd5; 7.d4 Be7; 8.Nc3 0–0; 9.Bg5 c4.

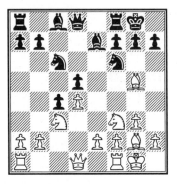

Lputian has always been partial to this aggressive move, which is also one of my favorites. After you master the central exchange lines with 9...cxd4, consider adopting this risky approach from time to time. **10.Ne5 Be6; 11.f4 Nxe5; 12.dxe5 d4; 13.exf6 gxf6; 14.Bh6 dxc3; 15.bxc3 Qb6+; 16.e3.** This is an attempt to improve on 16.Kh1 16...Rfd8; 17.Qc2 Bd5; 18.e4 Bc6; 19.Qe2 f5; 20.Rad1 Re8; 21.Qh5 Bxe4; 22.Bxe4 fxe4; 23.f5 Qf6; 24.Rf4 Kh8; 25.Rg4 Rg8; 26.Be3 Rxg4; 27.Bd4 Rg7; 28.Bxf6 Bxf6; 29.Qe2 Re8; 30.Qxc4 e3; 31.Re1 Rgg8; 32.Kg2 Re7; 33.Kf3 Rge8; 34.Re2 b6; 35.h4 h6; 36.Qc6 Kg7; 37.Kg4 h5+; 38.Kf4 was drawn in Rubinstein–Perlis, St. Petersburg 1909!

16...Qxe3+; 17.Kh1 Rfd8; 18.Qh5 f5; 19.Bg5 Qc5; 20.Rae1 Rd2; 21.Re5 Qd6; 22.Rfe1 Kh8; 23.Bxe7 Qxe7; 24.Rxf5.

White is still dreaming about a mating attack while Black simply attains a won ending.

24...Rxa2; 25.Rfe5 Qf6; 26.Be4 h6; 27.f5 Bd7; 28.Re7 Be8; 29.Bxb7 Bc6+; 30.Bxc6 Qxc6+; 31.R7e4 Rb8; 32.Qxf7.

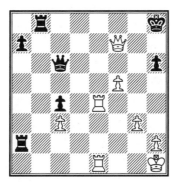

Black illustrates now that White's king has been at least as exposed as Black's. It is crucial to maintain an eye on one's own king safety while trying to create weaknesses in the enemy's camp. **32...Qxe4+. White resigned.**

SLAVOLUB MARJANOVIC

You would think that someone whose first name translates to Slav-lover would choose the Slav Defense, but Marjanovic, born in 1955, inherited the Tarrasch bug from Gligoric and has been an addict of the opening throughout his career. Here is a fine attacking game.

NATSIS VS. MARJANOVIC
Istanbul, 1980

1.d4 d5; 2.c4 e6; 3.Nc3 c5; 4.cxd5 exd5; 5.Nf3 Nc6; 6.g3 Nf6; 7.Bg2 Be7; 8.0–0 0–0; 9.Bg5 cxd4; 10.Nxd4 h6; 11.Be3 Bg4; 12.Qa4 Qd7; 13.Rfd1 Bh3; 14.Bxh3 Qxh3; 15.Nf3 Rfd8; 16.Bd4 Ne4; 17.Qb3 Nxd4; 18.Nxd4.

The weakness of the f2–square doesn't escape Marjanovic's vision! **18...Nxf2!; 19.Kxf2 Qxh2+; 20.Kf3 Rd6; 21.Nxd5 Qh5+; 22.Ke4 Re8!; 23.Qb5 Rdd8; 24.Ne6.**

A desperate attempt to close the e-file, but... **24...f5+!; 25.Kd3 Bg5; 26.Nd4 Qg4; 27.Kc3 a6; 28.Qc4 Kh8!** Black eliminates the threat of double discovered check. **29.Kb3 b5; 30.Qc6 Re4; 31.Nf3 Re3+; 32.Kc2 Qe4+. White resigned.**

JOHN NUNN

Dr. John Nunn is one of the greatest chess theoreticians. Born in 1955, he was a true prodigy, entering Oxford at the age of graduating in 1973. He was awarded his doctoral degree in 1978, by which time he had already joined the ranks of England's leading players.

Nunn's writings are among the most detailed analyses available on opening and endgame theory. It is hardly surprising that an endgame specialist would find the Tarrasch Defense appealing, and Nunn's endgame prowess served him well.

Of course, Nunn is also one of the Royal Game's most brilliant tacticians, as he showed in the following game:

VADASZ VS. NUNN
Budapest, 1978

1.Nf3 d5; 2.c4 e6; 3.g3 c5; 4.Bg2 Nc6; 5.0-0 Nf6; 6.cxd5 exd5; 7.d4 Be7; 8.Nc3 0-0; 9.Bg5 cxd4; 10.Nxd4 h6; 11.Be3 Re8; 12.Nxc6.

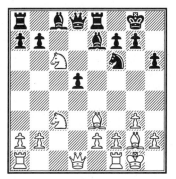

Giving Black the hanging pawns. White's plan is simply to occupy the c5-square with a knight and to pressure the c6-pawn. White has tried a number of other moves here:

12.Nb3 Be6.

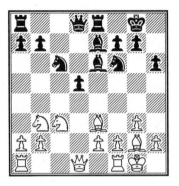

White's knights are not in useful positions.

A) 13.Bd4 Nxd4; 14.Nxd4 Bc5. (14...Qb6; 15.Qd2 Rad8 looks good, since 16.e3 can be met by 16...Bc5; 17.Nb3 Bb4.) 15.Qd3 Bg4; 16.e3 Re5; 17.h3 Bd7; 18.Nf3 Re8; 19.Rfd1 Qb6; 20.Rac1 Rac8; 21.Rc2 a5; 22.Kh2 a4; 23.Nd4 (23.Nxd5 Nxd5; 24.Qxd5 Be6 followed by ...Bxa2) 23...Qd6; 24.a3 Qe5; 25.Nf3 Qe7. White has the advantage, Daly–S.Arkell, English Championship 1990.

B) 13.Qd2 Bb4; 14.Rad1 Qc8; 15.Qc1 Bxc3; 16.Qxc3 Bh3; 17.Rfe1 Bxg2; 18.Kxg2 Ne4; 19.Qc1 Qf5; 20.Nd4 Nxd4; 21.Rxd4 Rac8 and Black is at least equal, Korchnoi–Illescas, Manila Interzonal 1990.

C) 13.Nd4 Qd7. (13...Nxd4; 14.Qxd4 Qa5 looks equal.) 14.Nxe6 fxe6; 15.Qa4 Red8; 16.Rad1 Rac8; 17.Bh3 b6; 18.Ne4 Kf7; 19.Nxf6 Bxf6; 20.b3 d4! and Black had a good game in Kestler–Bartelborth, Bundesliga 1984.

There are still more plans for White.

12.Re1 Bg4; 13.h3 Be6; 14.Qc2 Qd7; 15.Nxe6 fxe6; 16.Red1 Bb4; 17.Ne4 Qf7; 18.Nxf6+ Qxf6 is very comfortable for Black, Savon–Zolnierowicz, Baku 1988.

12.h3 is a waste of time. Black can exploit this with 12...Bd6!? and if the bishop is attacked by a knight at b5, it can retreat to b8, with the possibility of joining an attack on the kingside. Black will continue with ...Qe7, adding to the presence on the e-file.

12...bxc6; 13.Qa4.

13.Na4 Bf5; 14.Rc1 Qd7; 15.Nc5 Bxc5; 16.Rxc5 Be4? This is the wrong piece. Black should play ...Rab8 and then ...Ne4. 17.Qa4 Bxg2; 18.Kxg2 Rac8; 19.Rfc1 Re4; 20.Bd4 Qf5; 21.e3 Ree8; 22.Bxf6 Qxf6; 23.Rxc6 Rxc6; 24.Qxc6 and White won easily in Goehring–Borik, Bundesliga 1983.

13...Bd7; 14.Qc2 Qc8; 15.Rfd1 Bh3; 16.Bh1 Ng4; 17.Bd2. Now White maneuvers another piece toward the Black king. **17...Qe6; 18.Be1 Rad8; 19.e4 Qf6; 20.exd5 Ne3!**

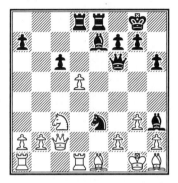

The f-pawn is indirectly pinned, because of the threat of ...Qf1#! **21.Qa4 Nxd1; 22.Rxd1 cxd5; 23.Nxd5 Qe6; 24.Ba5 Bc5; 25.Qc2.** 25.Bxd8?? would allow 25...Qe1+; 26.Rxe1 Rxe1#.

25...Bb6; 26.Nxb6 Qf5; 27.Rxd8 Rxd8.

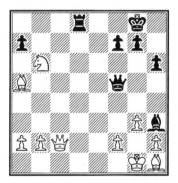

All of White's, pieces, except the cornered bishop, are hanging, so White resigned.

MURRAY CHANDLER

Another major figure on the British Tarrasch scene was Grandmaster Murray Chandler, who was born in New Zealand in 1960, but most of his career has been London–based. He served as a second to many excellent British players and has written many treatises on the opening.

KING VS. CHANDLER
Reykjavik, 1984

1.Nf3 d5; 2.d4 c5; 3.c4 e6; 4.cxd5 exd5; 5.g3 Nc6; 6.Bg2 Nf6; 7.0–0 Be7; 8.Nc3 0–0; 9.dxc5 Bxc5; 10.Bg5 d4; 11.Bxf6 Qxf6; 12.Nd5 Qd8; 13.Nd2 Re8; 14.Rc1 Bb6; 15.Re1 Be6; 16.Nf4 Bxa2.

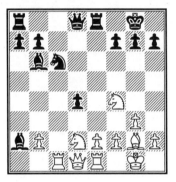

This is the risky alternative to 16...Bg4. **17.b3.** It is very unusual to see the bishop at a2 when White has a pawn at b3! Black realizes that there are several ways to defend the bishop, and one, a rook at c2, seems highly implausible here. Nevertheless, that is what Chandler achieves after a few moves! 17.Bxc6 bxc6; 18.b3 Ba5; 19.Rc2 Bxb3; 20.Nxb3 d3; 21.Nxa5 dxc2; 22.Qa1 Re4; 23.Rc1 Qg5; 24.e3 Qb5; 25.Qc3 Rb4; 26.Nd3 Rb1; 27.Nc4 Rxc1+; 28.Nxc1 Qb1; 29.Qd2 h6; 30.Kg2 a5; 31.Nxa5 Rxa5; 32.Qd8+ Kh7; 33.Qxa5 Qxc1; 34.Qf5+ allowed White to get away with a draw in Spraggett–Chandler, Hong Kong 1984.

17...Ba5; 18.Bd5. 18.Rc2 is a significant alternative, for example:

A) 18...Nb4; 19.Rb2 Rc8; 20.Nc4 g5!; 21.Nxa5 (21.Nh5 Rxc4!; 22.bxc4 Bxc4 and Black has compensation, for example 23.Qa4 b5; 24.Nf6+ Qxf6; 25.Qxa5 Na6 with enough for the exchange) 21...Qxa5; 22.Bxb7 gxf4; 23.Bxc8 Rxc8; 24.Qxd4 Nc2! wins for Black.

B) 18...Bxb3; 19.Nxb3 d3 is interesting. (19...Bxe1; 20.Qxe1 Rc8 is a less risky alternative.) 20.Rxc6! Bxe1; 21.Rc1 d2; 22.Rb1 a5. (22...Rc8 may be an improvement.) 23.Nd3 and White has demonstrated the superiority of the position in two high–level encounters.

B1) 23...Qg5; 24.Nbc5 Rad8; 25.Bxb7 h5; 26.Bf3 Qf5; 27.Kg2 h4; 28.g4 Qg5; 29.h3 Rd4; 30.Qb3 g6; 31.e3 Rdd8; 32.Ne4 a4; 33.Qxa4 Qe7; 34.g5 Rxd3; 35.Nf6+ Kf8; 36.Qxh4 Qd8; 37.Rb7 Black resigned in Karpov–Chandler, London 1984.

B2) 23...Rb8; 24.Ra1 b6; 25.Nxe1 dxe1Q+; 26.Qxe1 Rc8; 27.e3

Re5; 28.Nd4 Rec5; 29.h4 Qc7; 30.Ne2 g6; 31.Bf3 Rc2; 32.Kg2 Qc5; 33.h5 Kg7; 34.Ra4 Qe5; 35.Nd4 Rc1; 36.Qe2 Rb1; 37.Rc4 Rc5; 38.Qa2 Rxc4; 39.Qxc4 Qc5; 40.h6+ Kf6; 41.Qa4 Qc1; 42.Kh3 Qc8+; 43.g4 Rb4; 44.Qa1 Rc4; 45.Nc6+ Kg5; 46.Qe5+ f5; 47.Qe7+.

Black gave up, Spraggett–Ivanovic, Toronto 1984. So, we return to the game.

18...d3.

Now we see how Black secures the use of the c2–square. **19.e3** On 19.exd3 Rxe1+; 20.Qxe1 g5; 21.Ra1 Bxb3; 22.Bxb3 gxf4. Black has a better position, with a strong pin at d2 and a good square for the knight at d4.

19...Ne5!; 20.Kf1. 20.Bxb7 Rb8; 21.Bd5 Bxd2; 22.Qxd2 Qxd5; 23.Qxa2 Nf3+; 24.Kh1 Qb7 and Black has all the threats. **20...Rc8; 21.Ra1.** 21.Rxc8 Qxc8; 22.b4 Bxd5; 23.Nxd5 Qc6! and White is still in trouble. **21...Rc2.** The infiltration of the seventh rank is carried out under very unusual circumstances.

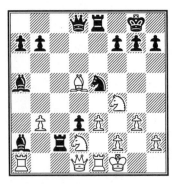

22.Rxa2 Rxa2; 23.b4 Bxb4; 24.Bxa2 Qa5; 25.Nxd3 Nxd3; 26.Qb3 Qf5; 27.Re2 Nc1; 28.Qc4 Rc8; 29.g4 Rxc4.

White resigned. If 30.gxf5 Rc2! White cannot avoid the loss of serious amounts of material.

RETURN TO THE WORLD CHAMPIONSHIP

The big boost for the Tarrasch came from Garry Kasparov, who used it successfully throughout his run for the World Championship title, until he ran up against Anatoly Karpov in the championship match. Karpov was well prepared, and scored seemingly at will against the Tarrasch. Actually, it was not the opening that let Kasparov down, but rather the fact that his endgame technique was not yet up to the level of Karpov.

GARRY KASPAROV

Garry Kimovich Kasparov was born April 13th, 1963 in Baku. He rose quickly to a prominent position in the chess world, and was already a superstar when he made the Soviet Olympiad side in 1980. He won his first Soviet Championship a year later, qualified for the candidates matches in 1982, and defeated Korchnoi, Belyavsky and Smyslov on his way to the first showdown with his "eternal rival" Anatoly Karpov. That match was suspended after six months in 1984/85, during much of which Karpov held a 5–0 advantage but could not bring home the final point.

Kasparov won the rematch later in 1985, and defended his title in 1986, 1987, and 1990 before breaking ranks with the World Chess Federation in 1993, defeating Nigel Short in London for the Professional Chess Association title. He defended that title in 1995 against Viswanathan Anand. Having temporarily exhausted the supply of human challengers, in 1996 he defeated the silicon beast Deep Blue, the product of IBM technology. A rematch in 1997 saw Kasparov go down in defeat!

We have already seen a selection of his games in the theory section. He is another fine game from one of his simultaneous exhibitions against a set of strong masters.

ZUEGER VS. KASPAROV
Simultaneous Exhibition, 1987

1.c4 Nf6; 2.Nc3 c5; 3.g3 e6; 4.Nf3 d5; 5.cxd5 exd5; 6.d4 Nc6; 7.Bg2 Be7; 8.0–0 0–0; 9.Bg5 cxd4; 10.Nxd4 h6; 11.Be3 Re8; 12.Rc1 Bg4; 13.h3. Now Black must decide on the most appropriate retreat for the bishop.

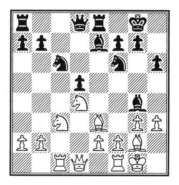

13...Be6!; 14.Kh2.

A prophylactic move, since sooner or later the pawn at h3 will need further defense. 14.Nxc6 bxc6; 15.Na4 Qa5; 16.Bc5 Ne4; 17.Bxe7 Rxe7; 18.Kh2 Rc8; 19.b3 c5 and Black had control of the fifth rank in Mitura–Zolnierowicz, Wisla 1992.

14...Qd7; 15.Nxc6. 15.Na4 Nxd4; 16.Bxd4 b6; 17.Nc3 Rac8; 18.e3 b5; 19.Qd3 b4; 20.Bxf6 Bxf6; 21.Nxd5 Bxb2; 22.Rxc8 Rxc8 and Black is a bit better, Clara–Lobron, Bundesliga 1985.

15...bxc6; 16.Na4 Bf5. 16...Rab8 is an acceptable alternative. 17.Bc5 Bf5; 18.b3 Bd6; 19.Bxd6 Qxd6; 20.e3 Nd7; 21.Qd4 Rb7; 22.Nc5 Nxc5; 23.Qxc5 Qxc5; 24.Rxc5 Rb6 was eventually drawn in Greenfeld–Frois, Novi Sad Olympiad 1990.

17.Bc5. 17.Nc5 Bxc5; 18.Bxc5 Ne4; 19.e3 Nxc5; 20.Rxc5 Be4; 21.Bxe4 Rxe4 is drawish Burger–Valvo, New York 1990. **17...Bd8; 18.Bd4 Ne4; 19.f3.** 19.Nc5 Nxc5; 20.Bxc5 Bf6; 21.Qd2 Be4; 22.e3

Bxg2; 23.Kxg2 a5 was drawn in Small–Salazar, Manila Olympiad 1992.
19...Ng5!; 20.Nc5 Qe7.

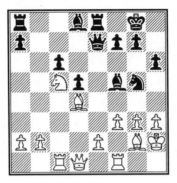

21.e4?! A premature break at e4 is often the source of serious trouble for White. **21...dxe4; 22.fxe4 Bg6; 23.e5 Bb6; 24.h4 Rad8!** The pin is very strong.

25.hxg5 Qxg5; 26.Qa4 Qh5+; 27.Kg1 Rxe5; 28.Bxe5 Qxe5.

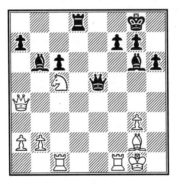

The tactics have left Black down a rook, but the pin at c5 and the exposed White king provide serious compensation when combined with the two pawns and bishop pair.

29.Qb4 Rd3!; 30.Rf2 Rxg3; 31.Qf4.

Black is not finished with the stunning tactical display.

31...Rxg2+!; 32.Kxg2 Qd5+; 33.Kg3 Bxc5. The bishop pair plus three pawns is worth much more than the rooks. **34.Rd2 Qh5; 35.Qg4 Qe5+; 36.Qf4 Qe7; 37.Rc3 Bb6; 38.Kg2 Qe1; 39.Rc1 Qe6; 40.Qg3 Be4+; 41.Kh2 Qf5.** White resigned.

TRUE BELIEVERS

There are some active players who have trusted the Tarrasch Defense for most of their careers. These players don't rely on the element of surprise. They have such great faith in the Tarrasch that they are willing to play it even against the best opposition, and fear no special opening preparation. Margeir Petursson and Miguel Illescas Cordoba are two such players.

MARGEIR PETURSSON

The Icelandic Grandmaster was born in 1960 and has been a leading player in that chess-loving country for many years. His special contribution to the Tarrasch is in the main lines with 9.Bg5 cxd4; 10.Nxd4, where he discovered that 10...Re8 is playable in addition to the normal 10...h6. Here is a sample of his artistry.

SCHUSSLER VS. PETURSSON
Gausdal Zonal (10), 1985

1.d4 d5; 2.c4 e6; 3.Nc3 c5; 4.cxd5 exd5; 5.Nf3 Nc6; 6.g3 Nf6; 7.Bg2 Be7; 8.0-0 0-0; 9.dxc5 Bxc5; 10.Na4.

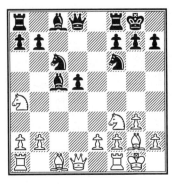

This is the main alternative to the development of the bishop at g5. White drives the bishop back to e7, and will concentrate on the c5-square.

10...Be7; 11.Be3. 11.Nd4 (11.b3 Bg4; 12.Bb2 Re8 gives Black a normal and good Tarrasch formation. 13.Rc1 Rc8; 14.a3 Ne4; 15.b4 b5; 16.Nc5 Nxc5 was agreed drawn in Kalinichev–Novik, Novosibirsk 1989) 11...Nxd4; 12.Qxd4 Qa5. (12...Ne4; 13.Bxe4 dxe4; 14.Qxe4 Bh3 is supposed to provide Black with counterplay, but I am skeptical that it is worth a pawn. 15.Re1 Qd7; 16.Be3 Bf5; 17.Qf4 looks better for White.) 13.Bd2 Qb5; 14.b3 Bf5; 15.Nc3 Qd7; 16.Rac1 Rfd8 is fully equal, Black eventually prevailed: 17.Bg5 Be6; 18.Rfd1 h6; 19.Bf4 b6; 20.Na4 Rac8; 21.Bf3 Bg4; 22.Rxc8 Rxc8; 23.Bxg4 Qxg4; 24.f3 Qh3; 25.Qb2 Nh5; 26.Rxd5 Nxf4; 27.gxf4 Rc6; 28.f5 Bg5; 29.Qe5 Rc1+; 30.Kf2 Rf1#. Slagter-De Jong, Postal 1990.

11...Re8. Petursson likes to get the rook to e8 as quickly as possible. This provides a home for the bishop at f8 and the rook can later take part in operations in the center and on the kingside. **12.Rc1** (12.Nd4 Bg4; 13.Rc1 transposes below.)

12...Bg4.

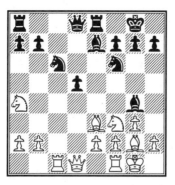

This is the usual Tarrasch strategy, though 12...Ne4 is a good alternative. White has many different plans here. Either a knight or bishop can be sent to occupy c5. White can play the knight to d4, leading to positions similar to the 9.Bg5 cxd4; 10.Nxd4 lines, where Petursson usually plays 10...Re8. The bishop at g4 can be forced to make an important decision after 13.h3.

13.Bc5. There are some less commital moves too.

A) 13.h3 Bh5; 14.Nd4 Qd7; 15.Nxc6 bxc6; 16.Re1 Bb4; 17.Bd2 Bf8; 18.Bf4 Re6; 19.g4 Bg6; 20.Qd4 Rae8 gave Black equal chances in Ree–Petursson, Reykjavik 1984.

B) 13.Nc5 Bxc5; 14.Bxc5 (14.Rxc5 Qd7; 15.Re1 Rac8; 16.Nd4 Ne5; 17.Rxc8 Rxc8; 18.Bg5 Ne8; 19.Bf4 Ng6; 20.Be3 Bh3; 21.Bh1 Nf6; 22.Nf3 b6; 23.Ng5 was agreed drawn in Szabo-Parma, Palma de Mallorca 1969) 14...Qd7; 15.Re1 Rad8; 16.Nd4 h5; 17.Nxc6 bxc6; 18.Bd4 saw Black equalize with the interesting maneuver 18...Nh7; 19.Qd2 Nf8 in Partos–Petursson, Biel Interzonal 1985.

C) 13.Nd4 Qd7! Black prepares ...Rad8 and ...Ne4. 14.Re1 (14.Nc3 Bb4; 15.Nb3 Rad8; 16.a3 Bf8 equalized in Zagorskis-Henao, Karvina 1992) 14...Bb4; 15.Nc3 h6; 16.Qa4 Bf8; 17.a3 Bh3; 18.Red1 Bxg2; 19.Kxg2 Re5; 20.h4 Rh5. Black had attacking chances in Nika–Madl, Thessaloniki Olympiad 1984.

D) 13.Bd4 Ne4; 14.Nc3 Qd7; 15.Be3 Rad8; 16.Nb5 Bf6; 17.Nbd4 Rc8. Black has an acceptable game, Ungureanu-Balashov, Bath 1973.

E) 13.Qb3 Qd7; 14.Bc5 Ne4; 15.Bxe7 Rxe7; 16.Rfd1 d4; 17.Qa3 Rae8; 18.Bf1 Qf5; 19.Nc5 Nxf2; 20.Kxf2 Re3; 21.Rd3.

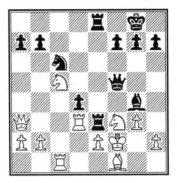

This exciting position is from Hulak–Marjanovic, Subotica 1984. Black lost his nerve and played 21...b6?, but after 21...Bxf3!; 22.exf3 (22.Rxe3 dxe3+; 23.Kg1 Bd5; 24.Nd3 Re4 wins for Black) 22...Qxf3+; 23.Kg1, the same idea can win, for example 23...b6!; 24.Nd7 (24.Rxe3 loses to 24...dxe3; 25.Nd7 Qf2+; 26.Kh1 e2) 24...h5; 25.Qb3 R8e7; 26.Qd1 Qe4; 27.Rxe3 Qxe3+; 28.Kh1 Nd8; 29.Nb8 h4; 30.Rc8 Qe4+; 31.Bg2 Qe1+; 32.Qxe1 Rxe1+; 33.Bf1 Rxf1+; 34.Kg2 Rd1; 35.Rxd8+ Kh7; 36.gxh4 Rd2+; 37.Kg3 Rxb2; 38.a4 Rb4; 39.Nc6 Rxa4; 40.Nxd4 a5 and only Black has any realistic winning chances.

F) Another idea is seen in the variation 13.a3 Qd7; 14.Re1 (14.Nc5 Bxc5; 15.Rxc5 Rad8; 16.Rc3. Black now takes advantage of the control of d4 with 16...d4!; 17.Rd3 Bf5; 18.Rxd4 Nxd4; 19.Bxd4 Bg4 and suddenly White is in serious trouble. 20.e3 Ne4; 21.Qe1 f6; 22.Nd2 Ng5; 23.h4 Ne6; 24.Bc3 Nc5; 25.Nc4 Qd3 led to White's resignation in Kalkman–Weyerstrass, Germany 1990) 14...Bh3; 15.Bh1 Ne4; 16.Nc3 Nxc3; 17.Rxc3 Bf6. Black had good counterplay in Jakobsen–Hansen, Naestved 1985.

13...Ne4.

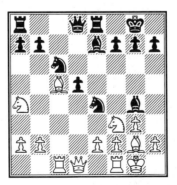

The knight now joins the battle for the c5-square, and creates a possible new home for the bishop at f6. **14.Bxe7 Qxe7; 15.h3 Bxf3.** Black does not mind parting with the minor exchange, since the knight at e4 remains strong unless White captures with the pawn, giving Black a dangerous passed pawn on the d-file.

16.Bxf3. 16.exf3 Nf6; 17.f4 Rad8!; 18.Nc5 b6; 19.Nb3 Qd7; 20.Nd4 Nxd4; 21.Qxd4 Rc8; 22.g4 Qb5; 23.g5 Ne4 is fine for Black. The tempo of the game can accelerate quickly, as the following example shows. 24.a4 Qb3; 25.Rfd1 Nc5; 26.Bxd5 Qxh3; 27.Bg2 Qg4; 28.Kh2 Rb8; 29.Bh3 Qf3; 30.Bg2 Qh5+; 31.Kg1 Nb3. White resigned, Hunger-Merker, Postal 1987.

16 ...Rad8; 17.Bg2 Rd6; 18.Nc5 Nxc5; 19.Rxc5 d4!

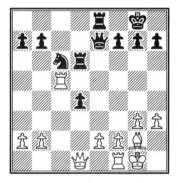

This typical space-gaining advance brings Black equalty. 20.Rc2 h5; 21.Rd2 h4; 22.g4 Red8; 23.Qa4 R8d7; 24.Rc1 Qg5; 25.Rcd1 b5; 26.Qa3 Ne5; 27.b3.

Black is faced with a variety of plans. The d-pawn can keep on marching, the f-pawn can advance to confront the pawn at g4. Petursson decides the time is right for sacrifice on the kingside, while the enemy queen is far away at a3. **27...Nxg4; 28.hxg4 Qxg4; 29.Kh2 Qf4+; 30.Kh1 Qxf2.** Black has three pawns for the bishop and a promising kingside attack, too.

31.b4 h3!; 32.Bxh3. 32.Be4 Re7; 33.e3 Qh4; 34.Bc2 Qg3! Black will be able to capture the e-pawn with the rook. **32...d3!; 33.Rxd3?** Surely 33.exd3 is better, but after 33...Qe3; 34.Bg4 Rh6+; 35.Rh2 Rxh2+; 36.Kxh2 Qf2+; 37.Kh3 Re7!; 38.d4 Re3+; 39.Qxe3 Qxe3+; 40.Kg2 Qa3 gives Black excellent winning chances in the endgame. **33...Rxd3; 34.exd3 Qf3+; 35.Kh2 Qe2+; 36.Kg3 Re7!**

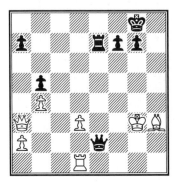

White resigned, as the postion is hopeless, despite the extra bishop.

MIGUEL ILLESCAS CORDOBA

Grandmaster Miguel Illescas Cordoba is the leading native–born player of Spain, a country with over a thousand years of chess tradition. He has been devoted to the Tarrasch throughout his career. We have already seen many fine examples of his play, but here is another.

BELIAVSKY VS. ILLESCAS CORDOBA
Linares, 1990

1.d4 d5; 2.c4 e6; 3.Nc3 c5; 4.cxd5 exd5; 5.Nf3 Nc6; 6.g3 Nf6; 7.Bg2 Be7; 8.0–0 0–0; 9.Bg5 cxd4; 10.Nxd4 h6; 11.Be3 Re8; 12.Qc2 Bg4; 13.h3 Bd7; 14.Rad1.

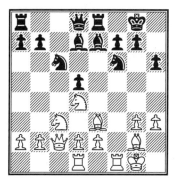

A typical position in the Classical Tarrasch has arisen. How should Black take the initiative. Illescas targets the weak h-pawn, using bishop, queen, and eventually, the rook at e8! **14 ...Qc8; 15.Kh2 Bf8; 16.Rfe1 Re5.** Black wants to play the rook to h5. White decides to jettison the h-pawn.

17.Rh1! 17.Nxc6 bxc6; 18.Bd4 Rh5; 19.Bxf6 looks good, but Black has a strong reply in Ftacnik's 19...Bxh3! 20.Bh4 *(20.Bf3 Bg2+)* 20...Rxh4! 21.gxh4 Bd6+! Checkmate in 8 moves! **17 ...Rh5; 18.Kg1 Bxh3; 19.Bf3 Re5.** Its task complete, the rook can return home. **20.Nxc6 bxc6.** 20 ...Rxe3 is interesting, since after 21.fxe3 bxc6 the chances are about even. But the text is stronger.

21.Bd4 Bf5!

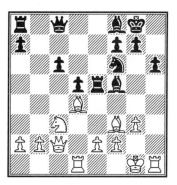

Black's counterattack on the White king secures the advantage. The point is that with the bishop at f5, instead of h3, Black can afford to retreat the rook to e6, and protect the kngiht at f6. My guess is that Belyavsky missed this intermezzo.

22.e4 Rxe4; 23.Nxe4 Nxe4; 24.Qe2 c5; 25.Be3 Qe6; 26.Kg2 d4.
A good move, but bringing the rook to e8 might have been stronger.
In any case Black has plenty of compensation for the exchange. **27.Bc1
Re8; 28.Qb5 a6; 29.Qb7 Qxa2; 30.Rde1 Nd6; 31.Qb6 Rc8; 32.Bf4
Nc4.** Now the b-pawn falls, and Black will have connected passed
pawns.

33.Qb7 Qxb2; 34.Qd5 Qc2; 35.Re2 Nb6; 36.Qb7 Qb3. The a-
pawn is still taboo. **37.Rhe1.** 37.Qxa6 c4; 38.Re5 Rc5; 39.Rxc5 Bxc5;
40.Qa5 Qb4 is terrible for White because the pawns advance quickly.
37...Qb5! 38.Bc1 Nc4; 39.Qd5 Bd7. 39...Bg6! would have been more
efficient. **40.Re7.** White returns the exchange, hoping to tie Black's
forces down to the defense of f7.

40...Bxe7; 41.Rxe7 Be8.

42.Be4? This is a logical move, but as it turns out White does not
build enough of an attack. This move should be delayed. First, the
other bishop should be delivered to the kingside.

42.Bf4!? is interesting.

A) 42 ...Nb6; 43.Qf5 Kf8 (43 ...c4; 44.Be5 c3; 45.Be4 Kf8; 46.Re6
and White should win!) 44.Rb7 Bd7; 45.Qh7 Rc6! 46.Qh8+ Ke7;
47.Qb8 c4; 48.Bc7 Rxc7; 49.Qxc7 Na8; 50.Qb8 Qc5; 51.Qxa8 c3;
52.Qg8 is better for White, though the situation remains complicated. White has an extra rook, but Black has 4 extra pawns, and one
is approaching the promotion square. 52 ...c2; 53.Rxd7+! Kxd7;
54.Qxf7+ Kd8; 55.Qg8+ Kc7; 56.Qxg7+ Kb6; 57.Qxh6+ Ka5; 58.Qc1
Kb4; 59.Be4 d3! White cannot take the pawn because of ...Qd5+.
60.Qb2+ Kc4; 61.f3 Qe3; 62.Qa2+ Kc3; 63.Qa5+ Kb2; 64.Qb4+ Kc1;
65.Bxd3 Qxd3; 66.Qe1+ Qd1; 67.Qe4 Qd2+; 68.Kg1 Kd1; 69.Kf1 a5
(69...c1Q 70.Qa4+ Qcc2; 71.Qa1+ Qdc1; 72.Qd4+ Q2d2 73.Qa4+ is
a swindle.) 70.g4 Kc1; 71.Qe5 Kb1; 72.Qb5+ Qb4; 73.Qd3 Kb2;

74.Qe2 Kb3; 75.Qd3+ Qc3; 76.Qb5+ Ka3 and there are no more checks, so Black wins.

B) 42 ...g5 is stronger, challenging the invader. If it retreats, then Black can get back to business and get the pawns rollng soon. Two other plans come to mind. Both are very complicated, so the sample variations are just a taste of the possibilities.

B1) 43.Bxg5 is an offer that can, and should, be refused. 43 ...Nb6 (43 ...hxg5; 44.Qxg5+ Kf8; 45.Rb7! Ne3+! 46.fxe3 Qd3; 47.Qh4 Qg6; 48.exd4 cxd4; 49.Qh8+ Qg8; 50.Qxd4 Rc2+; 51.Kh3 Qh7+ forces the queens from the board. 52.Qh4 Qxh4+; 53.Kxh4 Rd2; 54.Ra7 Bb5; 55.Bb7 Kg7 and White has the saving grace 56.Bxa6! Ra2; 57.Rxf7+ Kxf7; 58.Bxb5 with a probable draw.) 44.Qf5 c4; 45.Re5 gets very messy. 45 ...Qxe5; 46.Qxe5 Nd7; 47.Qe7 hxg5; 48.Qxg5+ Kf8; 49.Qh6+ Ke7; 50.Qh4+ f6; 51.Qxd4 c3; 52.Bb7 Rc5; 53.Qe3+ Kf8; 54.Bxa6 c2; 55.Qc1 Rc3; 56.Bb7 Nc5; 57.Bf3 Kg7 looks hopeless for White.

B2) 43.Qf5 43 ...Rd8; 44.Be4 gxf4; 45.Qh7+ Kf8; 46.Rb7 Qxb7 (46...f3+ 47.Bxf3 Bd7!? 48.Qxh6+ Ke8; 49.Qh8+ Ke7; 50.Qh4+ f6; 51.Qh7+ Kd6; 52.Qf7 Qxb7; 53.Bxb7 Be6; 54.Qxf6 Rb8; 55.Bxa6 Ne5; 56.f4 Rb2+; 57.Kf1 Ng4; 58.Qd8+ Kc6; 59.Qe8+ should draw.) 47.Qxh6+ Ke7; 48.Qg5+ Kd7 (48 ...f6; 49.Qxc5+ Rd6; 50.Bxb7 Bb5; 51.Qc7+ Ke6; 52.Bc8+ Kd5; 53.Bb7+ Bc6; 54.Bxa6 fxg3; 55.Bxc4+ Kxc4+; 56.Kxg3 Re6 is likely to end up as a draw.) 49.Bxb7 Nd6; 50.Bxa6 Ra8; 51.Be2 f5 (51 ...fxg3; 52.Qxc5 gxf2; 53.Qxd4 is headed toward a split point.) 52.Qxf4 Bf7; 53.Bd3 Bd5+; 54.Kf1 Ra1+ (54 ...Be4; 55.Bxe4 fxe4; 56.g4 Ra2; 57.g5 c4; 58.g6 is better for White.) 55.Ke2 Ra2+; 56.Kd1 Be4 (56 ...Kc6; 57.Bxf5 c4; 58.Bh7 Kc5; 59.g4 c3; 60.g5 Bb3+; 61.Ke1 Ra1+; 62.Ke2 Bc4+; 63.Kf3 Ra7; 64.g6 Bd5+; 65.Kg3 Ra1! 66.Qe5 c2; 67.Bg8 Ne4+; 68.Kh2 Rh1+; 69.Kxh1 c1Q+

70.Kg2 and now Black wins with the surprising tactical resource 70...Qc4! 71.g7 Nf6+; 72.Bxd5 Qxd5+; 73.Qxd5+ Kxd5; 74.Kf3 Kc4; 75.Ke2 Kc3; 76.Kd1 d3; 77.f3 d2; 78.f4 Kd3; 79.f5 Nd5; 80.g8Q Ne3#) 57.Bxe4 fxe4; 58.Qf6 d3; 59.g4 c4; 60.g5 Rc2; 61.g6 c3; 62.g7 Rd2+; 63.Kc1 Rc2+; 64.Kb1 Rb2+; 65.Ka1 d2; 66.Qd4 Rb8! is unpleasant for White.

We've spent a lot of time looking at this complex position, and the investigation has nevertheless been superficial. This gives you a taste of the complexities that can arise in the Classical Tarrasch. Illescas was fortunate in not needing to work this out at the board, because after the move chosen by his oppnent, the win is simple.

42...Kf8.

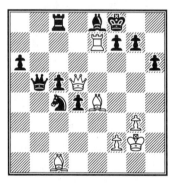

White resigned, because the rook cannot be saved. 43.Rb7 Qc6! 44.Rxf7+ (44.Bf4 Qxd5; 45.Bxd5 Rd8; 46.Bf3 d3 and the pawns are too much.) 44 ...Bxf7; 45.Qxc6 Rxc6; 46.Bxc6 d3 wins without difficulty.

INTO THE FUTURE

Our study of the Tarrasch Defense ends with a game played by a promising young player, showing that the future of the opening is in secure hands. This was played at the 1997 Hawai'i International by 15–year old Gabe Kahane, one of my students. Two of my 10-year old students used the Tarrasch successfully in their international debut in Holland at the end of the same year.

The Tarrasch is an excellent choice for young players, with its clear cut strategy and abundant tactical possibilities.

HEYL VS. KAHANE
Outrigger Prince Kuhio International, 1997

1.d4 d5; 2.Nf3 e6; 3.c4 c5; 4.cxd5 exd5; 5.Nc3 Nc6; 6.g3 Nf6; 7.Bg2 Be7; 8.0-0 0-0; 9.Bg5 cxd4; 10.Nxd4 h6; 11.Be3 Re8; 12.Rc1 Bf8; 13.a3 Bg4; 14.Re1 Qd7; 15.Nxc6 bxc6; 16.Na4.

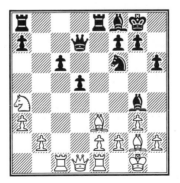

So far we have typical Tarrasch play. Watch how Kahane zeroes in on the kingside with ruthless efficiency.

16...Bh3! 17.Bf3. Retreating to h1 would have been wiser. **17...Ne4; 18.Bg2?** White suddenly changes his mind. Better to react on the queenside with 18.b4.

18 ...Bxg2; 19.Kxg2 Re5; 20.h3?! An unnecessary weakening of the kingside that is quickly exploited.

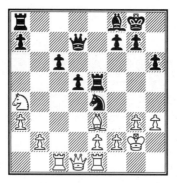

20...Nxg3!? 20 ...Rh5 would have been more accurate. **21.Kxg3 Qd6.** Threatening a nasty discovered check. **22.Kg2?** 22.Bf4! Rg5+; 23.Kf3 Rf5! 24.e3 g5; 25.Qd3 Qf6; 26.Rg1 Bg7 and White has nothing better than 27.Rxc6 Rxf4+; 28.exf4 Qxc6; 29.fxg5 hxg5; 30.Nc3 d4+; 31.Qe4! but even so Black is better after 31...Qc8.

22...Qg6+ 23.Kh2.

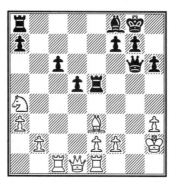

Black is attacking only with queen and rook, and now continues to sacrifice. **23...Rxe3! 24.Rc3.** 24.fxe3 Bd6+; 25.Kh1 Qg3 delivers mate next move. **24...Bd6+ 25.Kh1 Qe4+; 26.Kg1 Qf4! White resigned.**

A FINAL WORD

Well, I hope you have learned the secrets of the Tarrasch Defense well and are now ready to go out and confound your enemies at the chessboard. The repertoire you have been given here should serve you well, and requires very little maintenance.

Most of the ideas of the Tarrasch are general and it is not hard to figure out a good reply to any strange moves that may be thrown at you in competitions. I hope you enjoy playing these openings and am confident that they will serve you well. Have fun!

SELF–TEST

Test your understanding by examining the following positions. The proper reactions are illustrated in the cited games. Page numbers are given so that you can locate the beginning of each game.

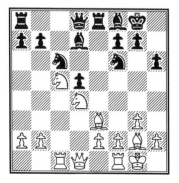

What is Black's correct move? (Kramnik–Illescas Cordoba, pg 61)

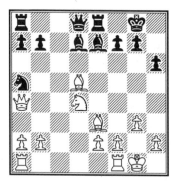

How should Black continue? (Belyavsky–Kasparov, pg 76)

270

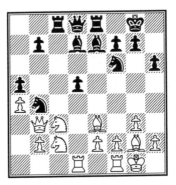

Black has a dynamic move here, what is it?
(Ristic–Petursson, pg 81)

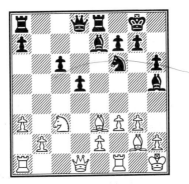

What is Black's plan here (Smyslov–Kasparov, pg 88)

Who has the better game? (Seirawan–Kasparov, pg 95)

Where should the bishop go? (Radulov–Spassov, pg 114)

Black has a strong move here. What is it?
(Larsen–Kasparov, pg 118)

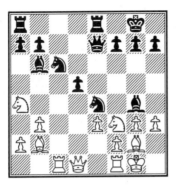

Can you work out all the tactics in this position,
with Black to move? (Meins–Schiller, pg 125)

Is ...d4 playable here? (Gurevich–Wilder, pg 127)

WHERE TO GO FROM HERE

After reading this book, you can go on to incorporate openings that you find interesting into your own repertoire. There are thousands of books available on specific opening strategies, and for proficiency you'll need to turn to the extensive literature on each opening. A selection of recommended opening books from many different publishers is available from Cardoza Publishing, as well as many of my new up-to-date titles on opening play, at www.cardozapub.com. My recent 1700 page trilogy, *World Champion Openings, Standard Chess Openings,* and *Unorthodox Chess Openings,* contains many more openings you may find of interest.

Additional information on the openings is available at http://www.chessworks.com, which is the web site of the author. Also, look for the new free online chess magazine where I am editor-in-chief, Chess City, www.chesscity.com. There will be loads of resources and information available here for free, and articles, columns, gossip, and much more from some of the best writers in the chess world.

Armed with the knowledge you gain in this book, you can also deepen your understanding of the ideas behind the openings by examining collections of games by the strong players who use those openings. You can find many books devoted to the games of the great masters. There are also plenty of sources on the Internet where you can find collections for free!

INDICES

INDEX OF VARIATIONS

boldface indicates primary game

INDEX OF SELECTED PLAYERS

boldface indicates biographical entry

KASPAROV EXPRESS™

SAITEK - *The World Leader in Intelligent Electronic Games*

VERSATILE AND FUN - An amazing 384 level/setting combinations includes fun levels for novices and challenging levels for experienced players. Economic powerful, and pocket size (approximately 5" x 61/2" x 1') this game is an unbeatable easy traveling companion.
GREAT INEXPENSIVE TRAVEL COMPANION! - Features different playing styles and strengths, 5 special coach modes, and teaching levels! Sensory-style chess board, peg type pieces, folding lid, LCD screen, take back and hint features, built-in chess clock that keeps track of time for both sides, and self-rating system. Memory holds an unfinished game for up to two years, gives you the complete package in an economical, handy travel-ready unit.

To order, send just $49.95 for the <u>Express</u>.

KASPAROV TRAVEL CHAMPION 2100

SAITEK - *The World Leader in Intelligent Electronic Games*

THE WORLD'S MOST POWERFUL HAND-HELD CHESS COMPUTER ANYWHERE! - This **super program** and **integrated training system** has an **official USCF rating of 2334!** This **awesome program** can beat over 99% of all chess players, yet it's still great for the novice. LCD shows principal variation, evaluation, search depth, and search mode counts.
64 SKILL LEVELS - 64 levels of skill and handicapping give you tons of **options** and **versatility**: Play against beginning, intermediate or advanced opponents (includes tournament time controls), play Blitz or Tournament, choose Active, Passive, or Complete style, or Tournament Opening Book, select **Brute Force** algorithm or the advanced Selective Search. Match your skill to the correct level for most **challenging** chess. You want it - it's all here!

To order, send just $129.95 for the <u>Kasparov Travel Champion 2100</u>.

282

KASPAROV CHESS GK2100™
SAITEK - The World Leader in Intelligent Electronic Games

THE BEST VALUE MONEY CAN BUY! - The **fabulous** Kasparov GK2100 is the **most popular** chess computer we sell. Using a super high speed **RISC** computer chip and rated at a **2334** USCF rating, you'll have consistent challenges and excitement. Coaching features and fun levels makes it suitable for novices; masters and experts will want to choose higher levels.

GREAT DESIGN - Packaged in a sleek, handsome cabinet suitable for your living room. No need to find a partner to play - **take on the Champion!**

POWERFUL PROGRAM FEATURES - **64 levels of play** include sudden death, tournament, problem solving and beginner's. Shows intended move and position evaluation, take back up to 50 moves, and user selectable **book openings library**. Also choose from **Active, Passive, Tournament, complete book, no book.** Select the high speed **Selective Search** or play against the powerful **Brute Force.** program. Thinks in opponents time for best realism. Shutoff, shut on memory - remembers game for 1 year!

GREAT FOR BEGINNERS AND MASTERS ALIKE! - This **awesome program** can beat over 99% of all regular chess players, yet it is still suitable for beginners and intermediate players: Simply set the skill level to the appropriate strength for the best challenges. Matching your skill to the correct level of play ensures a **challenging** and **exciting** game.

EVEN MORE FEATURES - Opening library of 35,000 moves, **large LCD** shows full information and keeps track of playing time. Modern ergonomic design goes well in living room.

To order, send $199.95 for the <u>Kasparov Chess GK2100</u>

283

CARDOZA PUBLISHING CHESS BOOKS

COMPLETE DEFENSE TO KING PAWN OPENINGS by *Eric Schiller* - Learn a complete defensive system against 1.e4. This powerful repertoire not only limits White's ability to obtain any significant opening advantage but allows Black to adopt the flexible Caro-Kann formation, the favorite weapon of many of the greatest chess players. All White's options are explained in detail, and a plan is given for Black to combat them all. Analysis is up-to-date and backed by examples drawn from games of top stars. Detailed index lets you follow the opening from the point of a specific player, or through its history. 240 pages, $16.95.

SECRETS OF THE SICILIAN DRAGON by *GM Eduard Gufeld and Eric Schiller* - The mighty Dragon Variation of the Sicilian Defense is one of the most exciting openings in chess. Everything from opening piece formation to the endgame, including clear explanations of all the key strategic and tactical ideas, is covered in full conceptual detail. Instead of memorizing a jungle of variations, you learn the really important ideas behind the opening, and how to adapt them at the chessboard. Special sections on the heroes of the Dragon show how the greatest players handle the opening. The most instructive book on the Dragon written! 160 pages, $14.95.

- MIDDLEGAME/TACTICS/WINNING CONCEPTS -

WORLD CHAMPION COMBINATIONS by *Keene and Schiller* - Learn the insights, concepts and moves of the greatest combinations ever by the greatest players who ever lived. From Morphy to Alekhine, to Fischer to Kasparov, the incredible combinations and brilliant sacrifices of the 13 World Champions are collected here in the most insightful combinations book written. Packed with fascinating strategems, 50 annotated games, and great practical advice for your own games, this is a great companion guide to *World Champion Openings*. 288 pages, $16.95.

WINNING CHESS TACTICS by *Bill Robertie* - 14 chapters of winning tactical concepts show the complete explanations and thinking behind every tactical concept: pins, single and double forks, double attacks, skewers, discovered and double checks, multiple threats - and other crushing tactics to gain an immediate edge over opponents. Learn the power tools of tactical play to become a stronger player. Includes guide to chess notation. 128 pages, $9.95

ENCYCLOPEDIA OF CHESS WISDOM, The Essential Concepts and Strategies of Smart Chess Play by *Eric Schiller* - The most important concepts, strategies, tactics, wisdom, and thinking that every chessplayer must know, plus the gold nuggets of knowledge behind every attack and defense, is collected together in one highly focused volume. From opening, middle and endgame strategy, to psychological warfare and tournament tactics, the *Encyclopedia of Chess Wisdom* forms the blueprint of power play and advantage at the chess board. Step-by-step, the reader is taken through the thinking behind each essential concept, and through examples, discussions, and diagrams, shown the full impact on the game's direction. You even learn how to correctly study chess to become a chess master. 400 pages, $19.95.

- BASIC CHESS BOOKS -

THE BASICS OF WINNING CHESS by *Jacob Cantrell* - A great first book of chess, in one easy reading, beginner's learn the moves of the pieces, the basic rules and principles of play, the standard openings, and both Algebraic and English chess notation. The basic ideas of the winning concepts and strategies of middle and end game play are shown as well. Includes example games of great champions. 64 pages, $4.95.

BEGINNING CHESS PLAY by *Bill Robertie* - Step-by-step approach uses 113 diagrams to teach novices the basic principles of chess. Covers opening, middle and end game strategies, principles of development, pawn structure, checkmates, openings and defenses, how to write and read chess notation, join a chess club, play in tournaments, use a chess clock, and get rated. Two annotated games illlustrate strategic thinking for easy learning. 144 pages, $9.95

- MATES & ENDGAMES -

303 TRICKY CHECKMATES by *Fred Wilson and Bruce Alberston* - Both a fascinating challenge and great training tool, this collection of two, three and bonus four move checkmates is great for advanced beginning, intermediate and expert players. Mates are in order of difficulty, from the simple to very complex positions. Learn the standard patterns and stratagems for cornering the king: corridor and support mates, attraction and deflection sacrifices, pins and annihilation, the quiet move, and the dreaded *zugzwang*. Examples, drawn from actual games, illustrate a wide range of chess tactics from old classics right up to the 1990's. 192 pages, $12.95.

MASTER CHECKMATE STRATEGY *by Bill Robertie* - Learn the basic combinations, plus advanced, surprising and unconventional mates, the most effective pieces needed to win, and how to mate opponents with just a pawn advantage. also, how to work two rooks into an unstoppable attack; how to wield a queen advantage with deadly intent; how to coordinate pieces of differing strengths into indefensible positions of their opponents; when it's best to have a knight, and when a bishop to win. 144 pages, $9.95

BASIC ENDGAME STRATEGY: Kings, Pawns and Minor Pieces *by Bill Robertie* - Learn the mating principles and combinations needed to finish off opponents. From the four basic checkmates using the King with the queen, rook, two bishops, and bishop/knight combinations, to the King/pawn, King/Knight and King/Bishop endgames, you'll learn the essentials of translating small edges into decisive checkmates. Learn the 50-move rule, and the combinations of pieces that can't force a mate against a lone King. 144 pages, $12.95.

BASIC ENDGAME STRATEGY: Rooks and Queens by Bill Robertie - The companion guide to *Basic Endgame Strategy: Kings, Pawns and Minor Pieces*, you'll learn the basic mating principles and combinations of the Queen and Rook with King, how to turn middlegame advantages into victories, by creating passed pawns, using the King as a weapon, clearing the way for rook mates, and other endgame combinations. 144 pages, $12.95.

EXCELLENT CHESS BOOKS - OTHER PUBLISHERS
- OPENINGS -

HOW TO PLAY THE TORRE *by Eric Schiller* - One of Schiller's best-selling books, the 19 chapters on this fabulous and aggressive White opening (1. d4 Nf6; 2. Nf3 e6; 3. Bg5) will make opponents shudder and get you excited about chess all over again. Insightful analysis, completely annotated games get you ready to win! 210 pages, $17.50.

A BLACK DEFENSIVE SYSTEM WITH 1...D6 *by Andrew Soltis* - This Black reply - so rarely played that it doesn't even have a name - throws many opponents off their rote attack and can lead to a decisive positional advantage. Use this surprisingly strong system to give you the edge against unprepared opponents. 166 pages, $16.50.

BLACK TO PLAY CLASSICAL DEFENSES AND WIN *by Eric Schiller - Shows you how to develop a complete opening repertoire as black.* Emerge from *any* opening with a playable position, fighting for the center from the very first move. Defend against the Ruy Lopez, Italian Game, King's Gambit, King's Indian, many more. 166 pages, $16.50.

ROMANTIC KING'S GAMBIT IN GAMES & ANALYSIS *by Santasiere & Smith* - The most comprehensive collection of theory and games (137) on this adventurous opening is filled with annotations and "color" on the greatest King's Gambits played and the players. Makes you *want* to play! Very readable; packed with great concepts. 233 pages, $17.50.

WHITE TO PLAY 1.E4 AND WIN *by Eric Schiller - Shows you how to develop a complete opening system as white beginning 1. e4.* Learn the recommended opening lines to all the major systems as white, and how to handle any defense black throws back. Covers the Sicilian, French, Caro-Kann, Scandinavia; many more. 166 pages, $16.50.

BIG BOOK OF BUSTS *by Schiller & Watson* - Learn how to defend against 70 dangerous and annoying openings which are popular in amateur chess and can lead to defeat if unprepared, but can be refuted when you know how to take opponents off their favorite lines. Greet opponents with your own surprises! Recommended. 293 pages, $22.95.

MIDDLEGAME/TACTICS/WINNING CONCEPTS -

CHESS TACTICS FOR ADVANCED PLAYERS *by Yuri Averbakh* - A great tactical book. Complex combinations are brilliantly simpified into basic, easy-to-understand concepts you can use to win. Learn the underlying structure of piece harmony and fortify skills through numerous exercises. Very instructive, a must read. 328 pages, $17.50.

BIG BOOK OF COMBINATIONS *by Eric Schiller* - Test your tactical ability in 1,000 brilliant combinations from actual games spanning the history of chess. Includes various degrees of difficulty from the easiest to the most difficult combinations. Unlike other combination books, no hints are provided, so you'll have to work! 266 pages, $17.95.

STRATEGY FOR ADVANCED PLAYERS by *Eric Schiller* - For intermediate to advanced players, 45 insightful and very informative lessons illustrate the strategic and positional factors you need to know in middle and endgame play. Recommended highly as a tool to learn strategic chess and become a better player. 135 pages, $14.50.

HOW TO BECOME A CANDIDATE MASTER by *Alex Dunne* -The book that makes you *think* is packed with tips and inspiration; from a wide variety of openings in 50 fully annotated games to in-depth middle and end game discussions, the goal is to take your game up to the Expert level. A perennial favorite. 252 pages, $18.95.

- ENDGAMES -

ESSENTIAL CHESS ENDINGS EXPLAINED VOL. 1 by *Jeremy Silman* - This essential and enjoyable reference tool to mates and stalemates belongs in every chess player's library. Commentary on every move plus quizzes and many diagrams insure complete understanding. All basic positions covered, plus many advanced ones. 221 pages, $16.50.

ESSENTIAL CHESS ENDINGS EXPLAINED VOL. 2 by *Ken Smith* - This book assumes you know the basics of the 1st volume and takes you all the way to Master levels. Work through moves of 275 positions and learn as you go. There are explanations of every White and Black move so you know what's happening from both sides. 298 pages, $17.50.

- ORDER YOUR BOOKS TODAY AND BE A WINNER! -